SWAMPSCOTT HIGH SCHOOL LIBRARY

FN #29
3/73

The Supreme Court Under Earl Warren

D1189443

The
Supreme Court
Under
Earl Warren

Edited with an Introduction by

Leonard W. Levy

A NEW YORK TIMES BOOK

Quadrangle Books

A NEW YORK TIMES COMPANY

THE SUPREME COURT UNDER EARL WARREN. Copyright © 1972
by The New York Times Company. All rights reserved,
including the right to reproduce this book or portions thereof
in any form. For information, address: Quadrangle Books, Inc.,
330 Madison Avenue, New York, N.Y. 10017. Manufactured in
the United States of America. Published simultaneously in
Canada by Burns and MacEachern Ltd., Toronto.

Library of Congress Catalog Card Number: 70–190122
International Standard Book Number: 0–8129–0240–8 (cloth)
                                    0–8129–6186–2 (paper)

The publishers are grateful to the contributors herein
for permission to reprint their articles.

To
HENRY STEELE COMMAGER
with deep respect,
affection, and gratitude

Contents

2. Judicial Attributes and Philosophies

3. Legal Scholars Evaluate the Warren Court

The Supreme Court Under Earl Warren

Introduction

WHEN EARL WARREN became Chief Justice of the United States in 1953, American constitutional law, like the nation that it served, stood poised at the brink between two worlds. One, which nothing short of lethal action could move or remove, deserved a speedy, contemptible death; it was the world of racism, political rotten-boroughs, McCarthyism, discriminations against the poor, puritanism in sexual matters, denial of the suffrage, and egregious infringements on the rights of the criminally accused. The other was a world struggling to be born, in which injustices would be remedied and the fundamental law of the land would have a liberating and egalitarian impact. The Supreme Court under Warren was a midwife to the newer world. Freedom of expression and association, and, even more importantly, racial justice, criminal justice, and political justice became the Court's preoccupation, its meat and drink. Not since the early nineteenth century when the great John Marshall presided had the Court made American constitutional law so generative, even transforming—indeed there were friends and foes alike who spoke of a judicial "revolution"; and not since Marshall's time had the Court, which periodically suffered withering criticism, been so vilified by its critics nor so rapturously acclaimed by its supporters.

Although the Court operates in the main as a judicial team rather than as individual stars, Warren was the symbol of his Court, literally its head, figuratively its heart. He drew the kudos as well as the aspersions, even the psychotic hatreds epitomized by the scream, "Impeach Earl Warren!" Those who cautiously approved of the law's new direction but worried about the swiftness and extent of change, blamed him for the Court's overreaching itself. Distinguished law-school professors pharisaically parsed his opinions: they clucked disapprovingly when they detected a missing or botched stitch, but in their concern for legal *petit point* they lost sight of Warren's grand enterprise and the functional nature of law. President Dwight Eisenhower, who had appointed him, grew to regret his choice of Warren and is supposed to have said it was the "biggest damn fool mistake I ever made." President Lyndon Johnson handed Warren the accolade as "the greatest Chief Justice of them all." Warren nevertheless always served with eight very able associates—sixteen altogether during his tenure—and they, as much as he, shaped the Court's controversial opinions, even when they bickered and dissented. The principle of majority rule, based on "one man, one vote," has always prevailed within the Court. It is a collective institution with a perpetual corporate life. Still, the public identified the Court with its Chief Justice, and he did in fact associate himself with its trailblazing decisions in every area of constitutional law except on the subject of obscenity. Although Warren was not responsible for the judicial "revolution," he was responsive to it, and in the crucial areas of civil rights and electoral representation he led it. That revolution might not have taken place without him. He certainly lent it respectability, the public influence of his high position, and, above all, perhaps, his universally recognized attributes—in the words of President Nixon, one of the most vociferous critics of the "Warren Court"—of "humanity . . . fairness, integrity, dignity."

When Warren retired on June 23, 1969, Nixon stood before the Court, a self-appointed representative of the American bar, to offer a muted tribute. It preceded a unique event in the Court's history: the retiring Chief Justice swearing in his successor, Warren E. Burger, Nixon's appointee. The President, offering his grudging respect to the departing Warren, declared that the sixteen years during which he had presided "without doubt, will be described by historians as years of greater change in America than any in our history. . . . Change with continuity," he ventured, "can mean progress," and quite remarkably he added that of the three great branches of the government, none had been more responsible "for that continuity with change than the Supreme Court of the United States." The nation already knew what the President belatedly, if only ceremonially, recognized, that the Constitution had triumphantly survived the change and still stood, despite all vicissitudes —but that it most definitely had not stood still: under Warren it had progressed.

In his extemporaneous response, the Chief Justice stressed the theme of continuity with change. Observing that the Court is a continuing body, he pointed out the stunning fact that the judicial careers of just seven men, including the still sitting Justice Hugo L. Black, connected without interruption the 180-year history of the Court. Then Warren added, "We, of course, venerate the past, but our focus is on the problems of the day and of the future as we conceive it to be." In one sense at least, he declared, the Court's position was similar to that of the President, for it often had the awesome responsibility of speaking the last word "in great government affairs" and of speaking for the whole American public. "It is a responsibility that is made more difficult in this Court because we have no constituency. We serve no majority. We serve no minority. We serve only the public interest as we see it, guided only by that Constitution and our consciences. . . ." The Court, Warren concluded, had applied constitutional principles, so broadly stated in the document, in a manner consistent with the public interest and with the future "so far as it can be discerned."

Warren's candid and simple valedictory in effect endorsed the view, stated by both the Court's admirers and critics, that the justices seemed to consider themselves as movers and shakers of the country's destiny rather than as impersonal spokesmen of "the law." Surely Warren would have agreed with Woodrow Wilson who declared that the country looked for "statesmanship" in its judges, because the Constitution was not "a mere lawyer's document" but the "vehicle of the nation's life."

In an article on "The Law and the Future," published in *Fortune* magazine in 1955, two years after his appointment as Chief Justice, Warren was characteristically expansive, warm, and idealistic. This public statement confirmed the tenor of his stewardship. His prime concern for the law, Warren noted, was that it adapt to changing circumstances by keeping its rules in harmony with the enlightened common sense of the nation. That meant to him that the Supreme Court faced "a single continuous problem: how to apply to ever changing conditions the never changing principles of freedom." The Constitution, existing for the individual as well as the nation, best fulfilled its mission, he asserted, by serving the unchanging cause of human justice. Significantly he fastened upon "the 462 words of our Bill of Rights" as "the most precious part of our legal heritage," yet he presided over the Court at a time, he said, when the Bill of Rights was under subtle and pervasive attack. Turning to needed reforms of our constitutional system, he noted that the proud inscription above the portals of the Supreme Court Building—"Equal Justice Under Law"—described a goal by no means secured for all citizens. The rights due them, particularly oppressed minorities and the poor, had been infringed, neglected, or unperfected. Our system of criminal justice was "pockmarked with . . . procedural flaws and anachronisms," making for unequal access to justice. "Suspects are sometimes arrested, tried, and convicted without being adequately informed of their right to counsel. Even when he knows of this right, many a citizen cannot afford to exercise it." The remark foreshadowed some of the most disputed reforms inaugurated by the Warren Court.

Freedom, like justice, the Chief Justice continued, requires constant vigilance. Making no allowance for exceptions, Warren declared that when the rights of any individual or group were "chipped away, the freedom of all erodes." Warren's statement implicitly recognized that the Supreme Court had a crucial responsibility, one that could not be evaded, to help regenerate and fulfill the noblest aspirations for which the nation stood. In effect he was saying that the law, though remaining constantly rooted in the great ideals of the past, must change in order to realize them. Thus, when posterity receives the Bill of Rights from the present generation, the document will not have the same meaning as it had when we received it from past generations. "We will pass on a better Bill of Rights," he asserted, "or a worse one, tarnished by neglect or burnished by growing use. If these rights are real, they need constant and imaginative applications to new situations." Such "constant and imaginative applications" earned for the Warren Court its reputation for "activism."

In this article, and throughout his tenure on the Court, Earl Warren recognized that what counts is not what the Constitution says, because it says so very little; what counts, rather, is what the Supreme Court has said about the Constitution—in over four hundred volumes of decisions thus far. The Constitution itself necessarily plays a secondary role in American constitutional law, because as Justice Jackson once observed, when the Court had to construe the First Amendment's injunction against establishments of religion, it was "idle to pretend that this task is one for which we can find in the Constitution one word to help us as judges to decide where the secular ends and the sectarian begins in education." Justices who look to the Constitution for more than a Delphic phrase delude themselves. They might just as well turn to the latest fiction for all the guidance they will find on most of the great cases that involve national public policy, whether the question relates to reapportionment, racial segregation, public school prayers, preliminary hearings, subversive activities, the rights of welfare recipients or of illegitimate children, criminal interrogation, the conditions for naturalization and expatriation, school busing, or juvenile courts. The Constitution contains not a word about these or most of the subjects of great import with which the Court must deal. The framers of the Constitution had a genius for studied imprecision and calculated ambiguity. Their document, expressed in very generalized terms, resembled Martin Chuzzlewit's grandnephew who had no more than "the first idea and sketchy notion of a face." It thereby permitted, even encouraged—in fact necessitated—continuous reinterpretation and adaptation.

With all its amendments the Constitution clearly delineates the structure of the American national government but only roughly maps the contours of power and the rights that it guarantees. We know unmistakably that there is to be a President whose term of office is four years; but what is "the executive power" with which he is vested? Chief Justice John Marshall once happily noted that the Constitution has none of the "prolixity of a legal code"; it has, rather, the virtue of muddy brevity. Very few of its approximately seven thousand words have any significance in constitutional law.

Almost without exception these are the purposefully protean or undefined words, like general welfare, due process of law, commerce among the states, equal protection, privileges and immunities of citizenship, direct taxes, and necessary and proper. Other words of crucial importance in constitutional law are not even in the Constitution, including clear and present danger, fair trial, war powers, self-incrimination, public purpose, separate but equal, fair return, separation of church and state, and the police power. They are all judicial glosses. Even the seemingly specific injunctions of the Bill of Rights do not always exclude exceptions to their rule, nor are they self-defining. What is "due" process of law, a "speedy" trial, an "impartial" jury, an "unreasonable" search or seizure, an "excessive" bail, a "cruel" or "unusual" punishment, or an "establishment" of religion? Freedom of speech and press may not be "abridged"—what is an abridgement?—but the guarantee of freedom of religion is that it may not be "prohibited." May freedom of religion be abridged or regulated in some way short of prohibition? And what indeed is the "freedom of speech" that is protected? Obscenity—whatever that may be—libel, direct and successful verbal incitement to crime, and other types of speech are certainly not, nor were they intended to be, within the constitutional protection. The point is that there are no meaningful constitutional absolutes. And there is no constitutional question, at least none that has come before the Court, which can be sliced so thin that it has only one side.

"Strict constructionists" to the contrary, the Supreme Court is and must be for all practical purposes a "continuous constitutional convention" adapting the original charter by reinterpretation. One who used that phrase was James Beck, a Solicitor General of the United States and a very conservative one at that. He described the duties of the Court as "political in the highest sense of the word as well as judicial." Scholars and even justices of the Supreme Court who have had an appreciation of the realities of the situation have used the phrase too. In very much the same sense, justices of the Supreme Court, including such distinguished ones as Brandeis, Frankfurter, and Black, have described the Court, sometimes despairingly, as a superlegislature. It is indeed, and cannot help but be so. The reason is simply that the Constitution, as Jefferson said in exasperation, is "merely a thing of wax" which the Court "may twist and shape into any form they please." Judge Learned Hand observed that when a judge must pass on a question of constitutional law, "The words he must construe are empty vessels into which he can pour nearly anything he will." Justice Felix Frankfurter—whom President Nixon on appointing Chief Justice Warren Burger held up as a model of the strict-constructionist jurist dedicated to self-restraint—once explained that the words of the Constitution are so unrestricted by their intrinsic meaning, or by history, or by tradition, or by prior decisions, "that they leave the individual justice free, if indeed they do not compel him, to gather meaning not from reading the Constitution but from reading life . . . the process of constitutional interpretation compels the translation of policy into judgment, and the controlling conceptions of the justices are their 'idealized political picture' of the existing social order." Nixon's search for conservative strict constructionists has been more than a candid attempt to alter the trend of decision; it is an acknowledgment that at the very apex of our government of laws and not of men, the men who interpret the laws, rather than the laws themselves, are decisive. That was what Earl Warren meant, in part, when on his retirement he noted that the Court consisted of nine independent men "who have no one to be responsible to except their own consciences."

The justices should, to the extent humanly possible, be aware of their own predilections and try to decide cases without consciously yielding to their own sympathies or deliberately reading the Constitution in the light of their own policy preferences. Yet even the best and most impartial of judges, those in whom the judicial temperament is most finely cultivated, cannot escape the currents that have tugged at them throughout their lives and inescapably color their judgment. Personality, the beliefs that make the man, has always made the difference in the Supreme Court's constitutional adjudication. Never has there been a constitutional case before the Court in which room was lacking for personal discretion. In constitutional law there simply are no legal rules that are objective or neutral or value-free, enabling every judge, regardless of his identity and without regard to the litigants, to apply those rules in the same way with the same results. The rules themselves, as Justice Holmes said, "reflect considerations of policy and social advantage." Legal erudition, legal rules, legal logic, legal research, and legal precedents do not decide cases involving the ambiguous clauses of the Constitution, the very clauses usually involved in those cases whose outcome helps to determine justice, the shape of public policy, and the degree of liberty or equality that exists in the United States. Although some judges can intoxicate themselves with a belief that precedents are controlling, their decisions prove that the justices are intellectually supple enough to find their way around encumbering precedents. Moreover, the Court always has available to it alternative principles of constitutional construction—broad or narrow—as well as alternative lines of precedent, with the result that the Court has "a freedom," in the words of the scholar Edward S. Corwin, "virtually legislative in scope in choosing the values which it shall promote through its reading of the Constitution." The Lord High Chancellor in *Iolanthe* might have characterized the Constitution and the Supreme Court when he humorously asserted, "The Law is the embodiment of everything that's excellent. . . . And, I, my Lords, embody the Law."

The most gifted judge who has a deep understanding of himself and a deeper strain of self-skepticism cannot avoid the fact that every case presents him with a choice of competing considerations that are necessarily value-laden. His "idealized political picture of the social order," as Frankfurter said, or his conception of the public interest in the present and his vision of the future, to paraphrase Warren, influence his judgment one way or the other. "We may try to see things as objectively as we please," Justice Cardozo wrote. "Nonetheless, we can never see them with any eyes except our own." Inevitably, then, our constitutional law is subjective in character and to a great degree result-oriented. We may not want judges who start with the answer rather than with the problem, but as long as mere mortals sit on the Court and must construe that majestic but muddy Constitution, we will rarely get any other kind. Not that the justices knowingly read their prejudices into law. Probably there has never been a member of the Supreme Court who consciously decided against the Constitution or was unable to square his opinions with it. Most judges convince themselves, or at least profess to believe, that they respond in the main to the clarity of words on parchment, as illuminated, of course, by historical or social imperatives. This fiction may be good for their psyches or for the public's need to believe that the men who sit on the nation's highest tribunal really are Olympians, untainted by the considerations that move lesser beings. Even those justices who start with the problem rather than with the result cannot transcend themselves nor make the obscure and inexact into simon-pure truth or impersonal principle. Even they cannot avoid the fact that constitutional law, more than any other branch of law, is a reflection of great public policies enshrined in the form of supreme and fundamental commands. It is truer of constitutional law than of any other branch that "what the courts declare to have always been the law," as Holmes put it, "is in fact new. It is legislative in its grounds. The very considerations which judges most rarely mention, and always with an apology, are the secret root from which the law draws all the juices of life. I mean, of course, consideration of what is expedient for the community concerned." Judicial self-restraint and strict constructionism are at best factors that merely temper the inescapable activism needed for decision in constitutional adjudication. But self-restraint and strict constructionism can also enable a member of the Court to achieve a pose which permits him to reach a desired result in an apparently impersonal way. The judicial process is overwhelmingly a means of rationalizing preferred ends. Judicial activism, not restraint, has been our experience with the Supreme Court literally from the time of its very first decision.

Activism has certainly characterized the Warren Court, a galloping, hyperthyroid activism. But that occupational disease of the highest judicial process is not at all what distinguished the Warren Court from its predecessors. Activism in the past was associated in the main with the Court's invalidation of federal or state acts and its construction of statutes in a manner that changed their meaning or robbed them of it. With respect to judicial review of congressional acts, classic examples of judicial activism are the Dred Scott case, the Income Tax case, the Child Labor case, or the sudden batch of cases in 1935–1936 when the Court struck down major legislation of the New Deal. With respect to judicial review of state enactments, classic examples of judicial activism are the Dartmouth College case, the Lochner case, or the 1936 Minimum Wage case. In these historic examples of judicial activism, the Court sought to redirect the course of public policy into more conservative channels by interposing its highly legislative judgments against those of the popularly elected and politically responsible agencies of government. In such cases the Court, in James Bradley Thayer's phrase, sought "to dwarf the political capacity of the people, and to deaden its sense of moral responsibility." What made the Warren Court so different is that it sought to *enlarge* the political capacity of the people and to heighten their sense of moral responsibility. The Warren Court invalidated few acts of Congress, roughly on the average of less than one a year, but significantly it did so exclusively on Bill of Rights grounds.

In 1955 the Court held in *Toth v. Quarles* that a provision of Congress' Uniform Code of Military Justice, which subjected a former serviceman to trial by court martial for a crime alleged to have been committed while in uniform, denied due process of law, that is, trial by jury after indictment by grand jury. The same grounds were invoked in a 1957 case and in three related cases of 1960. In these the Court struck down provisions of the Uniform Code of Military Justice by which Congress had subjected overseas civilians—employees and dependents of the armed forces —to trial by court martial in both capital and noncapital cases.

In *Trop v. Dulles,* decided in 1958, the Court held unconstitutional a provision of the Nationality Act of 1940 which automatically denationalized or divested of citizenship any citizen convicted by court martial for wartime desertion. The grounds of decision were not clear, because none of the opinions in the case mustered a majority. It seems, however, that the infirmity of the act resulted from its depriving the victim of the inviolable birthright of citizenship. The act also conflicted with the constitutional guarantee against cruel and unusual punishments by imposing statelessness on its victims. In 1963 the Court in the *Mendoza-Martin* case invalidated provisions of the same statute and of the Immigration and Nationality Act of 1952 which automatically denationalized citizens who left the country in wartime to avoid military service. The majority ruled that Congress had imposed loss of citizenship as a punishment without affording the procedural safeguards of the Fifth and Sixth Amendments. A year later the Court held in *Schneider v. Rusk* that another provision of the act, subjecting naturalized citizens to denationalization for staying abroad three years in their country of former citizenship or birth, violated the Fifth Amendment's due process clause by denying them equal protection of the laws. The Court reasoned that all citizens, naturalized as well as native born, possessed equal rights; to deny the naturalized citizen the right enjoyed by native-born citizens to remain abroad indefinitely created an unconstitutional status of second-class citizenship. In the 1967 case of *Afroyim v. Rusk* the Court held unconstitutional another section of the statute which forfeited the citizenship of anyone voting in a foreign election. Congress, the Court declared, had no power to deprive anyone of his citizenship, which is a constitutional right guaranteed by the first clause of the Fourteenth Amendment; citizenship may be knowingly and voluntarily relinquished but cannot be divested by Congress as a form of punishment for conduct that Congress dislikes.

In 1964 the Court sustained the right to travel abroad as part of the liberty guaranteed by the Fifth Amendment's due process clause. In this case, *Aptheker v. Secretary of State,* the Court voided a provision of the Subversive Activities Control Act of 1950 which made it a felony for a member of a communist organization to apply for or use a passport. In *United States v. Brown,* decided the next year, the Court found a bill of attainder in the provision of the Labor Management Reporting and Disclosure Act of 1959 which made it a crime for a member of the Communist party to serve as an officer or employee of a labor union. The decision in another 1965 case discredited the discreditable fact that in all of American history the Court had never, despite many appropriate opportunities, struck down an act of Congress on First Amendment grounds. In that unprecedented case, *Lamont v. Postmaster General,* freedom of speech and press furnished the basis for a ruling against the constitutionality of a 1962 statute requiring the Post Office Department to detain and destroy unsealed foreign mail classified as communist propaganda, unless the addressee indicated his desire to receive it by returning a reply card. In that same year the Court also held in the *Albertson* case that the registration orders under the Subversive Activities Control Act, requiring registration of members of the Communist party on forms compelling admission of membership, conflicted with the Fifth Amendment's protection of the right against compulsory self-incrimination. In related cases decided in 1968 the Court voided the registration provisions of the Federal Wagering Act and the Federal Firearms Act. In the first statute Congress, in an effort to control gambling, had required gamblers to register and pay a license or occupational tax. The Court found a violation of the self-incrimination clause, because anyone who complied with the registration provisions exposed himself to prosecution under state law for illegal gambling. In the companion case, the Court declared that compulsory registration of an illegally possessed weapon similarly exposed the registrant to prosecution, thus forcing him to incriminate himself.

In an opinion of 1967 the Court changed the meaning of the Magnuson Act by ruling that Congress, when seeking to safeguard vessels and waterfront facilities from subversion by establishing a loyalty-security screening program, did not authorize a Coast Guard commandant, in violation of the First Amendment's freedom of speech, to deny a license to a merchant seaman because of his allegedly subversive beliefs. Finally, in the *Jackson* case of 1968, the Court invalidated a section of the Federal Kidnaping Act which authorized the death penalty only if a jury should so recommend. The Court reasoned that since a defendant could not be sentenced to death if he confessed or waived jury trial, the death-penalty provision burdened the right of trial by jury protected by the Sixth Amendment.

This review of cases in which the Warren Court voided acts of Congress indicates a new trend in the history of the high tribunal. It had at last caught up with popular folklore by becoming the protector of civil liberties. Its dizzying interventionism in the exercise of judicial review, especially in state cases, was occasioned by an intense desire, in Warren's off-Court phrase, to safeguard "the most precious part of our legal heritage," the Bill of Rights, and to "pass on a better Bill of Rights . . . burnished by growing use." No predecessor of the Warren Court took so seriously or energetically its mission in that regard. In Justice Cardozo's writings is a passage that shines as the guiding star of the Warren Court's ministry: "The great ideals of liberty and equality are preserved against the assaults of opportunism, the expediency of the passing hour, the erosion of small encroachments, the scorn and derision of those who have no patience with general principles, by enshrining them in constitutions, and consecrating to the task of their protection a body of defenders. By conscious or subconscious influence, the presence of this restraining power, aloof in the background, but nonetheless always in reserve, tends to stabilize and rationalize the legislative judgment, to infuse it with the glow of principle, to hold the standard aloft and visible to those who must run the race and keep the faith." This judicial power, Cardozo added, found its chief value in "making vocal and audible the ideals that might otherwise be silenced, in giving them continuity of life and of expression, in guiding and directing choice within the limits where choice ranges. This function should preserve to the courts the power that belongs to them, if only the power is exercised with insight into social values, and with suppleness of adaptation to changing social needs."

Taken as a group, the cases in which the Warren Court voided acts of Congress are of greater symbolic than practical importance. None of them received much attention from the press or Congress. The cases which evoked great public interest and were most significant involved judicial review of state action, chiefly the racial discrimination and legislative apportionment cases whose transforming effects upon American life are not yet played out. Similarly, the state cases on censorship of obscenity and freedom of the press, on church-state relations and freedom of religion, and on criminal justice loom larger in the public mind and have had a more far-reaching influence than the cases in which the Court invalidated congressional legislation. Under the Warren Court the constitutional law of civil liberties and civil rights enjoyed a golden age in our history. Never before was the Court so bold and vigilant in its defense of constitutional freedoms in so many diverse fields. The various First Amendment liberties, the great procedural rights of the criminally accused, and equal justice under the law for racial minorities, for political lepers, and for the poor have flourished mightily in the pages of the Court's opinions, with considerable fallout in the world beyond.

Often the Court held "the standard aloft" when all other agencies of government, pressed by more expediential or parochial considerations, had lost sight of it. The controversial reforms in state criminal procedure would not have been necessary had local police officials, prosecutors, and courts done their jobs with respect for the Bill of Rights. The reapportionment revolution would not have been imposed by the Supreme Court had state legislatures and state courts discharged their obligations under their own laws and under the equal-protection clause of the Fourteenth Amendment. The Supreme Court would not have had to serve as a sword for the destruction of racial discriminations that had been compelled by law if Congress had passed civil rights acts or if the state legislatures and courts had not sustained local prejudices against constitutional rights. What made the Warren Court so different from its predecessors and vulnerable to criticism was its enthusiastic willingness to play St. George in defense of constitutional rights.

In short, the special character of the Warren Court derived from the fact that it was the first *liberal* activist court in our history. Because it was libertarian and egalitarian in its judicial activism, and because it dared to lead the way, redressing injustices to which state courts, policemen, and politicians both state and national had been stone blind, neglectful, or unable to redress, the Warren Court became the conscience of the country. Its moralistic admonitions and appeals to national ideals, joined to judicial "thou-shalt-nots," provoked feelings of guilt and resentment, even outrage. Even within its own ranks, the Court's departure from its traditional role as a defender of the status quo and its novel assumption of the role of St. George exposed it to scathing criticisms.

The trenchant, intramural discord in the Warren Court was reflected in bruising opinions by dissenting justices. In anguished and angry words they accused the majority, time and again, of making new law, departing from precedent, deciding on the basis of personal predilections, acting as a super-legislature, and disregarding conventional canons of constitutional construction. Years ago when William Jennings Bryan was asked what he thought about the income tax decisions, he replied in effect, "Read the dissenting opinions," which were as censorious as could be. The dissenting opinions on the Warren Court were equally censorious. The public, which has little understanding of and even less patience for constitutional niceties, cares only about the results of cases, and so the Court was accused in irresponsible and misleading terms of having coddled criminals and communists, outlawed God from the public schools, legislated morality and sociology in its desegregation decisions, and intruded into the political thicket of legislative apportionment. Dissenting opinions, sometimes quite openly, fed such charges, but the chief complaint of the dissenters turned on the overbreadth of many of the Court's opinions and the failure of the majority justices to confront complicated constitutional issues with appropriate professional expertise and consistency.

Consistency has rarely been a virtue of the Supreme Court, and under Warren its record in this regard was no worse than in the past. The question of consistency, or, rather, the lack of it, does point to a fact about the Warren Court that is often obscured by stressing its affirmations of Bill of Rights freedoms. On balance, liberal activism characterized the work of the Court during its sixteen years under Warren; but there were many decisions that libertarians deplored as encroachments on constitutionally protected freedoms.

The Warren Court is associated, for example, with a broad view of First Amendment rights, enabling obscene literature to escape censorship. Yet the Court's leading decision on the subject, in the *Roth* case, sustained the constitutionality of both state and federal obscenity laws; and in several other cases, convictions for violating state laws against obscenity were sustained. In one, the Court sustained a conviction for violating the United States postal laws against obscenity on the startling ground that the material was advertised in a pandering manner. If the rule of that case were applied literally, one might be jailed for hawking *Lady Chatterly's Lover* or *Ulysses,* even the *Bible,* by appealing to their prurient interest.

In the *Perez* decision dealing with the right to citizenship, the Court, though it subsequently overruled itself, supported the power of Congress to denationalize native-born citizens who voted in foreign elections. In *Zemel v. Rusk* the Court decided that the Secretary of State could ban passports for travel to Cuba, notwithstanding claims, based on due process and the First Amendment, of a right to travel freely. Against a First Amendment challenge based on freedom of expression, the Court in the *O'Brien* case of 1965 sustained a congressional statute making it a felony deliberately to destroy or mutilate a draft card. In four other First Amendment cases, decided in 1961, the Court upheld Sunday closing laws in the face of arguments that they used state power on behalf of sectarian purposes, thereby breaching the prohibition against establishments of religion; that they violated the religious freedom of observers of the Jewish sabbath; and that they denied sabbatarian merchants the equal protection of the laws. In the area of criminal justice, despite charges that it was handcuffing the cops, the Court in *Terry v. Ohio* sustained a "stop and frisk" law and the conviction obtained under it, although the police officer lacked probable cause to seize, search, and arrest. Reversing the conviction before it in the *Katz* case, the Court nevertheless indicated that evidence secured by electronic bugging, judicially authorized and not involving physical trespass, would not violate the Fourth Amendment.

The Court sustained the government in numerous internal-security cases. In *Barenblatt,* an important case dealing with the broad mandate of the House Committee on Un-American Activities, the Court sustained the investigating committee and the conviction of a witness who had refused, mainly on First Amendment grounds, to answer questions about his Communist party affiliations. In the related *Uphaus* case the Court upheld the conviction of a pacifist who refused to produce before a state investigating committee a list of guests at his summer camp, which was suspected of being a communist front. In three other cases the Court also supported the House Un-American Activities Committee against arguments that individuals had been improperly convicted for contempt by refusing to answer questions, concerning their subversive connections, that were unrelated to a legislative purpose, lacked pertinency, sought exposure for exposure's sake, and infringed both freedom of association and petition. In the *Koningsberg* case of 1961, the Court also upheld against First Amendment claims the denial of membership in a state bar association to a person who refused to answer questions concerning communist affiliations. In the same year in the *Scales* case, the Court also legitimized the membership clause of the Smith Act making criminal the knowing membership in any organization that advocates the overthrow of the government of the United States by force or violence. Against Fifth Amendment claims that the right against self-incrimination was violated, the Court's *Ullmann* decision sustained the constitutionality of a congressional immunity act forcing witnesses to testify concerning subversive activities; and in three cases the Court upheld the dismissals from public service of persons who refused to answer concerning their communist affiliations. In still other Fifth Amendment cases not dealing with internal security, the Court denied that the right against self-incrimination had been violated by blood tests to determine drunkenness; in *Breithaupt v. Abram* the police had taken the blood from an unconscious truck driver who had been involved in an accident, and in *Schmerber v. California* from a suspected drunk who protested the test.

In these various cases that do not square with the reputation of the Warren Court for unadulterated and consistent support of Bill of Rights claims against the government, the Chief Justice himself sided with the government in the obscenity, stop-and-frisk, Sunday-closing, travel-to-Cuba, electronic bugging, and immunity cases. In the others he dissented. In the late 1950's the liberal activist group on the Court met frequent defeat, particularly in internal-security cases, because of the defections of Justices Frankfurter and Harlan. When Justice Goldberg succeeded Justice Frankfurter at the beginning of the 1962–1963 term, the balance of power shifted for the remainder of the Chief Justice's incumbency to the liberal activists. In the preceding term, however, Justice Clark's votes insured two victories that will always be identified with the Warren wing. One, *Mapp v. Ohio,* overruled a 1948 precedent and extended the Fourth Amendment's guarantee against unreasonable search and seizure to the states, making the fruits of an illegal search as excludable as evidence in a state trial as it would be in a federal one. In the other precedent-shattering case, *Baker v. Carr,* the Court sustained the jurisdiction of federal tribunals to require state legislatures to redistrict themselves on an equitable basis. Both cases spawned a progeny of remarkable decisions in the 1960's. By the conclusion of Warren's tenure as Chief Justice the Court had incorporated into the Fourteenth Amendment most of the provisions of the Bill of Rights applicable to accused persons—indeed, all the essential ones except the right against excessive bail. In sum, the Court abolished the double standard that had formerly existed by requiring that state criminal procedures conform to federal ones. In the long line of reapportionment decisions following *Baker v. Carr,* the Court ordered an end to the existing malapportionment schemes in federal, state, and local governments that had reached such proportions as to mock the integrity of representative government. When Warren, nearing his retirement, was asked which were the most important decisions of his time, he chose, in rank order, the reapportionment cases, the school desegregation cases, and *Gideon v. Wainwright,* the case in which the Court, adding representation by counsel in all felony prosecutions to the list of incorporated rights, required the states to provide counsel to defendants too poor to hire their own.

Warren's choice of the most important decisions of his time was surprising only because he did not rank the school desegregation cases first. These were, after all, the only cases during his sixteen years of which it may be said that had the decisions gone the other way, the United States would have been morally bankrupt and unfit to survive under the pretense that it was a democracy. The nation would have been a far poorer place had the Court ducked the reapportionment issue and had it decided the criminal procedure cases wholly on the side of the government, but on the issue of racial justice, any opinion other than or even narrower than the one handed down by Warren would have been unthinkable, unbearable, unspeakable. Half the states of the nation at that time either required or permitted the segregation of Negro children in the public schools. Their apartheid laws were based on an 1896 opinion of the Supreme Court which expressed the racist sociology of that date; the holding was that the equal-protection clause of the Fourteenth Amendment was not violated by providing "separate but equal" public facilities to Negroes. The separate-but-equal doctrine was the linchpin of Jim Crow jurisprudence in America. Although it had been peripherally weakened by several opinions of the Court between 1938 and 1950, the doctrine still stood in principle as this nation's equivalent of the Nazi Nuremberg Laws, rationalizing a belief in the superiority of the white race.

Under Chief Justice Vinson the Court had evaded a direct confrontation with the doctrine, doubtless for fear of the consequences of disrupting the South's caste system based on race. Warren probably deserves the credit for marshaling a unanimous Court to back his opinion, unmarred even by separate concurring opinions, that the noxious doctrine was a relic of racial prejudice incompatible with the equalitarian principle of the Fourteenth Amendment. The Court, junking the doctrine, held that separate facilities were inherently unequal. Nevertheless the Court countenanced a year of delays and rearguments before handing down an order to implement its new position, and then—no doubt in deference to justices who were apprehensive about Southern threats of blood in the streets and wide scale resistance—the Court made a tragic, strategic error: returning the cases to the lower courts, it ordered them to work out desegregation schemes "as soon as practicable," to require the school systems to "make a prompt and reasonable start toward full compliance," and to issue such decrees that would put the schools on a racially nondiscriminatory basis "with all deliberate speed."

After his retirement, Warren in a public address declared that many people had told him that they opposed discrimination and favored equal treatment under the laws—but "Don't you think that we are moving too fast?" The question, replied Warren, was "an escape from responsibility" and assumed that the Court "had the right to ration freedoms, and that it should go slow enough so as not to offend anyone in doing so. Of course, no such power exists in law or morals. Either all rights of citizenship belong to them or they are entitled to none. . . ." Such rights, being personal, required immediate remedy; but the Court provided none. Its gradualist implementation order invited a variety of evasive schemes, such as pupil-placement laws, freedom-of-choice plans, public tuition payments for private schools, and even closure of the public schools. Some states, notably Arkansas, Louisiana, and Mississippi, invoked doctrines of interposition and nullification to repudiate federal law which was enforced at Little Rock and Oxford only by the use of federal troops. When Warren retired, the Court was still handing down decisions ordering compliance and striking down circumvention tactics. A decade after his monumental scrapping of the separate-but-equal doctrine, only about 2 per cent of the Negro pupils in the states of the former Confederacy attended school with white pupils. Although that figure increased fifteenfold when Warren left the bench, the reason had far less to do with judicial orders than with the orders of the Department of Health, Education, and Welfare, acting under Title VI of the Civil Rights Act of 1964; that is, compliance dramatically increased when the spigot controlling federal subsidies for education was turned off. Nevertheless, it was Warren's opinion in the 1954 case that sparked the civil rights revolution which led to the series of civil rights acts belatedly passed by Congress.

That opinion also marked the beginning of a profound commitment by the Warren Court to the achievement of racial justice. American constitutional law has always had a central interest to guard. Throughout most of American history that interest had been the rights of property; sometimes it has been the Union, the state police power, the rights of labor, or internal security. During Warren's chief justiceship that central interest was, broadly speaking, the Bill of Rights; more particularly it was racial justice. The unifying theme that runs through a variety of the Court's opinions is that all Americans, including Negroes, are entitled to the same constitutional rights. That theme was most directly expressed in the series of cases that extended the principle of the school desegregation decisions to all public facilities and places of public accommodation. The same theme appears in the decisions that voided: the listing of political candidates on the ballot by race, the practice in Southern courts of calling Negroes by their first names, the discriminatory punishment of interracial fornication, and the banning of interracial marriages. The theme manifested itself also in the Court's startling decision in the Mayer Company case that an 1866 civil rights act, passed under the Thirteenth Amendment, outlawed racial discrimination in the sale or rental of housing, private as well as public. Similarly, other decisions prevented states and municipalities from repealing or delaying the operation of open-housing laws.

The Court, by broadly reinterpreting the scope and application of virtually moribund statutes from the Reconstruction era, sustained the Department of Justice in its protection of civil rights by criminal prosecutions against police officers and even private citizens who murdered, beat, intimidated, or harassed any Negro in the exercise of any right guaranteed to him by the Constitution or federal laws. The Court also protected Negro voters by voiding racial gerrymanders, poll taxes, and discriminatory "understanding" and literacy tests, and by sustaining the constitutionality of the Voting Rights Act of 1965 which banned various tests and devices by which Southern states had prevented black citizens from exercising the right to vote. The Court also sustained the constitutionality of the Civil Rights Act of 1964, which outlawed racial segregation in sweeping terms; on that occasion the Court relied on a broad construction of the commerce powers of Congress. By contrast, the First Amendment's protection of freedom of association and of political expression was the basis of the decisions protecting the National Association for the Advancement of Colored People against reprisals and harassment from Southern states. When Negroes engaged in mass sit-ins and other public demonstrations verging on civil disobedience, the Court kept the civil rights movement alive by reversing the convictions for breach of the peace and trespass.

The theme of equal rights and racial justice even underscores the Court's various decisions on criminal procedures and reapportionment, because Negroes constitute a disproportionate number of the criminally accused and are increasingly concentrated in metropolitan centers. Racial justice, criminal justice, and political justice were interrelated though different facets of the Warren Court's dedication to passing on to future generations a better Bill of Rights, burnished by growing use and imaginatively applied to new situations.

Part 1

THE COURT AND ITS WORK

Editor's Preface

BY 1956 THE Supreme Court was under attack throughout the South because of the school desegregation decisions. Virginia instituted its program of "massive resistance" and voted to close any school that desegregated under federal court orders. Georgia declared the Supreme Court's decision "null, void, and of no effect," and Louisiana denounced the decision as unconstitutional. The revolt against the Court spread to other states and to the South's representatives in Congress. The Southern Manifesto of 1956, signed by almost all Southern Congressmen and all but three Senators, described the "unwarranted" decision as the result of the Court's substitution of "naked power for established law. . . . We regard the decision of the Supreme Court in the school cases as a clear abuse of judicial power. . . . We decry the Supreme Court's encroachment on rights reserved to the States and to the people, contrary to established law, and to the Constitution." Such was the context of Edmond Cahn's introductory piece in this section. In his calm, scholarly, and historical essay, Cahn, a foremost expert on jurisprudence, defended the court and its exercise of judicial review, showing that it had a responsibility to enforce the Constitution, especially its protections of individual rights. He argued too that the Court did not thwart the principle of popular representation. He saw the Court as "the nation's exemplar and disseminator of democratic values," a role no liberal would have described for the Court a generation earlier.

Cahn's article was published when the Court began its 1956–1957 term. William J. Brennan, Jr., took his seat at that time as a new justice, his nomination confirmed by every member of the Senate except Joseph McCarthy. At Harvard Law School Brennan had been a student of Felix Frankfurter, whom he joined as a member of the Court. Frankfurter is supposed to have said, "I always wanted my students to think for themselves, but Brennan goes too far." What Frankfurter meant was that he had lost control of Brennan, who drifted to the liberal-activist wing of the Court. In the article by Brennan reprinted here, he gives us an "Inside View of the High Court," describing its process.

The article by Bernard Schwartz, a distinguished scholar in the field of constitutional law, is a perceptive early estimate of Warren as Chief Justice. Schwartz notes that a member of the Supreme Court, the Chief Justice in particular, must be a statesman even more than a lawyer; he notes too that the libertarian predispositions of most of the justices, while championing the Bill of Rights, tended toward opinions that were broader than required by the actual disposition of the cases. In effect, Schwartz enters a caveat which became common among friendly professional critics of the Court: technical expertise and careful reasoning were essential if the Court's commands were to be respected.

Alan F. Westin, a lawyer and political scientist, in his two articles explains why liberals and conservatives switched positions in their attitudes toward the Court during the Warren years. Westin also stresses the influence of public opinion on the Court's decisions. Anthony Lewis, long the *New York Times's* specialist on legal affairs and the Court, explains in his article how and why the Court changed from its former role as protector of private property to keeper of the country's conscience. Lewis reviews the changing role of the Court by examining its work in three crucial areas—criminal procedure, racial justice, and reapportionment. He concludes that the Court has acted as the instrument of national moral values that have been unable to find other government expression. His article is also a useful introduction to an explanation of the dissenting views within a liberal activist Court.

Lewis M. Steel at the time of his article was a lawyer for the National Association for the Advancement of Colored People, but he spoke for himself rather than for his organization. Steel's piece is worth careful reading as an expression of the new militancy among Negro intellectuals. It is also an unexpected, slashing attack on the Supreme Court for its alleged conservatism and genteel white racism in the field of racial justice. Notwithstanding his immoderate tone, a reflection of the "rage" so fashionable among militants, Steel's position is substantially accurate and justifiable except in one respect. There is a very serious question, which he does not recognize, whether it was politically or practically possible for the Court to have gotten so far out in front of national public opinion that it would have lost popular support, been unable to implement its decisions, and jeopardized its own position.

The final article in this section, by Joseph W. Bishop, Jr., of Yale Law School, might just as well have been included in the last section where "Legal Scholars Evaluate the Warren Court." The article is placed here, however, because it provides a masterly summation of the work of the Court under Warren's chief justiceship. Bishop, though mildly critical of the Court's overbroad language, is judicious and full of commonsense observations. Like Lewis he focuses on criminal procedure, race relations, and reapportionment, the subjects on which the Court's public image, he says, was based. In these areas, he declares, "(1) the Court was right and (2) most people know it was right." He adds too that it was not at all as revolutionary as commentators usually depict it, and he exposes as substantially meritless common criticisms of the Court, for example, that it coddled criminals.

Brief for
the Supreme Court

by Edmond Cahn

THE UNITED STATES Supreme Court is in the party platforms again.
Ever since 1954 when the school segregation cases were decided,
the court has become a target of severe criticism. Decisions of
minor legal points that would ordinarily pass without special notice
are suddenly seen to possess deep and lasting significance. If a dissenting justice writes tartly of his colleagues' learning or wisdom,
he may rely on a large, attentive audience. As before in its history,
the court is passing through a hostile phase when criticism becomes
strident enough to seem substantial and extreme enough to suggest
alarm.

While Americans argue and squabble about the court, other nations are emulating it in every quarter of the globe. The latest
disciple is Italy. In June, 1956, the Italian Constitutional Court
held that censorship laws inherited from the old Fascist regime
were unconstitutional. In this, the very first decision of the new
tribunal, freedom of the press was at issue, and it won a momentous victory. Leading Italian jurists hailed the decree as mark-
ing a new chapter for democracy. It was, they declared, their
country's counterpart of Marbury v. Madison, in which Chief

From the *New York Times Magazine,* October 7, 1956, copyright © 1956
by The New York Times Company.

Justice Marshall established that a law contrary to the Constitution was void in our courts.

On every continent there have been judicial performances of this kind, in behalf of freedom and equality. For example, the judges of the Supreme Court of India endeavor courageously to enforce the guarantees of personal liberty which are set down in India's Constitution and, in doing so, they pay suitable attention to American sources and precedents. It is good tidings for the world that judges in New Delhi are reading Jefferson, Madison, Marshall, Holmes and Hughes.

Nevertheless, "judicial review," developed through 150 years of American experience, seems to be poorly understood at home. There are quite a number at home who assume that a native American does not need to read Jefferson, Madison, Marshall and the rest before expounding the Constitution and admonishing the justices. Perhaps that is why so many recent comments on Supreme Court decisions have been full of heat and noise. That the current state of misinformation and confused opinion can eventually become dangerous, I think no one will deny. It is high time to confront two basic fallacies about our Supreme Court.

Fallacy Number One: That contrary to what our more liberal Founding Fathers (such as Jefferson and Madison) intended at the time the Constitution was adopted, Chief Justice Marshall and his court later usurped the right to decide questions of constitutionality.

Many Americans feel a vague unease about the Supreme Court's role in our Government. Remembering from student days that John Marshall belonged to the Federalist party, that the Federalists emphasized stability and conservatism, and that Marshall and Jefferson eventually became bitter antagonists, good citizens are liable to find themselves distrusting Marshall's accomplishments.

Did not Jefferson, as President and ex-President, frequently lash out at the Supreme Court? Even if one grants that today, after a century and a half, it is too late to reopen the question of whether the court ought to determine constitutional issues, Americans who believe that the power was usurped in the first place are likely to examine the current of decisions with a suspicious eye.

When we accept "judicial review," are we betraying the ideals of Jefferson?

The historical record is easy to consult. Since Jefferson was representing the United States in Paris through the entire period of framing and adopting the Constitution and framing and submitting the Bill of Rights, we have his letters to his friends, which conveyed his wishes and anxieties during this critical epoch. When he received the text of the Constitution drafted in Philadelphia, he wrote his views to James Madison. In a famous letter dated Dec. 20, 1787, he expressed indignation that the Constitution did not contain a bill of rights because "a bill of rights is what the people are entitled to against every government on earth."

What were his remarks on the provision for a Federal judiciary? He said he would prefer that the judges either participate in the President's veto power or possess a separate veto power of their own. In effect, Jefferson suggested that the judges determine not only the constitutionality but also the political wisdom and desirability of laws passed by Congress. The suggestion, which proved stillborn, would have vested the Supreme Court with more power than anyone has dared claim for it during all the subsequent generations.

In 1788, the several states ratified the Constitution, but only on the understanding that it would be amended forthwith to add a bill of rights. The new United States Government got under way in New York City during the spring of 1789.

As leader in the House of Representatives, it was Madison's duty to systematize the many proposals and draft an acceptable list of amendments. He had written Jefferson a long, reflective commentary on bills of rights and their purposes but, transatlantic mails being what they were in those days, months elapsed before it reached Paris. Jefferson read the letter with dismay, and well he might, for in it Madison doubted that a bill of rights would have any practical worth in times of turmoil and popular passion; his tone seemed lackluster, hesitant, tepid.

What could one conceivably write in Paris to kindle more vigor and zeal in New York? As he sat frowning at Madison's letter, Jefferson remembered his friends George Wythe, John Blair and Edmund Pendleton, the three great judges who composed Virginia's High Court of Chancery. Perhaps their names, universally revered as the Romans once revered the name of Cato, would banish Madison's misgivings and stiffen his resolve. On March 15, 1789, Jefferson wrote:

"In the arguments in favor of a declaration of rights, you omit one which has great weight with me; the legal check which it puts into the hands of the judiciary. This is a body which, if rendered independent and kept strictly to their own department, merits great confidence for their learning and integrity. In fact, what degree of confidence would be too much for a body composed of such men as Wythe, Blair and Pendleton? On characters like these, the *'civium ardor prava jubentium'* [frenzy of the citizens bidding what is wrong] would make no impression."

This was the first time in their long trans-Atlantic correspondence that either had even alluded to the judiciary as an instrument to enforce the Bill of Rights. Manifestly, the concept could become supremely important to our fabric of government. But would Madison receive the letter in time to place Jefferson's concept before the Congress along with the proposed Bill of Rights?

In New York, where Congress had convened, Madison struggled under a burden of impatience. Aware that the people would never trust the new Federal Government until Congress voted the amendments, he was in a great hurry to have them considered and approved. Nevertheless, Congress, which was not in a hurry, continued from day to day discussing every imaginable subject but a bill of rights. Madison waited and fretted. Meanwhile, Jefferson's letter, with the vital message which Madison could scarcely anticipate, reposed in the Embassy's official pouch on a vessel moving slowly across the Atlantic.

By arrangement, Madison was scheduled to address the House of Representatives on June 8. Jefferson's letter arrived in New York on June 2—just in time to influence the speech and enhance the constitutional dignity of the Bill of Rights. When Madison rose to address the House on June 8, 1789, he asserted:

"If they [the fundamental rights] are incorporated into the Constitution, independent tribunals of justice will consider themselves in a peculiar manner the guardians of those rights; they will be an impenetrable bulwark against every assumption of power in the legislative or executive; they will be naturally led to resist every encroachment upon rights expressly stipulated for in the Constitution by the declaration of rights."

Thus the initial United States Congress, which voted to submit the Bill of Rights for ratification, was frankly and explicitly informed that the illustrious sponsors of the bill desired the judges to consider themselves active guardians of our fundamental freedoms.

If Jefferson could advise us today, he would be the first to insist that we in the twentieth century are not bound by anything he may have intended in the eighteenth. To the end of his life, he reiterated boldly that the Constitution belongs not to the dead but to every successive generation of living Americans. This has been the very life of the Constitution. To agree now with what Jefferson or Madison may have intended or may have communicated to the First Congress is only a comfort, not an obligation.

Nevertheless, this time we are entitled to the comfort. As we have seen, the foremost liberal minds among the Founding Fathers joined with the foremost conservatives in expecting the Supreme Court to enforce the Constitution and Bill of Rights. Concededly, no statesman ever assumed that the court could perform the function alone, without cooperation from the President, the Congress, the states, or—most necessary of all—the American people.

"Judicial review" is only one of many apt devices for converting promises on parchment into living liberties, and there are obvious limits to what a single device can achieve. But the historical record is evident; "judicial review" was no usurpation. The court's authority is not something stolen by lawyers' wiles. Historically it is legitimate.

Fallacy Number Two: That, contrary to the principle of majority rule, the Supreme Court has been thwarting the will of the people's representatives in Congress.

Twenty years have passed since Franklin D. Roosevelt's major controversy with the Supreme Court, years so compact with wars, changes and crises that even during Roosevelt's lifetime the outlines of the controversy had begun to fade in our memories. In retrospect, the twenty years seem like twenty distinct eras and the issues of 1936-37 like the small and simple issues of some outgrown, almost quaint society. The distance in time from 1937 is as nothing compared with the difference in historical conditions. Yet almost daily we hear the voices of lawyers, Congressmen and Governors assailing the Supreme Court in the nomenclature of that obsolete conflict. How they exert themselves to call up the spirit of 1937!

Twenty years ago, the conflict between legislative and judicial authority was real, profound and crucial. For decades, the court majority had been reading their own economic and social predilections into the text of the Constitution. In 1936 the process reached its climax. New Deal statutes, state and Federal, were falling like withered leaves in the glare of the judges' disapproval. The decisions of that year left enormous gaps in the powers of government, areas where urgently necessary action was forbidden to the nation and the states alike.

Conflict between the two departments became inevitable. Even if one combines the New Deal period with all the preceding years back to 1865, one finds the Supreme Court striking down an average of more than one Act of Congress for every year from 1865 through 1936. Many of the invalidated statutes were essential in the highest degree; many of the decisions left impassable blocks on the road to social and economic reform. Public discontent cumulated and became peremptory. No wonder that today we witness such strenuous attempts to summon the ghost of 1937!

Here again, the historical record is quite manifest. Ever since 1937, the Supreme Court has followed a deliberate, consistent policy of reducing and withholding its jurisdiction. It has employed every known device in the tool-chest of procedure to avoid friction with Congress. When the present court has erred—as it has in the opinion of liberals—the error has served invariably to favor and sustain Congressional action.

With invalidations at the rate of more than one a year from 1865 to 1936, it is impressive to contrast the average from 1937 to 1956: one Act of Congress held invalid every six or seven years. Moreover, as even hostile critics would concede, not a single one of the post-1937 instances has affected an important legislative power.

Our Constitution is not proffered to individual or local option;

it binds everyone, legislators and judges, the governors as well as the governed. It protects and, by like token, controls all persons, officials and departments.

It establishes principles that do not always bow to a majority vote; as a nation we have resolved that, just as there are fields of human experience where the popular majority is entitled to have its way even when it is wrong, there are other fields (e.g., religion) where it is not entitled to have its way even when it is right. To the Supreme Court we have committed a part—by no means all— of the responsibility for preserving the fabric of government and our own civic freedoms.

Yet what of the fact that the judges are appointed to life tenure? Surely they cannot pretend to respond promptly, as elected representatives may, to the currents of popular opinion. The judges cannot so pretend; they know, or ought to know, that their duty may require them to disregard the people's wishes. They are judges, not delegates. Theirs is the obligation to expound the Constitution objectively, impartially and justly—to the utmost limits of human capacity and individual endowment.

Popular majorities are volatile aggregations, they melt and reassemble, shift and change. The Constitution was conceived advisedly to channel the majority's temporary impulses in the interest of the historic tradition, the social conscience and the future welfare of the country. To enforce the Constitution, though at the cost of nullifying an Act of Congress that clearly conflicts with it, is to keep America's covenant with the *abiding* majority.

Who of us would be naive enough to confide the Supreme Court's vast authority to nine lawyers in robes if they were required to compete at the polls for election and re-election? Suppose, for a moment, that a Justice's future tenure were to depend on continued support from party leaders or from the President who appointed him. The supposition is worth making. It explains demonstratively why, like the Founding Fathers, we are determined to have thoroughly independent judges who will fulfill their conscientious duty, no matter whom they antagonize.

Independence does not necessarily imply aggressiveness or conflict. Continuing as it does to deal very tenderly with Congressional legislation, the present Supreme Court deserves none of 1937's anachronistic charges and epithets. These days, if a Congressman wishes to discover some pretext for discontent, he can no longer charge that the court arrogantly nullifies Acts of Congress. At worst, he can only complain that the court misunderstands and misinterprets them.

In a few cases, the complaint seems right, in most it seems baseless. But, right or wrong, it can scarcely justify a very livid display of resentment, for if the court does happen to misinterpret a piece of Federal legislation, Congress need only pass another act to make its intent explicit, and the Justices will accept the correction graciously. Nevertheless, when incidents of the kind do occur, they may provoke as much rhetoric and clamor as though the judiciary had collided head-on with the Congress.

In consequence, the public receives a distorted picture of the court's work. One simply cannot compose a true mosaic of the Supreme Court out of episodes of conflict and sporadic clashes. Fragments like these are bright enough, but too discrete, too often untypical.

Even to begin understanding the court's role in our Government, one must at least observe how frequently and usefully the court cooperates with the Congress. And one must also notice how the court serves to educate the Congress. When the process of education succeeds, it may provide the subtlest dramas and the most gratifying dénouements.

At bottom, the Supreme Court is the nation's exemplar and disseminator of democratic values. The role has been thrust on it. Americans have become accustomed to look to the court for symbols and emblems, standards and ideals, lines below which communal action ought not to sink, goals toward which communal action ought to strive. Though, like other preceptors, this one has committed some sorry blunders and has occasionally underestimated its audience, its prestige remains indubitable.

Let me present one specimen to show how the educative process develops.

Act I (1929). Rosika Schwimmer, Hungarian-born radical and pacifist, seeks to become a naturalized American citizen. The naturalization law, passed by Congress in 1906, requires every applicant to swear to "support and defend the Constitution."

Though the law says nothing about bearing arms in defense of the country, the official examiners ask her, as they ask all other applicants, whether she would be willing to do so.

On her negative answer and pacifist reasoning, the Supreme Court decides she is not entitled to citizenship. Three justices dissent, including Holmes, who says, "Some of her answers might excite popular prejudice, but if there is any principle of the Constitution that more imperatively calls for attachment than any other it is the principle of free thought—not free thought for those who agree with us but freedom for the thought that we hate."

Act II (1931). Douglas C. Macintosh, Canadian-born Chaplain of Yale Graduate School and Dwight Professor of Theology, applies for naturalization. He is willing to swear that he would bear arms in defense of the country, except in any war which might be unjust and contrary to his higher duty to God. The Supreme Court holds against him.

This time four Justices dissent—Hughes, Holmes, Brandeis and Stone. Chief Justice Hughes writes a noble dissenting opinion. He insists Congress never intended to authorize an oath that violated the spirit of our institutions. Laws for military draft have always recognized religious scruples. "The essence of religion is belief in a relation to God involving duties superior to those arising from any human relation." The great Chief Justice calls this "our happy tradition."

Act III (interlude to 1946). In six successive Congresses, bills are proposed to reverse the Schwimmer and Macintosh holdings by providing expressly for religious objections. All such efforts fail. In 1940 Congress codifies the naturalization laws and leaves the oath as silent as before on the entire question of bearing arms. Meanwhile, Holmes, Brandeis and Hughes retire from the court; Stone remains and becomes Chief Justice.

Act IV (1946). James L. Girouard, Canadian-born Seventh Day Adventist, applies for naturalization. In his registration for the draft, he has claimed exemption from combatant service only. Many Seventh Day Adventists serve as noncombatants in the medical corps; they object on religious grounds to combatant service. In the Supreme Court, Chief Justice Stone—to the astonishment of many—becomes spokesman for the denial of naturalization. In all sincerity, he reasons that the events in Act III show Congress' approval of the Macintosh decision as correctly interpreting the intent of the statute. Hence, he concludes, the court is bound.

To this Justices Reed and Frankfurter agree. But Justice William O. Douglas, speaking for the majority of the court, holds in favor of Girouard. Eloquently he supplements the earlier arguments of Holmes and Hughes. As for the circumstances in Act III, what did they prove? We ought not, he said, "place on the shoulders of Congress the burden of the court's own error." Thus, at long last, the ethical ensign is raised too high for Congress to overlook it.

Act V (1952). In a new naturalization statute, Congress finally discharges its duty. It expressly requires applicants to take an oath to bear arms in defense of the United States and makes exception for those who object on grounds of "religious training and belief." Objectors of this type can promise to do noncombatant work or other work of national importance.

But, under the new law, what shall be considered "religious training and belief?" A very subtle and nebulous phrase, yet Congress easily finds a definition: it is "belief in a relation to a Supreme Being involving duties superior to those arising from any human relation." (Whoever was alert during Act II will recognize the source of these words.) Thus, in respect of the naturalization oath, we return proudly to what Chief Justice Hughes called "our happy tradition."

The voices of the republic are not mere discord. Conflicts there must be from time to time, for when all conflicts cease, the spirit of political institutions dies. Yet amid the quiet harmonies, the rasps and the strange dissonances that accompany the American system, conflicts should not be confused with the principal theme. The theme is liberty and justice and compassion.

Inside View of
the High Court

by William J. Brennan, Jr.

THROUGHOUT ITS history the Supreme Court has been called upon
to face many of the dominant social, political, economic and even
philosophical issues that confront the nation. But Solicitor General Cox only recently reminded us that this does not mean that
the Court is charged with making social, political, economic or
philosophical decisions. Quite the contrary. The Court is not a
council of Platonic guardians for deciding our most difficult and
emotional questions according to the Justices' own notions of what
is just or wise or politic. To the extent that this is a governmental
function at all, it is the function of the people's elected representatives.

The Justices are charged with deciding according to law. Because
the issues arise in the framework of concrete litigation they must
be decided on facts embalmed in a record made by some lower
court or administrative agency. And while the Justices may and
do consult history and the other disciplines as aids to constitutional
decision, the text of the Constitution and relevant precedents dealing with that text are their primary tools.

It is indeed true, as Judge Learned Hand once said, that the

From the *New York Times Magazine,* October 6, 1963, copyright © 1963
by The New York Times Company.

judge's authority "depends upon the assumption that he speaks with the mouth of others: the momentum of his utterances must be greater than any which his personal reputation and character can command; if it is to do the work assigned to it—if it is to stand against the passionate resentments arising out of the interests he must frustrate—he must preserve his authority by cloaking himself in the majesty of an overshadowing past, but he must discover some composition with the dominant trends of his times."

However, we must keep in mind that, while the words of the Constitution are binding, their application to specific problems is not often easy. The Founding Fathers knew better than to pin down their descendants too closely. Enduring principles rather than petty details were what they sought. Thus the Constitution does not take the form of a litany of specifics. There are, therefore, very few cases where the constitutional answers are clear, all one way or all the other, and this is also true of the current cases raising conflicts between the individual and governmental power—an area increasingly requiring the Court's attention.

Ultimately, of course, the Court must resolve the conflicts of competing interests in these cases, but all Americans should keep in mind how intense and troubling these conflicts can be. Where one man claims a right to speak and the other man claims the right to be protected from abusive or dangerously provocative remarks the conflict is inescapable. Where the police have ample external evidence of a man's guilt, but to be sure of their case put into evidence a confession obtained through coercion, the conflict arises between his right to a fair prosecution and society's right to protection against his depravity. Where the orthodox Jew wishes to open his shop and do business on the day which non-Jews have chosen, and the Legislature has sanctioned, as a day of rest, the Court cannot escape a difficult problem of reconciling opposed interests. Finally, the claims of the Negro citizen, to borrow Solicitor General Cox's words, present a "conflict between the ideal of liberty and equality expressed in the Declaration of Independence, on the one hand, and, on the other hand, a way of life rooted in the customs of many of our people."

If all segments of our society can be made to appreciate that there are such conflicts, and that cases which involve constitutional rights often require difficult choices, if this alone is accomplished, we will have immeasurably enriched our common understanding of the meaning and significance of our freedoms. And we will have a better appreciation of the Court's function and its difficulties.

How conflicts such as these ought to be resolved constantly troubles our whole society. There should be no surprise, then, that how properly to resolve them often produces sharp division within the Court itself. When problems are so fundamental, the claims of the competing interests are often nicely balanced, and close divisions are almost inevitable.

Supreme Court cases are usually one of three kinds: the "original" action brought directly in the Court by one state against another state or states, or between a state or states and the Federal Government. Only a handful of such cases arise each year, but they are an important handful. A recent example was the contest between Arizona and California over the waters of the lower basin of the Colorado River. Another was the contest between the Federal Government and the newest state of Hawaii over the ownership of lands in Hawaii.

The second kind of case seeks review of the decisions of a Federal Court of Appeals—there are 11 such courts—or of a decision of a Federal District Court—there is a Federal District Court in each of the 50 states.

The third kind of case comes from a state court—the Court may review a state court judgment by the highest court of any of the 50 states, if the judgment rests on the decision of a Federal question.

When I came to the Court seven years ago the aggregate of the cases in the three classes was 1,600. In the term just completed there were 2,800, an increase of 75 per cent in seven years. Obviously, the volume will have doubled before I complete 10 years of service. How is it possible to manage such a huge volume of cases? The answer is that we have the authority to screen them and select for argument and decision only those which, in our judgment, guided by pertinent criteria, raise the most important and far-reaching questions. By that device we select annually around 6 per cent—between 150 and 170 cases—for decision. That screening process works like this: When nine Justices sit, it takes five to decide a case on the merits. But it takes only the votes of four of the nine to put a case on the argument calendar for argument and decision. Those four votes are hard to come by—only an exceptional case raising a significant Federal question commands them.

Each application for review is usually in the form of a short petition, attached to which are any opinions of the lower courts in the case. The adversary may file a response—also, in practice, usually short. Both the petition and response identify the Federal questions allegedly involved, argue their substantiality, and whether they were properly raised in the lower courts. Each Justice receives copies of the petition and response and such parts of the record as the parties may submit. Each Justice then, without any consultation at this stage with the others, reaches his own tentative conclusion whether the application should be granted or denied.

The first consultation about the case comes at the Court conference at which the case is listed on the agenda for discussion. We sit in conference almost every Friday during the term. Conferences begin at 10 in the morning and often continue until 6, except for a half-hour recess for lunch. Only the Justices are present. There are no law clerks, no stenographers, no secretaries, no pages—just the nine of us. The junior Justice acts as guardian of the door, receiving and delivering any messages that come in or go from the conference.

The conference room is a beautifully oak-paneled chamber with one side lined with books from floor to ceiling. Over the mantel of the exquisite marble fireplace at one end hangs the only adornment in the chamber—a portrait of Chief Justice John Marshall. In the middle of the room stands a rectangular table, not too large but large enough for the nine of us comfortably to gather around it. The Chief Justice sits at the south end and Mr. Justice Black, the senior Associate Justice, at the north end. Along the side to the left of the Chief Justice sit Justices Stewart, Goldberg, White and Harlan. On the right side sit Justice Clark, myself and Justice Douglas in that order.

We are summoned to conference by a buzzer which rings in our several chambers five minutes before the hour. Upon entering the conference room each of us shakes hands with his colleagues. The handshake tradition originated when Chief Justice Fuller presided many decades ago. It is a symbol that harmony of aims if not of views is the Court's guiding principle.

Each of us has his copy of the agenda of the day's cases before him. The agenda lists the cases applying for review. Each of us before coming to the conference has noted on his copy his tentative view whether or not review should be granted in each case.

The Chief Justice begins the discussion of each case. He then yields to the senior Associate Justice and discussion proceeds down the line in order of seniority until each Justice has spoken. Voting goes the other way. The junior Justice votes first and voting then proceeds up the line to the Chief Justice who votes last. Each of us has a docket containing a sheet for each case with appropriate places for recording the votes. When any case receives four votes for review, that case is transferred to the oral argument list. Applications in which none of us sees merit may be passed over without discussion.

Now how do we process the decisions we agree to review? There are rare occasions when the question is so clearly controlled by an earlier decision of the Court that a reversal of the lower court judgment is inevitable. In these rare instances we may summarily reverse without oral argument. The case must very clearly justify summary disposition, however, because our ordinary practice is not to reverse a decision without oral argument. Indeed, oral argument of cases taken for review, whether from the state or Federal courts, is the usual practice. We rarely accept submissions of cases on briefs.

Oral argument ordinarily occurs about four months after the application for review is granted. Each party is usually allowed one hour, but in recent years we have limited oral argument to a half-hour in cases thought to involve issues not requiring longer argument. Counsel submit their briefs and record in sufficient time for the distribution of one set to each Justice two or three weeks before the oral argument. Most of the members of the present Court follow the practice of reading the briefs before the argument. Some of us often have a bench memorandum prepared before the argument. This memorandum digests the facts and the arguments of both sides, highlighting the matters about which we may want to question counsel at the argument. Often I have independent research done in advance of argument and incorporate the results in the bench memorandum.

We follow a schedule of two weeks of argument from Monday through Thursday, followed by two weeks of recess for opinion writing and the study of petitions for review. The argued cases are listed on the conference agenda on the Friday following argument. Conference discussion follows the same procedure I have described for the discussion of certiorari petitions. Of course, it is much more extended. Not infrequently discussion of particular cases may be spread over two or more conferences.

Not until the discussion is completed and a vote taken is the opinion assigned. The assignment is not made at the conference but formally in writing some few days after the conference. The Chief Justice assigns the opinions in those cases in which he has voted with the majority. The senior Associate Justice voting with the majority assigns the opinions in the other cases. The dissenters agree among themselves who shall write the dissenting opinion. Of course, each Justice is free to write his own opinion, concurring or dissenting.

The writing of an opinion always takes weeks and sometimes months. The most painstaking research and care are involved. Research, of course, concentrates on relevant legal materials—precedents particularly. But Supreme Court cases often require some familiarity with history, economics, the social and other sciences, and authorities in these areas, too, are consulted when necessary.

When the author of an opinion feels he has an unanswerable document he sends it to a print shop, which we maintain in our building. The printed draft may be revised several times before his proposed opinion is circulated among the other Justices. Copies are sent to each member of the Court, those in the dissent as well as those in the majority.

Now the author often discovers that his work has only begun.

He receives a return, ordinarily in writing, from each Justice who voted with him and sometimes also from the Justices who voted the other way. He learns who will write the dissent if one is to be written. But his particular concern is whether those who voted with him are still of his view and what they have to say about his proposed opinion. Often some who voted with him at conference will advise that they reserve final judgment pending the circulation of the dissent. It is a common experience that dissents change votes, even enough votes to become the majority. I have had to convert more than one of my proposed majority opinions into a dissent before the final decision was announced. I have also, however, had the more satisfying experience of rewriting a dissent as a majority opinion for the Court.

Before everyone has finally made up his mind a constant interchange by memoranda, by telephone, at the lunch table, continues while we hammer out the final form of the opinion. I had one case during the past term in which I circulated 10 printed drafts before one was approved as the Court opinion.

The point of this procedure is that each Justice, unless he disqualifies himself in a particular case, passes on every piece of business coming to the Court. The Court does not function by means of committees or panels. Each Justice passes on each petition, each item, no matter how drawn, in longhand, by typewriter, or on a press. Our Constitution vests the judicial power in only one Supreme Court. This does not permit Supreme Court action by committees, panels, or sections.

The method that the Justices use in meeting an enormous caseload varies. There is one uniform rule: Judging is not delegated. Each Justice studies each case in sufficient detail to resolve the question for himself. In a very real sense, each decision is an individual decision of every Justice. The process can be a lonely, troubling experience for fallible human beings conscious that their best may not be adequate to the challenge. "We are not unaware," the late Justice Jackson said, "that we are not final because we are infallible; we know that we are infallible only because we are final." One does not forget how much may depend on his decision. He knows that usually more than the litigants may be affected, that the course of vital social, economic and political currents may be directed.

This then is the decisional process in the Supreme Court. It is not without its tensions, of course—indeed, quite agonizing tensions at times. I would particularly emphasize that, unlike the case of a Congressional or White House decision, Americans demand of their Supreme Court judges that they produce a written opinion, the collective expression of the judges subscribing to it, setting forth the reasons which led them to the decision. These opinions are the exposition, not just to lawyers, legal scholars and other judges, but to our whole society, of the bases upon which a particular result rests—why a problem, looked at as disinterestedly and dispassionately as nine human beings trained in a tradition of the disinterested and dispassionate approach can look at it, is answered as it is.

It is inevitable, however, that Supreme Court decisions—and the Justices themselves—should be caught up in public debate and be the subjects of bitter controversy. An editorial in The Washington Post did not miss the mark by much in saying that this was so because "one of the primary functions of the Supreme Court is to keep the people of the country from doing what they would like to do—at times when what they would like to do runs counter to the Constitution. . . . The function of the Supreme Court is not to count constituents; it is to interpret a fundamental charter which imposes restraints on constituents. Independence and integrity, not popularity, must be its standards."

Certainly controversy over its work has attended the Court throughout its history. As Professor Paul A. Freund of Harvard remarked, this has been true almost since the Court's first decision:

"When the Court held, in 1793, that the State of Georgia could be sued on a contract in the Federal courts, the outraged Assembly of that state passed a bill declaring that any Federal marshal who should try to collect the judgment would be guilty of a felony and would suffer death, without benefit of clergy, by being hanged. When the Court decided that state criminal convictions could be reviewed in the Supreme Court, Chief Justice Roane of Virginia exploded, calling it a 'most monstrous and unexampled decision.

It can only be accounted for by that love of power which history informs us infects and corrupts all who possess it, and from which even the eminent and upright judges are not exempt.' "

But public understanding has not always been lacking in the past. Perhaps it exists today. But surely a more informed knowledge of the decisional process should aid a better understanding.

It is not agreement with the Court's decisions that I urge. Our law is the richer and the wiser because academic and informed lay criticism is part of the stream of development. It is only a greater awareness of the nature and limits of the Supreme Court's function that I seek. I agree fully with the Solicitor General: It is essential, just because the public questions which the Court faces are pressing and divisive, that they be thoroughly canvassed in public, each step at a time, while the Court is evolving new principles. The ultimate resolution of questions fundamental to the whole community must be based on a common consensus of understanding of the unique responsibility assigned to the Supreme Court in our society.

The lack of that understanding led Mr. Justice Holmes to say 50 years ago:

"We are very quiet there, but it is the quiet of a storm center, as we all know. Science has taught the world skepticism and has made it legitimate to put everything to the test of proof. Many beautiful and noble reverences are impaired, but in these days no one can complain if any institution, system, or belief is called on to justify its continuance in life. Of course we are not excepted and have not escaped. Doubts are expressed that go to our very being. Not only are we told that when Marshall pronounced an Act of Congress unconstitutional he usurped a power that the Constitution did not give, but we are told that we are the representatives of a class—a tool of the money power. I get letters, not always anonymous, intimating that we are corrupt. Well, gentlemen, I admit that it makes my heart ache. It is very painful, when one spends all the energies of one's soul in trying to do good work, with no thought but that of solving a problem according to the rules by which one is bound, to know that many see sinister motives and would be glad of evidence that one was consciously bad. But we must take such things philosophically and try to see what we can learn from hatred and distrust and whether behind them there may not be a germ of inarticulate truth.

"The attacks upon the Court are merely an expression of the unrest that seems to wonder vaguely whether law and order pay. When the ignorant are taught to doubt they do not know what they safely may believe. And it seems to me that at this time we need education in the obvious more than investigation of the obscure."

"Warren Court" —An Opinion

by Bernard Schwartz

ON THE north and south walls of the Supreme Court Chamber are carved two marble panels depicting processions of historical lawgivers, beginning with Menes, the first Pharaoh of Egypt. Of the eighteen figures on the panels, only the last one is a judge, and he is the one American represented: John Marshall. This is more than mere coincidence; it sharply illustrates a basic difference between American law and that in other countries. It was Marshall who established the role of the Supreme Court as the authoritative expounder of the Constitution, and, in consequence, the court, more even than the political branches, has been *the* lawgiver in our system.

The role of the highest court as lawgiver has been dramatically underlined by the historic decisions rendered during recent weeks. These decisions, seen by many to mark a basic shift in the court's approach to constitutional issues, have focused attention once again upon the primordial part played by our unique supreme judicial institution.

More than that, they have reemphasized most strikingly the significance of the individual makeups of the men who sit on the

From the *New York Times Magazine,* June 30, 1957, copyright © 1957 by The New York Times Company.

supreme bench. It is the change in personnel under the Eisenhower Administration that has led to the present shift in the high tribunal's jurisprudence. Paradoxically perhaps, it has been the justices appointed by a relatively conservative President who have been responsible for the most liberal Supreme Court decisions handed down in over a decade.

Of the four court appointments made thus far by President Eisenhower, the most important, without any doubt, has been that of Earl Warren as Chief Justice. For it has been more than mere formalism that, ever since Marshall's day, has made it customary to designate the high court by the name of its chief. And each court has stood for different approaches to constitutional questions, approaches which are intimately associated with the personalities of the titular heads of such courts.

Thus, it is as the Warren Court that the present tribunal will be known to legal historians. It will bear the hallmark of Earl Warren as unmistakably as did prior courts those of his predecessors.

One who looks only to the bare legal powers of the Chief Justice will find it hard to understand this underscoring of his pre-eminence. Aside from his designation as chief of the court and the attribution to him of a slightly higher salary, his position is not legally superior to that of his colleagues. In Justice Clark's recent words, "the Chief Justice has no more authority than other members of the court."

This approach to the Chief Justiceship, while true in a formalistic sense, overlooks the extralegal potential inherent in that position. The Chief Justice may be only *primus inter pares;* but he is clearly *primus.* Somebody has to preside over a body of nine men, and it is the chief who does preside, both in open court and in the even more important work of deciding cases in the conference chamber. It is the Chief Justice who directs the business of the court. He controls the discussion in conference; his is the prerogative to call and discuss cases before the other justices speak.

In this respect, his role has been well said to be that of striking the pitch, as it were, for the orchestra. It is his example that will, most often, set the tone of the entire conference session.

In addition, it has become settled by custom that it is for the Chief Justice to assign the writing of court opinions. This function has been called the most important that pertains to the office of chief. In discharging it, a great Chief Justice has been compared to a general deploying his army. It is he who determines what use will be made of the court's personnel; his employment of the assigning power will both influence the growth of the law and his own relations with his colleagues.

Charles Evans Hughes' manner of presiding over the court has been compared to Toscanini leading an orchestra. It is premature to make the same claim for Earl Warren's leadership. Still, though Warren does not as yet conduct with all the skill of a Toscanini, it cannot be denied that he has brought more authority to the Chief Justiceship than has been the case since Hughes. Before Warren the dominant theme on the high bench was discord; all too often the court presented a far from edifying spectacle of internal atomization.

To be sure, judicial dissension has not turned into sweetness and light merely because of Warren's appointment to the central chair. Sharp divisions and dissents exist even on the Warren bench. But these differences are no longer, as they all too often were before Warren, reflections of personal antagonisms. Intellectual issues have once again come to be dealt with purely as such. Today, for almost the first time since Hughes' retirement, dissonance has ceased to be the major court characteristic.

The restoration of its institutional ethos to a court that was sorely in need of it has, indeed, been Earl Warren's primary contribution thus far. And it is one which outranks any that he has been able to make to our substantive law. It may be, as John Winthrop said in 1644, that "Judges are gods upon earth." But a pantheon that speaks with nine inconsistent voices can hardly inspire the listener with the feeling of divine certainty.

It may seem strange that Warren has been able to restore unity to a bench of judges, when he himself had no judicial experience whatever prior to his appointment. The lack of such experience was, in fact, the main objection raised against Warren, especially among the organized bar.

If the President were going to choose other than an established judge, however, he could hardly have selected a man more qualified for the present needs of the court than Warren. Starting at the bottom of the California political ladder, he became a successful prosecuting attorney, then was elected Attorney General, and finally Governor. He was the only man ever elected to three successive terms as California's Governor, his third election being achieved (under California's cross-filing system) with the nomination of both major parties. The popularity of his administration made him a national figure, Republican Vice Presidential candidate in 1948, and an oft-mentioned Presidential possibility.

What are the primary assets of a successful Governor? He must be a leader, able to guide men toward attainment of his program. He must be capable of working effectively with men whom he cannot coerce, such as members of the Legislature, whose cooperation is essential. He must be an effective conciliator of diverse viewpoints, never letting intraparty strife destroy the essential unity of purpose needed for political success. He must be an able administrator, capable of controlling all the different facets of the modern executive branch. Above all, he must have a reputation for fairness and integrity and the aura of competence and prestige that Americans have come to expect in those vested with high office.

All these attributes were possessed by Governor Warren and it was their possession that permitted him to make his outstanding record. They are precisely the attributes that have enabled him successfully to make the transition from the executive mansion to the high court.

It is a mistake to conceive of the Chief Justiceship solely in terms of learning in the law. Of course, the Supreme Court is a law court. But it is, and has been since Marshall, unique among courts. Public, not private, law is the stuff of its litigation. Elevation to it requires adjustment from preoccupation with the restricted, however novel, problems of private litigation to the most exacting demands of judicial statesmanship. On such a tribunal the judge must be even more the statesman than the lawyer.

This is particularly true of the man who sits at the center of the court. The main monument of Warren's judicial statesmanship is, of course, the 1954 decision in the school segregation case. It was under Warren's lead that the court seized the vital constitutional issue by the bit (the same issue which had been meticulously avoided under Warren's predecessor) and unanimously outlawed school segregation.

The element of unanimity cannot be overemphasized. It was no mean feat for the court's neophyte (as he then was), vested only with the moral prestige of the Chief Justiceship, to induce eight individualists, accustomed to arriving at decisions in their own ways and never hesitant at articulating their separate views, to join in the unanimous decision—without even a single concurring voice to detract from the majesty and forthrightness of his opinion.

Though Warren's chief contribution to the court has been on the administrative side, his influence on the substantive law dispensed by the high tribunal should not be overlooked. In this respect, Warren's approach has differed drastically from that of his predecessor. In cases involving conflicts between government and the individual, Fred Vinson was usually on the side of officialdom. Warren, on the other hand, starts with a strong predisposition in favor of the individual.

It has been under Warren's leadership that the Vinson court, almost invariably on the side of governmental authority, has been replaced by a tribunal inclined to look on claims of violation of individual rights with a far more friendly eye. This has been dramatically illustrated by the decisions of the past few weeks. "When the generation of 1980 receives from us the Bill of Rights," Warren has said, "the document will not have exactly the same meaning it had when we received it from our fathers." The Bill of Rights as it is being interpreted by the Warren Court already has a different meaning than that handed down to it by its predecessor.

One cognizant of the values involved in the Bill of Rights cannot help but feel sympathetic toward the protective zeal now shown by the high court. It is not, all the same, mere caviling to point out that judicial predisposition toward the libertarian result may be a two-edged sword. Properly employed, it can restore the essential balance between liberty and authority, which the Vinson court had upset in favor of governmental pretensions.

Carried to its extreme, however, judicial libertarianism can lead the court to assume undue authority over the other branches. This could make for a renaissance of the high tribunal as supreme censor of legislative and executive action—a role the court has renounced ever since the "switch in time that saved nine" that effectively put an end to the court-packing plan of twenty years ago.

What was it that the Supreme Court had done in the years before 1937 to which much of the country objected so strongly? It was the erection by the justices of their personal predilections into constitutional dogmas which could not be touched by the Legislature. It is true that the old court's action in that respect was almost entirely limited to the economic field; yet that was so because it was in that field that legislative action was upsetting the justices' preconceptions.

Today, none of the justices has difficulty in accepting governmental regulation that would have seemed all but revolutionary to the court majority before 1937. In the economic area, then, deference to the other branches accords with the personal convictions of the present court. The same is not true in the area of personal rights. Here, legislative restrictions run counter to the libertarian predispositions of most of the justices. But are these justices any more justified in writing their private predilections into the Constitution than were their pre-1937 predecessors?

Consistency in a court committed to the overriding values of democracy is not only consistency in seeking the libertarian result in all cases. Even restrictions on individual freedoms must be upheld when they are required for the preservation of other, more vital interests of society. If there is a danger in the recent tendency of the Warren court, it is that the justices may overlook this and permit their personal libertarian convictions to override even necessary restrictions on individual rights.

As yet, this danger is more theoretical than real. The actual holdings in recent decisions are not nearly so extreme as the reaction they have aroused. What is true, nevertheless, is that the court's language in these cases has been much broader and less restrained than the bare decisions themselves. The responsibility for the immoderate recent dicta must be laid, in large measure, at the door of the Chief Justice. It is the chief's job to restrain his colleagues against extreme language, unwarranted by the actual case. Instead, Warren himself has been as guilty as any of uttering unduly broad dicta.

In the recent Watkins case the court's bare holding was that the scope of authority of a Congressional committee must be spelled out with unambiguous clarity by the resolution creating it, and witnesses must be shown clearly the relevance of questions asked. These are needed checks upon legislative inquisitions and do not impair Congress' essential investigatory function. But Warren, who delivered the opinion, did not stop with this holding. He seized the occasion to read an essay upon abuse of investigatory power and the relation of such power to various constitutional provisions —all of which was unnecessary to the court's narrow holding.

The deficiencies in the Watkins opinion may be traced, at least in part, to Warren's lack of prior judicial experience. A master of the judicial craft does not adjudge in advance, by an omnibus answer to an omnibus question. He deals only with the particular instance; and he waits till it clearly arises. He is, in Cardozo's phrase, cautious, even timid, fearful of the vivid word, the heightened phrase. He dreams of an unworthy breed of scions, the spawn of careless dicta. Even in a case like Watkins', he realizes that he is not a judicial gladiator making a last stand against the Congressional lions.

The administrative side and the judicial side—these are but two faces of a single coin, which is the specie of a great Chief Justice. If Warren has in part proved deficient in his judicial side, he has already displayed greater eminence as an administrator than any court head since Hughes. And it was more a great statesman than a great common-law judge that the high bench needed after Hughes' retirement. Harlan Fiske Stone, Hughes' successor, was an outstanding judge. Yet his lack of administrative ability helped all but to destroy the court's effectiveness as a collegiate tribunal.

Warren may not be Stone's equal in purely legal qualifications. But his skill as a statesman has already done much to repair the damage done to the court's prestige under his predecessors.

When the Public Judges the Court

by Alan F. Westin

IN THE PAST three years, the Supreme Court has been denounced for "judicial misbehavior" by a wide assortment of critics, ranging from the American Bar Association and Southern officialdom to state court judges and the Daughters of the American Revolution. Bills and constitutional amendments have been sponsored in Congress to limit the Court's jurisdiction, and to make the justices think twice before extending their "offensive" doctrines.

To listen to many of the wisest commentators on our constitutional politics, this imbroglio is not strikingly different from situations which the Supreme Court has encountered ever since the days of Chief Justice John Marshall and his self-declared archfoe, Thomas Jefferson. But is it? In my opinion, this battle between Court and critics is distinctly different from any other in our history.

In each previous struggle over the proper role for the Federal judiciary in our governmental system, a property issue has been at the heart of the controversy. While the doctrines of the justices have always been a matter of debate, there were five notable periods when the Supreme Court became a leading political issue,

From the *New York Times Magazine*, May 31, 1959, copyright © 1959 by The New York Times Company.

and prompted campaigns by powerful blocs in Congress to alter the Court's personnel or its powers.

The year 1821-24 and 1831-33 saw protests against the Court's interference with state regulation of banks, land titles, companies and other parts of the mercantile establishment. Arguments during 1857-60 dealt with the Court's treatment of slavery as a property matter and the impact of the slave system upon the economies of the West, North and South. The years 1896-1912 were marked by protests against the Federal judiciary's insulation of corporate enterprise from both state and national measures aimed at monopoly, taxation and labor relations. Finally, 1934-37 centered on the Supreme Court's barriers to social welfare legislation and to national management of the national corporate economy. In all of these episodes, powerful economic interests were directly involved in defense of their privileges.

The current debate over the Court's role has no comparable economic basis. The reason for this lies in the character of the decisions that have precipitated protest. While the Supreme Court under Chief Justices Vinson and Warren has not been a "pro-business" Court, as in the days of Chief Justices Marshall or Taft, neither has it been "anti-business." In matters directly affecting business, as in labor relations, anti-trust and tax issues, the Warren Court has been simply an enunciator of the "social capitalist" *status quo* in American politics.

Instead of property issues, the present controversy deals with matters of liberty and equality. Where the outcome of disputed cases in the past decided what people could do with their property, free from Government restraint, the new cases decide what people can advocate and organize to promote, which people are consigned to be "more equal than others," and what procedures Government may follow in apprehending and prosecuting the non-propertied antisocial elements in our population.

Where the beneficiaries of the Court's rulings were once land speculators, planters, railroads and public utility holding companies, the new befriended are Negroes, syndicate leaders, Communists, balky college professors, rapists and Government employes accused of disloyalty.

Accompanying this shift in the issues has been an equally fundamental shift in the groups who attack and defend the judiciary. Previously, it was the spokesmen for liberalism and majority rule—from Jeffersonians to New Dealers—who denounced the Supreme Court. They did so on the rational liberal theory that the Court was an insufferable restraint upon majority will. In a democratic society, they argued, judges with life tenure had no right to substitute their notions of good policy for the wishes of the people acting through their elected representatives—Congress, the President, and state governments.

Yet, in the Nineteen Fifties, liberal groups are defending the judiciary as a wise agency to check mass passions and to protect natural rights from invasion by the "political" branches of Government.

A similar reversal has taken place in the conservative camp. Previously, liberal critics were opposed by propertied groups who declared, in rational conservative doctrine, that the Supreme Court was a badly needed brake upon populist democracy. Yet, in the Nineteen Fifties, the critics of the Court are led by groups we ordinarily associate with conservatism—the American Legion, the D.A.R., the American Bar Association, state and local law-enforcement officers, Southerners, right-wing Republicans and Democrats in Congress, and the like. Their cry now is that the Supreme Court is tampering with the wise conclusions of the people's representatives, and they denounce the notion that any doctrine of higher right permits the judiciary to intervene.

Finally, this is the first conflict not to present basically a party-line division. Previously, Jefferson, Jackson, Lincoln, Bryan and Roosevelt led the bulk of their party faithful against the disputed judicial doctrines. The party dominated by property interests being protected by the Court defended the justices. Today, with property issues absent, there are no party positions. Eisenhower remains aloof. Stevenson supports the Court. Congressional Republicans and Democrats are divided. In this controversy, conservatives among the two parties face liberals from the two parties.

What do these changes import for the present controversy over judicial review? On this score, I think it may be wiser to ask questions and supply speculations than to issue firm conclusions.

First of all, why have liberal and conservative elements changed positions? Have the ideological bases of these classic camps undergone a transformation in the Nineteen Fifties? I think the answer is less spectacular than that. An overwhelming majority of liberals now defend the Supreme Court and judicial review because the justices are handing down rulings on liberty and equality issues which accord with liberal beliefs. Conservatives are opposing the Court because it has become "dangerously unsound" on these matters.

It is clear that whether a group's ideological toe has been pinched is the first determinant of whether the pinching institution will be praised or damned. Since the five major crises over judicial review in our past found the Court steadfastly devoted to conservative positions, the simple explanation of the first liberal switch toward judicial review is that liberals have had to wait from 1790 until the Nineteen Fifties to find a set of justices to whom they could attach their allegiance.

A second question is why a majority of justices came to make this shift of positions possible. On this subject, since justices do not allow themselves to be polled or given Rorschach tests, the area of speculation is remarkably wide.

Perhaps, like nature, Supreme Court justices abhor a vacuum. Since 1937, a majority of justices have been committed to the concept of "judicial self-restraint" in matters of economic regulation by the elected branches of government. For two decades, not a single Federal tax measure, regulation of commerce, national welfare program or labor law has been declared unconstitutional.

While there was some talk within the Court between 1937 and 1953 of applying a different, more interventionist, standard of review for liberty and equality cases, a majority of the Court generally applied self-restraint across the board. Appointees who looked forward to enunciating high constitutional principles must have chafed under these self-imposed bonds.

By itself, I doubt whether this yearning for glory would have precipitated the departures of 1953-59. The personal discomfort coincided, though, with urging by powerful elements, including the Eisenhower Administration, to advance from the "gradualist" approach of the Vinson Court on equality matters and overturn the whole separate-but-equal doctrine of racial segregation. Growing sentiment in condemnation of the Court's "ducking" of fundamental issues, rising anti-McCarthyite spirit in the nation after 1954 and the arrival on the Court's docket of liberty cases which represented the most excessive and least necessary aspects of the internal security programs—all these factors pressed in upon the Court.

However, the Supreme Court, or even a majority, is not something with a life of its own. Justices are distinctly individuals, with viscera and predilections inside them rather than gears or I.B.M. cards. Thus one has to consider personalities as well as "forces" to reach satisfactory explanations of judicial behavior.

Chief Justice Vinson and Justices Jackson, Reed, Minton and Burton were judges who either found the case for authority persuasive in most liberty cases or else felt that the Supreme Court ought to exercise self-restraint in these as well as property cases.

In place of these justices, the Eisenhower Administration has installed Chief Justice Warren and Justices Harlan, Brennan, Whittaker and Stewart. While there are important differences in constitutional philosophy among these men, ranging from the liberal interventionist credo of Warren and Brennan to the legal institutionalist focus of Harlan, the Eisenhower appointees as a group are different from the justices they replaced.

Trained in law school when legal realism was at its height, and free from personal involvement in the anti-Court, judicial self-restraint fight of the Nineteen Thirties, these men approach the post-1954 cases with a freer and less self-conscious perspective than their predecessors.

However, I think the earlier justices, had they still been on the Court when the outer limits of the internal security issue were reached, between 1954 and the present, would also have been impelled to take a more active position than they had previously. Justice Frankfurter, for example, has found a way to vote against Government action and for defendants far more after 1954 than he had before. Justice Jackson would very likely have done the same.

In support of this hypothesis, it is useful to remember that courts have a way of defending liberty after a crisis has passed its peak. A delay in constitutional showdowns occurs on the theory that only when the dangers of excess are demonstrable and hysteria has diminished will the public heed the justices' call to constitutional ideals.

It is also pertinent to note that the liberty and equality issues, while similar in being non-propertied, do not represent identical problems for the Supreme Court. This has led to two different configurations within the Court. On cases dealing with segregation and its implementation the justices have presented a 9-0 face to the nation. Here, liberal interventionism is the judicial credo.

In liberty matters the present Supreme Court has a four-man interventionist core made up of Chief Justice Warren and Justices Black, Douglas and Brennan. Justices Frankfurter, Harlan and Whittaker have joined the four-man liberal phalanx in many of the disputed liberty cases, but usually with opinions which adopted more limited grounds for the result in the cases. Justice Clark has been in dissent in virtually all liberty cases. This leaves Justice Stewart, who has not participated in enough cases as yet to indicate exactly what his position represents, but seems to lean to the Frankfurter-Harlan group. Thus, close divisions are destined to be the rule in the liberty cases, with a divided court mirroring non-sectional public divisions on these questions.

A third question to consider is what effect these changes in the fight over judicial review will have upon the Supreme Court's power position, or, put another way, whether the Court can find as powerful a constituency to support it today as in the past.

Most Americans are not used to thinking that the Supreme Court has a constituency, like Congressmen with their electoral districts or the President with the national electorate. Yet the Supreme Court, despite life tenure for its members and a tradition of judge-worship in the population, remains a highly vulnerable institution. Decrees from the high tribunal are realistically enforced only if the President and Congress acquiesce in them and public opinion supports—or is not actively opposed to—the basic trend of decision.

Who will support the Court today? It seems to me that business conservatives have been uncommitted so far in the present Court controversy and are likely to remain so as long as the Court does not add anti-business decisions to its disputed doctrines. To be sure, a few men associated with business organs, such as David Lawrence, have joined in the attack upon the justices, but I think it is more significant to note that corporate spokesmen and business associations, such as the N.A.M., have chosen to stay out of this campaign.

Can the Court depend upon liberals, plus residual Court-worship in the population, to defend it against the nonbusiness conservatives? As Congressional events in 1958 showed, the Court's critics are far from few. With the unending animus of the Southerners (and Southern political power in Congress) to lead the drive, the Court is faced with more than a temporary round of dissent.

On the other hand, it would be a mistake to underestimate the strength of the Court's defenders in the new political atmosphere of post–World War II America. With the importance of Negro voters constantly growing in urban politics outside the South, and with white groups such as Jews continuing to identify themselves strongly with the anti-segregation issue, the Court's equality decisions are likely to be supported not just by liberal groups but by the urban machine leaders of both our political parties.

I think the Court has a somewhat rockier road for its liberty decisions, and it would not be at all surprising to see Congress reverse several specific rulings such as those dealing with the Smith Act, passport policy or state sedition laws. Even on the liberty side, however, the Court is not altogether defenseless. Distaste for McCarthyism, a desire for more careful scrutiny of internal security measures and concern for fair procedure seem to be steadily increasing since 1954.

Indeed, the existing sense of moderation is indicated in the fact that many local bar associations have dissented from the American Bar Association's criticism of the Supreme Court, that the A.B.A.'s resolution was really rather mild and that the president of the A.B.A. has felt it wise to stress publicly that the A.B.A. had no intention to attack the Court but only to suggest stronger anti-subversive machinery.

I do not mean to give the impression that a determinist tide rules the future of the present conflict over judicial review. Much will depend on how wisely and well the justices decide specific cases, when they choose to intervene and when to leave issues to the political branches of government, and whether the Court displays that basic craftsmanship in opinions without which a judge appears naked to those who do not agree with the results in cases.

The debate will also be affected by many factors not under the control of the justices at all, such as whether the nation can find a President who understands what the justices are saying and will place the prestige of the White House behind the Court's decisions.

At present the Court seems firmly fixed in its course. For the interventionist justices there are the lures of making high national policy and promoting liberal goals to spur them onward. For the justices who lean toward judicial self-restraint there are other compelling factors. Concerned with the prestige of the Court, they realize that the Court cannot draw back from its desegregation approach without compromising its basic position.

On the liberty side they realize that the arrival of radical anti-subversive measures, threatening the traditional values of fair procedure and ordered liberty, has impelled them to take the distinctly moderate stands inaccurately described by angry critics as sweeping doctrines. There is nothing which can stiffen a good judge's back more firmly than erroneous charges by groups which equate assumption of inescapable responsibility with a "treasonous" arrogation of power.

Whatever this examination of the history of American judicial review indicates about the present or the future, one thing seems clear. French proverbs to the contrary notwithstanding, the more things change, the less likely they are really to be the same. History may teach the justices that they are not the first to face fundamental attacks, but this Court will have to find its own path to success in dealing with "status" issues which have replaced property politics of past generations.

Also on the Bench: "Dominant Opinion"

by Alan F. Westin

DURING THE past six months, hardly a day has gone by without some influential figure in American public life denouncing the United States Supreme Court. Twenty-five United States Senators and 75 Representatives in this period have delivered speeches in Congress attacking the Court's constitutional outlook. Hostile editorials have appeared in over 150 newspapers. Arthur Krock of The New York Times has complained that the Court's "big brother" attitude constitutes a clear case of "judicial usurpation." Police officials and state judges have attacked the justices for "handcuffing" law enforcement.

The American Bar Association has heard its outgoing president lash the Court for gravely undermining "property rights," "internal security," "good citizenship," and other key values of our system. Many Catholic and Protestant church leaders have criticized the justices for rulings allegedly "secularizing" national life and "protecting immorality" from prosecution, and a shudder of apprehension greeted the Court's recent announcement that it would review two cases involving Bible reading and Lord's Prayer recitation in public schools. When asked recently what businessmen thought of

From the *New York Times Magazine*, October 21, 1962, copyright © 1962 by The New York Times Company.

the Court, the general counsel of one major corporation replied: "Well, it pays to be a Negro or a Communist if you want justice from the Warren Court. Business doesn't get it."

Is this criticism only a continuation of the protests that Southerners, conservatives and fundamentalist religious leaders have been aiming at the Court since the middle nineteen-fifties? Does the recent increase in their volume point to another Court-curbing debate in 1963, comparable to the fight over the Jenner-Butler Bills in 1958? Most important of all, how is the public responding to the Court's disputed rulings of the nineteen-sixties, and does the Court respond in turn to the public?

Any discussion of Supreme Court criticism must start with the recognition that the justices are subject to many direct and indirect controls under our constitutional system. Constitutional amendments and Congressional legislation can reverse unpopular rulings. The Constitution specifically gives Congress control over the Court's appellate jurisdiction and this can be used to cut off the Court's review of specific areas of controversy. Presidents are usually able to appoint new justices and can deliberately seek to change the voting balances within the Court through these appointments. State and Federal officials can mount embarrassingly effective resistance to the Court's orders, ranging from subtle inaction to open defiance, since the justices must usually look to elected officials to enforce their orders. The bar and bench can raise influential protests against the Court's legal arguments and its professional competence. And every Supreme Court, finally, is acutely sensitive to any continuous, widespread mistrust of its decisions by the general public.

Reflecting these realities, no Supreme Court in American history has ever defied for long the sustained will of "dominant opinion" in the nation. When the Court has met the determined will of these dominant forces—as it faced the Radical Republicans in 1866-68 or the New Deal in 1936-37—the existing Court majority has always modified its disputed doctrines to uphold the measure insisted upon by dominant opinion. As Reed Powell said, the Court knows how to execute the "switch in time that saves nine."

The troublesome question in these political-judicial crises, of course, is how to define and measure "dominant opinion." Clearly, the justices do not have to consult public opinion polls about their decisions, or party platforms or even the results of specific elections in which the voters hear debate over issues being considered by the Court. By "dominant opinion," we mean the active consensus of an era as represented in the "passionate truths" held by the majority of elected state and Federal officials; the leaders of the most influential economic, civic and religious groups, and those mass media trusted by the politically active public.

When wholesale criticism of its doctrines begins to dominate these key sectors, the Court must reconsider its checks on dominant opinion or else risk reprisals on charges of being "arrogant, unrepresentative and willful."

But the justices must also decide whether any given flood of attacks really represents dominant opinion or something less than that. If opinion in the nation is broadly divided over the Court's disputed doctrines, or if the Court is really the target of critics who are in dissent from the dominant opinion of their era, then the Court is not in ultimate crisis and the justices can pursue their views of the Constitution in the normal traditions of judicial independence and defense of "unpopular" constitutional rights.

Finally, it must also be realized that the storms that rage over the Court involve only a few of its rulings. Of the 250-275 cases it decides on their merits each year, fewer than a dozen normally make up the "constitutionally sensitive" cases that stir fundamental debate. Yet all the skill and wisdom displayed in the vast majority of its rulings will not alter the fact that it is by these sensitive cases that the Supreme Court will be judged, in its day and by history.

With these factors in mind, the constitutionally sensitive decisions of the present Court which have aroused so much criticism in the nineteen-sixties can be considered under four major headings: the continued application of earlier, disputed constitutional rulings; the Court's extension of existing doctrines beyond their previous boundaries; the entry of the Court into new fields of controversy; and its performance in the wide range of cases involving issues of internal security.

The first set of decisions under debate involves constitutional positions laid down by Court majorities before 1960. The present Court has simply been applying these. In segregation cases during

1960-62, for example, the Court struck down state racial discrimination practices at about the same pace as between 1954-59—drawing a similar volume of protest from Southern segregationists and their "hard conservative" allies like William Buckley Jr., who jointly deplore judicial interference with Southern "gradualism" in race relations. New issues, such as the sit-in demonstrations, have not yet been reached.

In cases involving Federal powers of taxation, spending and regulation of industry, the Court has continued to uphold Congressional measures despite the protests of corporate spokesmen that many of these activities are constitutionally forbidden to the national government. In the area of labor-management relations, the Court has continued to uphold Federal and state power over collective bargaining relationships—with Federal pre-eminence—again despite complaints from business and conservatives that these are either private or local matters.

On each of these issues, it seems clear that the present Court is moving in lockstep with the active consensus of this era. Public opinion and national political majorities support judicial activism in behalf of Negro civil rights and judicial self-restraint in matters of industrial relations and welfare programs. On these questions, the South, business and "hard conservatives" are the voice of pre-1929 and pre–World War II America. History has simply outrun their constitutional positions.

The second group of rulings under attack is made up of decisions in which the present Court has been extending significantly constitutional positions first adopted by earlier Court majorities. In the field of church-state relations, for example, the Court's ruling in 1961 that an oath of belief in God could not be required for holding state office, and the 1962 decision striking down a nondenominational prayer composed by the Regents in New York for the public schools, carried judicial review of public religious practices on to new ground.

The same is true with respect to state police methods and trial rules. While the Court has grappled with the meaning of "due process" for decades, a major step was taken in 1961 with its ruling that all evidence obtained illegally by police must be excluded from state criminal trials. Again, in dealing with government censorship of books and films, the Court of the nineteen-sixties has broadened considerably the area of constitutionally-protected expression.

These increased "interferences" with the action of elected officials account for much of the recent rise in Court criticism. The school prayer case set off more denunciation of the justices than any ruling since the segregation cases rallied Southern officialdom against the Court. When Congressman Glenn Cunningham of Nebraska commented this year that the Court's motto seemed to be "Obscenity, yes; prayer, no," he expressed the level of bitterness that many critics feel.

In matters of religion, censorship and law enforcement, national opinion and civic groups are deeply divided. This means that the Court has not received anything like the mandate from dominant opinion that it had had in the field of segregation or Federal regulation of industry. If anything, I think the balance of opinion probably tips to the side of the critics. It may be in instinctive recognition of this, therefore, that the Court has actually adopted quite guarded and flexible positions in these areas and has consciously refused to accept the absolute doctrines urged by Justices Black, Douglas, Brennan and Warren.

Thus the Court majority has *not* held that movies must be free from all censorship, or that every religious expression in public schools violates the Constitution or that state criminal procedure must conform exactly to Federal practice. The majority has chosen to advance more slowly, probing to see how far and how fast civil libertarian positions, previously rejected by local political majorities, can now be installed and obeyed because the Supreme Court says they should be.

The third main area in dispute involves the Court's wholly new departure in the state legislative apportionment case of 1962. Over the sharp protests of Justices Frankfurter and Harlan that the Court had deliberately avoided this "political thicket" for many years and should keep out of it still, six members of the Court voted that the citizen denied equal protection of the laws by discriminatory districting was entitled to judicial relief.

With the prospect that Federal judges will now oversee the constitutional fairness of apportionment in 50 states, critics have charged that this is an unprecedented invasion of States Rights and an improper intrusion by judges into the elective politics of the nation. Since the ruling threatens the present rural-conservative advantages in districting and promises to strengthen the representation of urban-suburban areas, the first public response divided largely along that line. Yet the significant thing is how much public support at the grass-roots level the Court's ruling seems to be gathering day by day.

Before the decision, only liberal stalwarts were seriously pressing for judicial intervention in this area. Many students of American politics had seemed resigned to gross gerrymandering as a permanent blemish on our democracy. But once the Court stepped in and unclogged the political process, a heavy flow of editorial and public support has developed for making districts fair—preferably by the states themselves but under minimum standards set by the courts. The alarmed cries of conservative critics seem to be falling on unappreciative ears.

The fourth and final group of decisions under attack is in the charged area of internal security, where critics contend that the justices have been steadily "hamstringing" the nation's fight against subversion. Last May, for example, the Chairman of the Senate Judiciary Committee, Senator James Eastland of Mississippi, stated that between 1953 and 1962, the Court had "sustained the position advocated by the Communists" in 46 out of 70 cases involving "Communist or subversive activities." By such decisions, the Senator said, the justices are "lending aid and comfort to the conspiracy" seeking to destroy this nation. Similar charges are heard often from some bar associations, civic groups and law-enforcement officers, and, of course, as the constant theme of the Radical Right.

Apart from their outrageous premise that judicial protection of constitutional rights is adopting a "Communist position," these attacks have a distinctly ironic character. During the Court-curb debates of 1958, internal-security stalwarts roundly denounced the Court for a dozen or more rapid-fire rulings in 1956-57 that upset Government anti-subversive prosecutions. The Court had questioned the scope of investigations by the House Committee on Un-American Activities, state investigations of "subversion" unconnected with state employes, state loyalty criteria for admission to the practice of law, Federal authority to withhold statements made to the Government by witnesses now testifying in Federal trials, the scope of Federal prosecutions of Communists under the Smith Act and dismissals of state employes for claiming the Fifth Amendment.

Civil libertarians greeted these decisions with cheers and many read them as high constitutional roadblocks against official "McCarthyism." But a storm of protest arose from conservatives. Congress swiftly passed a statute limiting the breadth of the ruling giving defendants access to witnesses' statements in Government files. Hostile Congressional investigations were held on several other rulings and a sharp Court-curb bill was defeated in the Senate by a 41-40 vote. As late as 1962, Congressional forces were still working to "undo" the Court's "mischief" of 1957; this spring saw the passage of an act reversing the Court's 1957 definition of a key Smith Act term.

By 1962, the Court majority had reacted by distinguishing or diluting virtually all of the bold and assertive rhetoric of the 1957 rulings. While the Court majority did not overrule earlier decisions, it permitted the House Un-American Activities Committee, Federal Smith Act prosecutors, state legislative investigators, state employment officials and state bar admission committees to do almost exactly what the 1957 rulings had seemed to forbid.

The Court's shift came not through the appointment of new justices but through a change in emphasis by Justices Frankfurter and Harlan. In 1956-57, they had voted with Chief Justice Warren and Justices Black, Douglas and Brennan to provide a majority for striking down extreme Government internal security measures. After 1957, however, Justices Frankfurter and Harlan voted with Justices Clark, Whittaker and Stewart to form a majority that upheld Government power in cases paralleling those of 1956-57.

What prompted this shift? The 1956-57 cases had reviewed internal security actions taken during the hysterical peak of the early nineteen-fifties. In 1957, anti-McCarthy sentiment was strong in the nation and the moment seemed ripe for judicial intervention against anti-Communist measures that were "popular" but, in the mind of the Court's majority, cut dangerously and unnecessarily into American civil liberties. So the Court freed some convicted people, wrote stirring opinions reaffirming our libertarian heritage, and warned Government to take more care in the future.

But when many officials of the states and nation responded by deliberately repeating their anti-Communist programs, when the public did not make such conduct politically unprofitable and when Court curb measures gained ominous momentum, the showdown was at hand. Should the Court transform the warnings of 1956-57 into flat commands outlawing these Government measures? And could the Court make such rulings stick?

To many Americans, and to Warren, Black, Douglas and Brennan, the answer was clear—of course, the Court should strike down "unconstitutional action," or else what are courts and the Constitution for? But for some of the justices, this answer was not enough. The insulation and isolation of the judiciary from elective responsibility, the need to encourage respect for the Constitution within the political process itself and the presence of sustained support for measures the justices might think desperately unwise but constitutionally on the border lines—these considerations are often paramount in moments of political-judicial crisis. Such factors were probably in the minds of Frankfurter and Harlan, leading them to follow the course of judicial self-restraint and to limit rather than extend the scope of the 1956-57 doctrines.

Could the Supreme Court have held fast to the larger implications of its 1956-57 rulings? The Court *did* remain firm on some sharply criticized rulings, such as those involving passport procedures, Federal loyalty-security programs and state sedition laws. Could it have maintained more? Given the ambiguous, if not hostile, position of the Eisenhower Administration toward the libertarian rulings of 1957 and given the strength of the Court's critics in Congress, an assertion of the full Warren-Black-Douglas-Brennan position would probably have produced swift reversals and even broad Court-curbs. Yet, though post-war generalship is easy, it is hard to believe that as complete a retreat as the Court carried out after 1957 was inescapable.

The Court could have asserted itself more, and even if some of its libertarian rulings had been reversed by Congress or by amendment, the debates stirred by this action would have turned the attention of the public to civil liberties in the cold war in a more systematic and educative way than has been achieved by the mere re-assertion of anti-Communist crusades by some elected officials.

Looking over the present Court's performance in these four major areas under dispute, many people may deny that any justices have been affected by dominant opinion in this way—for if they had, it would have to be considered either as timidity on their part or as a betrayal of the independent status given to the Court by the Founding Fathers for the protection of the Constitution. These people would explain that constitutional cases must be decided as a matter of right and wrong, with the law-trained Justices "finding" the meaning of the Constitution through use of constitutional records, prior decisions and basic canons of construction. These "findings" should be announced in utter disregard of dominant opinion.

Such an approach confuses the usual function of the justices as the nation's highest law court with its more complicated, more vital but less regular role as keeper of our constitutional checks and balances. In this latter capacity, the justices must function as constitutional statesmen, applying the brilliant but ambiguous phrases of 1789 or 1868 to economic, military, political, social and inter-group conditions then undreamed of. The Court must also try to apply to modern circumstances those continuing conflicts that the framers of the Constitution knowingly locked into our political system—conflicts between majority rule and minority rights, Federal authority and local control, the private domain and the public sector. In these areas, it should be remembered, the terms of the Constitution involve such highly elastic concepts as "due process of law," "equal protection of the law" and "establishment of religion."

As constitutional statesmen, the justices must arrive at some ultimate accommodation with dominant opinion. The imperatives of democracy and the need for broad confidence in the Court require this. But the justices must seek to influence dominant opinion as well. The creative challenge is to find exactly the right combination of judicial command, creative suggestion and respectful non-interference that will lead those entrusted with political power in the states and nation to live by the expanding ideals of the American Constitution.

When the Supreme Court opened its 1962-63 term, Justice Frankfurter was already in retirement. Justices Byron White and Arthur Goldberg took their seats at the two opposite ends of the bench, symbolizing by their physical location that the Court's doctrinal boundaries, for the moment, are as undetermined as the constitutional philosophies of the new Kennedy appointees. These two men now hold the Court's balance of power, and with their votes could come important changes in the direction or emphasis of the Court's rulings on sensitive issues.

In this situation, both supporters and critics of the Court can be sure that their efforts to mold dominant opinion in the nation on the great constitutional questions will have a profound impact on the Court of the nineteen-sixties. The justices are listening, and is this not as it should be in a constitutional democracy?

Historic Change in the Supreme Court

by Anthony Lewis

A HISTORIC term of the Supreme Court is drawing to a close. It rates that adjective because of a single momentous decision—the decision in *Baker v. Carr,* opening the doors of the Federal courts to legal attacks on the apportionment of seats in state legislatures.

The apportionment case was decided just three months ago, on March 26. But it has already started to remake the political map of the United States. In Georgia and Alabama, Federal courts have ordered rural forces to relax their ancient hold on the legislatures. In Maryland the legislature, acting under a judicial ultimatum, has redistricted its lower house for the first time in forty years. In two dozen other states legal or political action is under way on reapportionment.

A lawyer who has been a student of the Supreme Court's work for many years remarked soon after March 26 that the decision in *Baker v. Carr* had been "inevitable." Then he added: "But twenty years ago, or even ten, it would have been inconceivable."

From "inconceivable" to "inevitable" in a decade or two—so swiftly does the course of decision run. But why the change? That

From the *New York Times Magazine,* June 17, 1962, copyright © 1962 by The New York Times Company.

is the great question posed by the apportionment case. What had happened to Court or country that made the justices see the issue differently in 1962 from the way they might have, indeed had, seen it a few years earlier?

In this respect the apportionment case is part of the larger question of change in the Supreme Court. For of course it is not the only example of a revolution in constitutional doctrine in recent years. Two others come quickly to mind: the standards of fairness imposed on state criminal proceedings and, best known to the public at large, the Court's attitude toward racial segregation.

Perhaps it would be useful to approach the general question of the changing role of the Supreme Court by a particular examination of each of these areas—criminal procedure, segregation, apportionment. Seeing what the Court has done there, and considering why, may suggest some general reasons for the great shift in the Supreme Court's place in the American system of government over the past twenty-five years.

Recall, first, the dominant mood of the Supreme Court a generation ago. The issues then were the right of the states to set maximum hours and minimum wages, the right of the Federal Government to use its tax and commerce power to deal with the Depression. In short, the Court's concern seemed to be with property, not what we today would call human liberty.

It was in that setting, in 1936, that the Court for the first time in history set aside a state criminal conviction because the defendants had been mistreated. The case was called *Brown v. Mississippi,* and it is worth recalling the facts set out in Chief Justice Charles Evans Hughes' opinion.

Three Mississippi Negroes were charged with murder. One was hanged from a tree and told he would hang there until he confessed; at the trial he still bore the marks of the rope on his throat. The two others "were laid over chairs and their backs were cut to pieces with a leather strap with buckles on it. . . . In this manner the defendants confessed the crime, and as the whippings progressed or were repeated, they changed or adjusted their confession in all particulars of detail so as to conform to the demands of their torturers."

The Supreme Court decided that convictions based on confessions obtained by such methods denied the "due process of law" guaranteed by the Fourteenth Amendment.

Since 1936, in a steady progression of cases, the Court has struck at the use of coerced confessions. It has outlawed psychological as well as physical coercion. And in many other aspects of criminal law, despite protests from state officials and from dissenters within the Court, new restraints have been put on the states.

In 1956, over strong dissent, the Supreme Court said that a state which allows appeals in criminal cases cannot deny the right just because a prisoner is too poor to buy a trial transcript; it must supply the transcript or an adequate substitute. The Conference of State Chief Justices charged gloomily that the decision threatened "an almost complete breakdown in the work of state appellate courts," but nothing like that has occurred.

Just a year ago the Court, again by a narrow division, overturned the well-established rule that state courts were free to admit illegally seized evidence. It has put down for argument next year the question whether it should now require the states to supply free counsel to impoverished defendants in all criminal cases, abandoning the present rule assuring counsel only in cases involving the death penalty.

The course has been clear in the area of criminal law: despite resentment at new restrictions on the freedom of the states, and despite some misgivings within the Court from time to time, the Supreme Court has moved steadily in the past twenty-five years to impose uniform national standards of fairness on state criminal proceedings. State law enforcement faces Federal judicial scrutiny today to a degree unthinkable a generation ago.

Why?

It seems evident, first, that in moving against the third degree and other forms of unfairness and inequality in the criminal law, the Court was reflecting a national moral sentiment. Perhaps this arose from the experience of totalitarian brutality in other countries. Whatever the reason, Americans were plainly less willing to tolerate police misbehavior in any state, regardless of the political niceties of Federal-state relations, than they were in earlier years. Many Americans have a national conscience that is injured by any state's misbehavior. And more and more the national ideal is prevailing over state orientation.

A second point to be made is that, if higher national standards were to be imposed on law enforcement in this country, the Supreme Court was the only agency that could do the job.

The inmates of state prisons hardly had the kind of political power likely to spur legislative reforms. State courts tended to be dominated by local feelings and dislike for criminals. One of the happy effects of intervention by the Supreme Court has in fact been growing sensitivity on the part of local courts and political groups to the needs of fairness in criminal procedure. Intervention has spurred self-reform.

In 1938, two years after *Brown v. Mississippi,* there came a significant decision in the racial area. For the first time the Supreme Court emphasized the "equal" aspect of its 1896 rule that a state could provide "separate but equal" facilities for Negroes. Over bitter dissent, the Court held that Missouri did not meet the rule by sending Negroes to an out-of-state law school; it must provide legal training within its own borders.

There followed a series of unanimous decisions on higher education tightening the "separate-but-equal" standard. Finally, in 1950, the Court all but made segregation a legal impossibility. It held that Texas had not provided equality by establishing a separate law school for Negroes. In directing the (white) University of Texas Law School to admit a Negro applicant, Chief Justice Fred M. Vinson wrote:

"[The white law school] possesses to a far greater degree those qualities which are incapable of objective measurement but which make for greatness in a law school. Such qualities, to name but a few, include reputation of the faculty, experience of the administration, position and influence of the alumni, standing in the community, traditions and prestige."

It took no great thinker to realize that, when such intangibles were placed in the scale, no segregated school for Negroes was ever likely to be found "equal." Four years later the Court cut through the legal web and held that segregated schools were inherently unequal and denied the "equal protection of the laws" guaranteed by the Fourteenth Amendment.

The school decision followed other great victories for the Negro in the Supreme Court—cases establishing the right to vote and serve on juries and buy property without discrimination. But schools were by far the most inflammatory issue in the South, and the Court was well aware of that. Nevertheless, it decided against segregation, and unanimously.

Why?

Once again no complicated motive need be sought. The Supreme Court was reflecting a national moral consensus on segregation— perhaps anticipating a feeling that had not yet fully taken shape.

In 1896, in establishing the "separate but equal" rule, the Supreme Court had relied on the sociology of its day. It said there was nothing invidious to the Negro in segregation unless "the colored race chooses to put that construction upon it."

But after Adolf Hitler and South Africa, no court could say with a straight face that separation of human beings on account of race or color was a stamp of inferiority only if the segregated so regarded it. Most of the world knew, and the United States was at least coming to know, that segregation was intended as a demonstration of one race's superiority over another.

Moreover, there was again the fact that unless the Supreme Court acted there would be no action. Discrimination made the Negro politically powerless in his own state. Ever since Reconstruction, Congress had happily left to the Supreme Court the enforcement of constitutional guarantees against racial discrimination. The Federal legislative path to reform was blocked by the South's power in the Senate. Closing of the judicial path might produce intolerable social pressures.

The Senate Majority Leader, Mike Mansfield, made the point during the recent Senate civil-rights debate. Our recent constitutional history, he said, "makes clear that progress toward the equalization in practice of the ideals of human freedom will not be halted indefinitely. When one road to this end fails, others will unfold. If the process is ignored in legislative channels, it will not necessarily be blocked in other channels—in the Executive Branch and in the courts."

Finally, the problem of legislative districts. It is an old problem; rural areas have refused for decades to relinquish the power given to them by unrepresentative districts in state legislatures.

In 1946 the Supreme Court seemed to close the doors of the Federal courts to the aggrieved city-dwellers. Justice Felix Frankfurter said the districting question would lead the courts into a "political thicket." The cure, he said, would have to be a political struggle by the disenfranchised.

A dozen times since 1946 the Court had held to the hands-off attitude on apportionment and related questions. Then, last March, it abruptly changed direction. The extraordinarily swift reaction to *Baker v. Carr* helps to suggest why the Court decided as it did.

Here, in contrast with the much less than deliberate speed with which school segregation has been abandoned, the Supreme Court's lead has been followed with exuberant enthusiasm by lower Federal and even state judges and by political figures. No recent constitutional decision has had such widespread effects so fast.

It seems evident that on the issue of legislative apportionment a moral explosion was waiting to be set off. Almost everyone, including the beneficiaries of the evil, knew that an evil existed. But Justice Frankfurter's advice to work for political change was useless; the political system provided no way of escape. The Supreme Court supplied the key, opening the way for political as well as legal forces to work for orderly change.

Perhaps in 1946 it still seemed possible that the rural oligarchies in control of state legislatures would listen to reason. But by 1962 that hope had passed. It was plain that only the Supreme Court could cure the disease of malapportionment eating away at the vitals of American democracy.

There, then, are our three examples of dramatic change in Supreme Court doctrine during the past quarter-century. Surely they do suggest some generalizations about why the Court has shifted as it has in its own view of its role.

One constant in the three examples was the ethical element. In intervening in behalf of the abused criminal suspect, the Negro, the has been responding to what it deemed to be a moral demand—a citizen disenfranchised by malapportionment, the Supreme Court demand of the national conscience. Moreover, the national conscience had found no way to express itself except through the Supreme Court. The Court moved in only when the rest of our governmental system was stymied, when there was no other practical way out of the moral dilemma.

The conclusion is that the Supreme Court has tended in recent years to act as the instrument of national moral values that have not been able to find other governmental expression. If the Court has changed, it is because we have changed.

The unhappy recent history of the world has rearranged Americans' hierarchy of values, and so it should be no great surprise that the Supreme Court emphasizes interests different from those of the past. We are more concerned, now, about abuse of official authority, mistreatment of racial minorities and sabotage of democracy than we are about the state powers in a federal system.

This is not to say that everyone agrees on moral goals, much less ones that are judicially attainable. The nine justices cannot be expected to march in happy unanimity toward a legal heaven whose definition all applaud.

Only in the field of race relations—where, ironically, public reaction has been the most divisive—have the justices been regularly in agreement. They have apparently found the moral imperative more obvious. But even here it seems doubtful that unanimity can long be preserved as the Court reaches the difficult questions of how to distinguish "private" from "public" discrimination.

Outside the racial area the Court has been deeply divided. Justice Frankfurter has been the principal spokesman for the view that the Court should be hesitant to impose its moral ideal in a complex political structure. He dissented not only from *Baker v. Carr* but, for example, from last year's decision outlawing illegally seized evidence in state criminal trials.

This does not mean that Justice Frankfurter likes unfair apportionments or illegally seized evidence—far from it. He is simply a believer in the independent power of the states, wisely or unwisely used, and such a skeptic about the perfection of judges that he hesitates to bind government to rigid judicial formulas.

Justice Frankfurter, of course, is not alone in his doubts about an expansive role for the Supreme Court as keeper of the national conscience. Most of today's critics of the Court are disaffected only because they dislike some particular result—say, the outlawing of school segregation. But there are some who, like Justice Frankfurter, have deeper and more general philosophical objections.

One is that judges are not necessarily competent to make broad moral judgments. Law school trains a man to work his way through conflicting principles in construing a contract or a statute. But does it equip Supreme Court justices, or the lower court judges who must carry out their decisions, to pass judgment on great social questions such as race relations and legislative districting, where there are few guidelines—few easily defined principles?

Even more strongly pressed is the thesis that reliance on the courts to cure society's ills saps the strength of democracy. The late Judge Learned Hand put it most colorfully when he said that he did not care to be ruled by "a bevy of Platonic guardians."

The more citizens rely on the courts, it is argued, the less will they fight issues out where they ought to be fought out in a democracy—in the political forum. Justice Frankfurter has often spoken admiringly of Britain as a country where misuse of official power is quickly argued out and corrected in the legislative arena, Parliament.

Those who believe in the moral role that the Supreme Court has increasingly come to play would not deny the difficulty of the job it gives to judges. But they make the point that it is a duty compelled by a written Constitution. The Framers of the Constitution and its amendments deliberately chose to use phrases such as "due process" and "equal protection"—phrases that express no more than moral ideals, that must be given content by each generation. It is our judges who have been designated to supply that content, and their sources of inspiration must be national values.

Justice Frankfurter, for all his concern about judicial power, sees no escape from a judge's duty to give the Constitution concrete meaning. "It must be an impersonal judgment," he once wrote. "It must rest on fundamental presuppositions rooted in history to which widespread acceptance may fairly be attributed. . . . But in the end judgment cannot be escaped."

Another time, Justice Frankfurter spoke of the Supreme Court's right to enshrine in the Constitution "those liberties of the individual which history has attested as the indispensable conditions of an open against a closed society"—in short, deep-rooted national ideals of liberty.

And this is not Great Britain. It is not a small, homogeneous, centralized country with a tradition of parliamentary supremacy and a deep commitment to official impartiality and decency. This is a sprawling country divided by regional and other animosities, with an unhappy tradition of corrupt and partisan officials, especially on the local level. It has a national legislature too often driven by sectional interests, and in any case too busy, to spend much time bringing local action into harmony with national ideals.

It is a country, also, that has always looked to its courts for moral inspiration. It has looked especially to the Supreme Court, whose very remoteness and freedom from sectional and political pressures have made Americans value it as a forum for the defense of human liberty.

The Court has not been a Platonic dictator and could never successfully be that. When it has tried to stand against the tide of history, as in the Nineteen Thirties, it has failed. Its great success has been as a moral goad to the political process—when it has urged politicians to do what they have avoided doing but knew in their hearts they should, as in race relations and apportionment.

There is every indication that the Supreme Court more and more sees its constitutional function in those terms. Slowly but perceptibly, with occasional retreats but with the over-all direction clear, the Court is taking up the role of conscience to the country.

Nine Men in Black
Who Think White

by Lewis M. Steel

THE UNITED STATES Supreme Court has begun a new term embroiled in a controversy, involving the President, Congress and the Court itself, over the appointment of a new Chief Justice. The battle has been portrayed as a contest between liberals and conservatives, civil rights supporters and racists.

Whatever the validity of these characterizations, the rhetoric employed by the Court's rightist critics has followed a time-worn script, evoking from the egalitarians similarly stale defenses. A hard analysis of the Court's race-relations record, however, discloses that the defenders have been pushed into supporting an institution which has not departed from the American tradition of treating Negroes as second-class citizens.

Historically, the Supreme Court has been the enemy of the American black man. During the 15 years in which Earl Warren has presided as Chief Justice, the Court has eliminated from the law books some of its more atrocious decisions. But never has it indicated that it is committed to a society based upon principles of absolute equality.

From the *New York Times Magazine,* October 13, 1968, copyright © 1968 by The New York Times Company.

Popular belief has it that the Court deserves the major credit for awakening the nation to its civil rights responsibilities in 1954, when the justices decided that enforced segregation in our public schools violated constitutional precepts. With resolute firmness, according to both detractors and supporters, the Court has continued to strike down segregation and discrimination on every occasion. And, according to the traditional viewpoint, both the executive and legislative branches of our Government have lagged behind the Warren Court.

Because I believe, along with the National Advisory Commission on Civil Disorders, that "our nation is moving toward two societies, one black, one white—separate and unequal," I feel that all our institutions must be re-examined. A re-evaluation of the role of the United States Supreme Court discloses that it has struck down only the symbols of racism while condoning or overlooking the ingrained practices which have meant the survival of white supremacy in the United States, North and South. The Court has time and again taken the position that racial equality should be subordinated—or at least balanced against—white America's fear of rapid change, which would threaten its time-honored prerogatives. Only where racial barriers were overtly obnoxious—and, therefore, openly contradictory to the American creed of equality—has the Court deigned to move. Yet its decisions have allowed a confused, miseducated and prejudiced white public to believe that its black fellow citizens have been given their full rights.

To understand the Supreme Court's role in the civil rights movement and its peculiar obligation to insure equality for Negroes, it is imperative to understand the Court's role in establishing segregation in America. In the post–Civil War years, the Supreme Court led the nation away from the Reconstruction Congress's program for full citizenship for the freedmen. Congress passed five civil rights acts between 1866 and 1875. The 1875 act contained some strong public-accommodations sections that forbade racial discrimination in inns, public conveyances, theaters and other places of public amusement. When the act was first tested in the Supreme Court eight years later, the public-accommodations sections were struck down as unconstitutional; the opinion completely ignored the intent of Congress in passing the act and in proposing to the states the 13th and 14th Amendments. The Supreme Court thus opened the door for the passage of Jim Crow legislation.

Then, in 1896, the Court endorsed the establishment of a quasi-slave caste system by ruling that the states could require the segregation of public facilities as long as Negroes were provided equal accommodations. Three years later, the Court allowed Georgia to support a white high school while failing to provide secondary education for Negro children. This action destroyed even the myth of equality. Finally, in 1906, the High Court ruled that Congress had no constitutional authority to pass laws which would protect Negroes from harassment by whites solely on racial grounds.

Taken together, these cases meant that, in the Supreme Court's view, Congress could not protect Negroes from attack by their former masters and that state legislatures could pass laws which compelled a caste system.

Until 1954, the Supreme Court left its handiwork virtually alone. True, in the grandfather-clause and white-supremacy cases it disapproved of obvious measures to disfranchise Negroes completely, and in 1947 it prohibited the judicial enforcement of racially restrictive covenants attached to land deeds. But these decisions had no effect on the totally segregated society. Nor did they secure the vote to Negroes terrorized by white oppression. And, significantly, in 1950 the Court declined to review its own insidious creation, the separate-but-equal doctrine, when requested to do so in a case involving the right of a Negro student to attend the University of Texas Law School.

Long before the Court undertook any serious review of its constitutional doctrines in the field of race relations, other American institutions were re-evaluating their stands. During World War II and shortly thereafter, various agencies created machinery to make it appear that racial equality had become a part of our public policy. Thus, Presidential executive orders forbade racial discrimination by the recipients of Government contracts, the armed forces ordered the integration of military units and certain states enacted a variety of antidiscrimination laws. The reasons for these faint-hearted shifts in public policy have been discussed by the Advisory Commission and others. The war against Nazi Germany had raised the issue of racism and heightened the expectations of Negroes, who, because of labor shortages, were offered good jobs for the first time. Additionally, policy makers realized that the continuation of America's brand of apartheid could damage our standing with the newly emerging nations. Most important, black Americans came out of the war determined to fight for their rights at home.

Seen in the light of these pre-1954 shifts in attitude, the school-desegregation case did little more than bring the Court up to date. Until the 1954 decision, the gains won by Negroes were more in the nature of favors to be dispensed or withdrawn at the pleasure of the white overlords. Being gifts, not rights, these pre-1954 "reforms" stood as paper testaments only. Segregated Army units still fought in Korea; Negroes were still condemned to unequal job opportunities in defense plants and were openly segregated in the public schools of Northern states which had antisegregation laws.

In 1954, the Court was in a position to serve notice on the American people that equality was an absolute right of all citizens, that this right came before all other rights and that its further subversion could not be tolerated. By taking this stance, the Court could not only have gone a long way toward relieving its conscience but it could also have established itself as a true constitutional court, dedicated to an impartial search for just principles, irrespective of race.

Instead, the Court chose to act in the manner of the practical political reformer. Rather than ordering sweeping desegregation, it ordered another hearing. A year later, the Court ruled that the South did not have to desegregate its schools immediately, it merely had to do so "with all deliberate speed." Never in the history of the Supreme Court had the implementation of a constitutional right been so delayed or the creation of it put in such vague terms. The Court thereby made clear that it was a white court which would protect the interests of white America in the maintenance of stable institutions.

In essence, the Court considered the potential damage to white Americans resulting from the diminution of privilege as more critical than continued damage to the underprivileged. The Court found that public reasons—the offense to white sensibilities—

existed to justify the delay in school desegregation. Worse still, it gave the primary responsibility for achieving educational equality to those who had established the segregated institutions.

This decision to delay integration and ignore racially discriminatory mechanisms was more shameful than the Court's 19th-century monuments to apartheid. For, by the mid–20th century, there was no basis on which the Court's nine educated men could justify a segregated society. Scientific racism had been discredited and America had been exposed to the full implications of racism in Nazi Germany.

Moreover, the United States had proclaimed itself the guarantor of freedom by taking up the sword against international Communism. From a judicial standpoint, crimes against humanity had been defined and punished at Nuremberg. American justices had shown themselves to be capable of harshness when judging another people guilty of ghettoizing and destroying an ethnic group. Their failure to take an equally strong position when reviewing the sins of their own countrymen—whose institutions, according to the Court itself, damaged "the hearts and minds" of Negro children "in a way unlikely ever to be undone"—will long remain as a blot on the record of American jurisprudence.

Unfortunately, however, the Court's treatment of public-school desegregation was only the beginning of a pattern of conduct. Its handling of subsequent race cases indicates that it remains the Supreme Court of white America.

After its 1955 decision requiring "all deliberate speed," the Court did enter a series of decrees which slowly struck down segregation in public transportation and in public facilities and recreational areas. These decisions, however, were directed only at overt discriminatory practices in the Southern and border states.

In the field of education, the Court refused to review a series of conservative lower-court decisions which upheld what school officials described as accidental segregation in Gary, Ind., Kansas City, Kan., and Cincinnati. As a result, the schools of the North have become segregated faster than Southern schools have been desegregated. Moreover, in the South and border states, Supreme Court reviews of lower-court decisions have been so timid that only 15 per cent of all Southern black children attend other than totally segregated schools. True, the Supreme Court ordered last May that discrimination be eliminated "root and branch" from school systems. But this decision, coming 14 years after *Brown v. Board of Education* in 1954, will yield small dividends unless the Court also agrees to tackle the question of *de facto* segregation. And nothing the Court has done to date indicates that this step is on the agenda.

The Court has also reflected the views of the white community in first protecting Negro protest marches, then removing its protection after significant changes had taken place in American attitudes. When Negroes and their white supporters began demonstrating, they were considered to be humble supplicants seeking succor from white America. Toward the middle of the nineteen-sixties, civil rights demonstrators, rather than playing a humble role, proclaimed that they would not be moved. Negroes had become assertive in a society which considered such behavior anathema, and repression became the order of the day. White America, without any basis in fact, decided that demonstrations and riots were synonymous.

The Court's change in attitude was foreshadowed in *Cox v. Louisiana* in 1965, in which it reversed the convictions of Negro demonstrators but warned that the right to protest could be limited. The new approach was not based on a fundamental difference between recent demonstrations and earlier ones; nothing had occurred which would indicate that civil rights advocates had abandoned their philosophy of peaceful protest. The new restrictions against demonstrations were first applied in *Adderley v. Florida* in 1966. The Court held that, although there was no violence, a peaceful protest outside a police station could be curtailed. The inconsistency between this and earlier cases can be explained only in terms of a judicial concession to white anxieties.

Significantly, the Court's new approach was reflected in decrees detrimental to the moderate civil rights organizations it originally protected. Thus, the Court, which had earlier intervened to save the National Association for the Advancement of Colored People in Alabama, allowed the Georgia state courts to threaten the group's existence by awarding a huge money judgment against it in a suit seeking damages for picketing. In failing to sustain the

N.A.A.C.P., the Supreme Court allowed the state courts to apply completely arbitrary rules of law. Even in the darkest days of anti-labor judicial decrees, the unions were never dealt with more harshly.

As public opinion in opposition to civil rights demonstrations mounted, the Supreme Court's position further hardened. In 1967, it allowed an obviously unconstitutional Alabama state-court injunction to serve as a vehicle for the jailing of the Rev. Martin Luther King.

This spring, in an even more damaging decision, the Court ruled in *Cameron v. Johnson* that a Federal court was correct in refusing to interfere with the prosecution of Mississippi civil rights demonstrators accused of nothing more evil than maintaining an orderly picket line.

These decisional changes were achieved by an extremely simple expedient. The majority of the Supreme Court justices began to accept the protestations of good faith made by racist public officials, where only a few years earlier the majority had evinced a willingness to look beyond self-serving statements to ascertain the facts. Indeed, the Court has had dissenters who have vainly and loudly protested the majority's new anti-Negro attitude in the realization that such decisions mean a surrender to racists.

As the Court began to rule against Negroes seeking to reverse state convictions, it also decided that civil rights advocates could not seek relief from oppressive state prosecutions by removing their cases to the Federal courts; the justices were willing to assume the impartiality of courts which were strongholds of segregationists. By narrowing Federal jurisdiction, the Court achieved substantially the same effect as its predecessors did when they decided in the 19th century that laws intended to protect Negroes were unconstitutional.

Similarly, after developing rules that Negroes could not be excluded from juries, the Court negated much of its progress. In *Swain v. Alabama,* it upheld the right of Southern prosecutors to challenge and remove all Negroes while selecting a jury. The Court overlooked the fact that a Negro had never sat on a civil or criminal jury in the county in question and accepted at face value the prosecutor's declaration that he would allow Negroes to serve under certain circumstances.

Supporters of the Court's civil rights record can point only to the field of housing when seeking a pattern of pro–civil rights decisions, and the pattern fades when viewed critically. Since it struck down the judicial enforcement of restrictive covenants in land deeds in 1947, the Supreme Court has ruled favorably in California's Proposition 14 case and has upheld an 1866 law as a general prohibition against housing discrimination based upon race. The Proposition 14 case, decided in 1967, involved an amendment to the California Constitution which would have prohibited all state and local fair-housing laws and ordinances. The Court ruled this amendment unconstitutional. When, in the spring of this year, the Court upheld the 1866 law, it gave Negroes the right to sue individuals who refused to sell or rent property to them because of their race. Significantly, this ruling came after Congress had passed a fair-housing act. Once again, therefore, the Supreme Court, contrary to popular belief, was not the ground-breaker in racial reform. Moreover, neither the Proposition 14 case nor the endorsement of the 1866 law will significantly weaken ghetto walls. Most black Americans, having low incomes, will not be able to utilize these rulings, just as they were not able to profit much from the 1947 restrictive-covenant decision.

In 1967, the Supreme Court could have played a significant role in attacking ghetto housing. The case before it was *Green Street Association v. Daley*. The petitioners, Negro residents and a neighborhood association, complained that public officials in Chicago were using urban-renewal funds to create "a no-Negro buffer zone" around a white shopping center. In essence, the complaint alleged that the urban-renewal program, financed with public funds, was actually a program for Negro removal. The petitioners also said that the city was relocating Negroes only in ghetto areas, thus perpetuating housing segregation.

The complaint was dismissed by a Federal district court in Chicago and the decision affirmed by the circuit court. The Supreme Court, which could have ruled that these facts, if proved, would entitle the petitioners to relief under the 14th Amendment, declined to review the case. Again this year, when Negroes charged that highway construction in Nashville was being used to discriminate against the black community, the Supreme Court declined to review adverse lower-court decisions.

Favorable action in either of these cases would have done far more to aid the ordinary black man than all the other housing cases put together. For today, the effect of Government—local, state and Federal—on housing is far greater than that of individuals.

Those in the legal profession who defend the Court's record do so on the ground that the traditional relationship between the states and the Federal Government must be preserved. According to this theory, the liberties of all Americans are better preserved if the Federal Government is strictly limited in its right to oversee the affairs of the states; the restrictions, the theory says, prevent the creation of a monolithic centralized police state. According to these thinkers, an "activist" Supreme Court would be reliant on Federal power to enforce its writ in the states, thereby tipping an already precarious balance.

But what is this argument really worth? If basic civil rights can be denied on a systematic basis to any definable segment of the population, that segment is living in a police state. The justification of the Court's record presumes that constitutionally guaranteed freedoms should be analyzed from the point of view of the white American majority.

In effect, the argument is based on the premise that any threat, real or imagined, to the civil liberties of whites should be forestalled, even at the price of denying to black men the rights which may be hypothetically threatened by Federal intervention. For example, whites are afraid that *their* public school systems would be damaged by integration because black children attending segregated black schools perform at a lower academic level. Though the lower performance by Negroes has been brought about by the white community's treatment of Negroes as inferiors, integration has been delayed to save the white public schools at the further expense of black children.

Another argument in favor of judicial nonintervention is based upon the premise that in a democracy the people, through their legislatures, have the primary responsibility to redress grievances.

This belief is also comforting only to the majority that completely controls the legislative process.

The fact is that the fabric of our country is threatened, not by theoretical considerations of the Federal-state relationship, but by the pervasive racism found by the Advisory Commission. "States' rights" is a phrase invented by the advocates of the status quo to stand as a philosophical bar to change. That politicians should grasp such a doctrine is to be expected; after all, politicians like to be able to tell their constituents that local problems are the result of outside interference. But Supreme Court justices should have no constituency; they are appointed for life to sit as judges over all the people.

In fields other than race relations, the Court has, to a much greater extent, acted without regard for popular opinion. Consider, for example, Supreme Court rulings in the fields of reapportionment, separation of church from state, obscenity, criminal law and the protection of Communists or others with unpopular political beliefs. In these areas, the Court has taken an active role in bringing about needed reforms. By and large, decisions in these fields have not been based upon a compromise between constitutional concepts and society's desire to preserve established institutions.

The reapportionment decisions show the differences in the handling of racial and nonracial cases. In cases involving only the one-man, one-vote principle applied to a political entity, the Court was not interested in the reasoning behind a challenged apportionment plan. It was enough that the power of some voters at the polls was diminished. But when Negroes began to challenge the use of gerrymandered districts or at-large elections to reduce the power of their votes, the Supreme Court backed away. For Negroes, it soon became clear, proof of the dilution of their votes was not sufficient; they also had to prove the subjective intent of legislators to limit their voting power.

A review of decisions affecting religion, obscenity and political belief also illustrates the differences between racial and nonracial cases. In first ruling that public-school authorities could not require the recitation of prayers in school and then broadening the scope of this ruling, the Court ignored massive outcries that it was ordaining a godless society. The pious—and America is a church-going country—were equally upset by a rash of decisions which effectively throttled the censor's authority to control what we read and see. Nor did the Court heed pleas that the necessity for the maintenance of law and order required the electronic invasion of homes and the use of confessions obtained before an accused could consult with a lawyer. Red-baiting was equally ineffective when the Court was faced with statutes and administrative fiats ostensibly designed to protect the United States against internal subversion. Supreme Court decisions in these fields demonstrate that public opinion need not influence the judicial interpretation of constitutional rights.

The Court has not been so bold in race relations. Since the Civil War, it has allowed itself to be swayed by the prejudices and mores of whites and, more recently, by their fears that equality for Negroes would adversely affect them. In the 19th century, an activist Supreme Court helped the Southern states defeat Congress's plan to rid this country of all the remnants of slavery. In recent years, a cautious Supreme Court has waltzed in time to the music of the white majority—one step forward, one step backward and sidestep, sidestep.

Each justice obviously has some effect on the direction of the Court's dance, so the power struggle over the appointment of a new Chief Justice cannot be entirely dismissed. However, the pattern of decisions in the field of civil rights indicates that it is not the thinking of individual justices, but the philosophy of the entire Court on civil rights that must be reoriented if the Court is to move out of the shadow of the 19th century.

Racial equality, of course, is dependent upon more than just Court decisions. Severe readjustments in political power and a redistribution of wealth must take place in order to avert catastrophic racial conflict. When the forces of reform are reduced to fighting for one judicial appointment to a Court that has inadequately interpreted the constitutional mandate of equality, it is evident that the advocates of the status quo are achieving their purpose no matter what the outcome of the power struggle.

The Warren Court Is Not Likely to Be Overruled

by Joseph W. Bishop, Jr.

THE JUDGMENT of history may well be that the Supreme Court was the distinctive feature of the polity of the United States, as extraordinary as the dual kingship of Sparta or the Mameluke slave-sultans of Egypt. Since 1803, when the Court decided *Marbury v. Madison,* it has been settled that "a law repugnant to the Constitution is void." In practice this means that five of nine lawyers (not all of them statesmen, or even politicians) have the power, in the name of the Constitution, to nullify acts of the President, the Congress and the states and sometimes to compel them to do the five Justices' will. Charles Evans Hughes (before he went on the Court) phrased it with characteristic directness and accuracy: "We are under a Constitution, but the Constitution is what the judges say it is." If the judges see in it things not visible to the eyes of laymen, or even other lawyers, the only recourse of those aggrieved is to persuade the Court to overrule itself, which is difficult, or to amend the Constitution, which is still more difficult.

Whether this enormous power can fairly be deduced from the language of the Constitution, and whether the framers of that in-

From the *New York Times Magazine,* September 7, 1969, copyright © 1969 by The New York Times Company.

strument intended to confer it on the Justices, has been the subject of vast learned controversy, much of it highly polemical, still continuing and unlikely ever to be resolved. The proposition that a law repugnant to the Supreme Court is void is certainly not self-evident. Andrew Jackson and Abraham Lincoln strongly disputed it. Franklin Roosevelt not only accepted the Court's power with very ill grace but vigorously, though unsuccessfully, attempted to do something about it. Other countries with written constitutions have no such doctrine. In trying to explain it to Frenchmen and Germans, and even Englishmen, I have encountered difficulty resembling that which a higher mathematician would face if he tried to teach me that on the planets circling Alpha Centauri two plus two is sometimes three and sometimes five but only occasionally four.

No matter; the power exists—in large part because the Court has used it sparingly and generally prudently. John Marshall, indeed, first invoked it in order to extricate the Court from an embarrassing predicament, by holding that an act of Congress which gave the Court jurisdiction of a hot political potato was inconsistent with the Constitution and therefore void. Rarely have the Justices pushed their prerogative so far as to remind Congressmen that under Article III of the Constitution the Court has appellate jurisdiction "with such Exceptions, and under such Regulations as the Congress shall make." The Court's most clearly disastrous interpretation of the Constitution, in Dred Scott's case, was overruled at Appomattox.

There have been, of course, long periods when the Court did nothing in particular and generated correspondingly little interest and controversy among the nonlawyer part of the American public. But there have also been periods of galvanic activity when it played a major role—perhaps *the* major role—in the governmental process. One such was John Marshall's tenure as Chief Justice. Another was the Hughes Court of the nineteen-thirties. The decisions of those Courts were epochal, but it is doubtful that either of them was half so well known to its contemporaries, or excited half so much public enthusiasm and detestation, as the Court over which Earl Warren presided from 1953 until last June. It would be hard to find many ordinary people who know what the Supreme

Court held in *Marbury v. Madison* or even *Schechter Poultry Corporation v. United States* (which shot down the blue eagle of F.D.R.'s National Recovery Administration). But most literate Americans know, and probably have strong opinions about, the decisions of the Warren Court in the school desegregation case (*Brown v. Board of Education*), the reapportionment case (*Baker v. Carr*) and the right-to-counsel cases (notably *Gideon v. Wainwright* and *Miranda v. Arizona*).

The Court's friends think it has rejuvenated the Constitution, turned its guarantees into something more than Fourth-of-July rhetoric and extended them to people to whom the Bill of Rights had never before been of much use. The school of opinion whose views crystallized in vociferous demands for Earl Warren's impeachment saw the Court as a gang of elderly hippies in judicial robes, persecuting religion and encouraging license on a scale unheard of since Nero's time. It had abandoned the Republic to the depredations of anarchists, atheists, black revolutionaries, pornographers and muggers; nothing could save us but prompt impeachment of the Chief Justice and restoration of the Constitution to its original condition.

Although I use the term myself as a convenient bit of shorthand, it should be stressed at the outset that it is inaccurate to label the Supreme Court of 1953-1969 as "the Warren Court." Seventeen Justices sat on the Court during these years, most of them men of strong intellect, strong personality and strong convictions. When the Chief Justice, former Governor of California and aspirant to the Republican nomination for President, came to the Court, he joined five of Franklin Roosevelt's appointees (Black, Reed, Frankfurter, Douglas and Jackson) and three of Harry Truman's (Clark, Burton and Minton). Only the Chief himself and the durable Justices Black and Douglas sat during the entire 16 years. The others were succeeded by four men of generally liberal persuasion (Brennan, Goldberg, Fortas and Marshall), two who cannot even roughly be classified as conservative or liberal (Stewart and White) and only two who could with approximate fairness be described as conservatives (Harlan and Whittaker).

President Eisenhower is reported to have called Warren's appointment "the biggest damn-fool mistake I ever made," which is saying a good deal. If it was a mistake, it was not all that big, for it is unlikely that the Court's decisions would have been greatly different if Warren had turned out to be precisely what Eisenhower supposed him to be. The Chief Justice has one vote out of nine. He is raised a little above his brethren in that he is paid $62,500 a year instead of $60,000. He rates a limousine and an additional law clerk, but is entitled to no extra ruching on his robe. He does preside over oral arguments and the conferences at which decisions are reached; if he is one of the majority, he determines who shall write the opinion of the Court.

These levers of power, such as they are, may contribute something to the dominance of a strong Chief Justice, such as Hughes. But there is no evidence that Warren exercised any such commanding influence over his brethren. The theory that his persuasiveness produced an unusual harmony among the Justices during his tenure is simply not borne out by the facts; there were actually *more* dissents than usual during those years. The unanimity of the Court's opinion in the original school desegregation case has sometimes been credited to his statesmanship, but I think it far more probable that the cause of that unanimity is to be found in the merits of the question.

Regardless of whether the Court of 1953-1969 is called the Warren Court, or the Black-Douglas Court, or the Brennan Court (from Eisenhower's standpoint, Brennan was probably a worse blunder than Warren, for he is at least as "liberal" and "activist" and 15 years younger) or simply the Goddamn Supreme Court, there is little doubt that it was the object of more heartfelt execration by conservatives than any other Supreme Court in our history —vials of wrath even fuller than those which liberals poured out on the Court of 1935. Some of the indignation might have been averted or at least mitigated without any sacrifice of principle, for the opinions of the Justices sometimes displayed an unfortunate and undiplomatic tendency to preach, to throw in arguments and authorities which were as unnecessary to the result as they were calculated to infuriate conservatives and irritate moderates.

Brown v. Board of Education could well have rested on the single, simple and straightforward ground that "separate educational facilities are inherently unequal," without adducing the "modern authority" of assorted psychologists and sociologists, most of them (with the outstanding exceptions of Kenneth Clark and Gunnar Myrdal) fairly obscure in 1954 and equally so today, to show that segregation retarded the mental development of Negro children. The holding of *Miranda v. Arizona,* that a man being questioned by the police is entitled to be told that he can remain silent and that he can have a lawyer, would surely have upset the cops and their friends much less if the Chief Justice had foregone a lengthy, lurid and probably somewhat overdrawn essay on the physical and psychological "brutality" of police inter-rogators. At the same time he managed to annoy the down-with-the-Cossacks faction of liberals by holding up the F.B.I. as an exemplar of fairness. (And from the rather special standpoint of connoisseurs of classic murders, there was a certain irony in the Court's heavy reliance on *Bram v. United States,* which reversed the conviction of a man who had butchered three harmless people with an ax.)

Some of the Court's unhappy public relations must be blamed on sheer bad luck. It was not the Justices' fault that Danny Escobedo, whose case laid down the not-very-startling rule that a man who is being questioned by the police is entitled to a lawyer when he asks for one, happened to be the sort who was pretty sure to get himself in further serious trouble with the criminal law almost as soon as he was sprung from the Illinois pen. Even worse luck was the Fortas debacle. The rest of the Court, of course, had nothing to do with either the rise or fall of Mr. Justice Fortas, and indeed seems to have given him scant sympathy. Nonetheless he was, on and off Capitol Hill, a highly visible and vulnerable symbol of the "Warren Court." As Dickens proved in what may be the greatest scene in "Pickwick," when the Reverend Mr. Stiggins appears at the monthly meeting of the Temperance Association far gone in rum-and-water, nothing gladdens the public heart so much as the fall from grace of the excessively righteous—and Mr. Justice Fortas had treated the public to some of the most righteous homilies ever delivered from the highest bench. When the news was told in Gath and published in the mass media of Ashkelon, the liberals did not openly join in the rejoicings of the Philistines, but neither did they look particularly downcast.

All this said, I concede that no sugar coating could have been thick enough to make some of the Court's major decisions—notably in the sensitive areas of electoral equality, race relations and criminal procedure—palatable to large segments of the population, including a great many highly vocal politicians. But in these areas it is my judgment (which I readily admit to be only that of an ordinary citizen, for I am not by trade a Supreme Court watcher and handicapper) that (1) the Court was right and (2) most people know it was right.

Earl Warren's own judgment was that the single most important decision of the 16 years was *Baker v. Carr*. Most political scientists and politicians would agree with him. By 1962, when the Court at long last decided that it had the right and duty to hear a voter's complaint that his vote was unconstitutionally debased by an antiquated Tennessee statute's allotment of members of the legislature among the state's counties, legislative malapportionment had become a scandal and an affront to democracy. In Tennessee, a vote in Moore County was worth 19 in Hamilton County—and Tennessee was not a particularly horrible example. There were several states in which a rural vote weighed a hundred times as much as an urban or suburban one. Congressional districts were somewhat less bad, but there were half a dozen states in which some members of the House represented three times as many voters as other Congressmen.

Felix Frankfurter was, of course, right when he called the situation a "political thicket," but he was wrong when he warned the Court not to enter it. The plain fact was that if the Court would not treat the disease, it would go untreated and maybe kill the patient, for the rustic politicians whose dominance of state legislatures malapportionment had made possible could hardly be expected to pass reform legislation which would abolish their power and themselves. As Mr. Justice Clark said, "I would not consider intervention by this Court into so delicate a field if there were any other relief available to the people of Tennessee."

In fact, although the Court shortly extended to Congressional districts and local governments the requirement that "a State make an honest and good faith effort to construct districts, in both Houses of its legislature, as nearly of equal population as is practicable," the Justices' ventures into what Frankfurter and Harlan called "a massive repudiation of the experience of our whole past" and also an assertion of "destructively novel judicial power" has not proved a catastrophe. The inferior Federal judges, who bear the brunt of enforcing the one-man-one-vote rule, have, of course, had to grapple with ferocious geographic and demographic problems, complicated by the introduction of computers and such peculiar concepts as election districts in the shapes of doughnuts and dumbbells. They have nonetheless managed greatly to reduce the incidence of rotten boroughs without much actual resort to such drastic remedies as ordering elections at large.

The change in the quality of state legislatures has naturally been startling and alarming to conservatives: Many of the states are actively considering, for example, reforms of their laws on divorce and abortion which would have been unthinkable a few years ago. The earnest efforts of Ev Dirksen and like-minded politicians to overrule *Baker* and its progeny by amending the Constitution are unlikely to succeed, for the simple reason that the people who benefited from reapportionment greatly outnumber those who lost by it. Indeed, the Court's intervention has been so successful that it may be encouraged to do something about another time-honored and cherished political racket, the gerrymander. (But the outstanding example of over- and under-representation, the United States Senate, is beyond the Court's reach, for the provisions which give two Senators to New York and California and two also to Alaska and Nevada, are entrenched in the Constitution itself, as part of the original bargain, and cannot be changed without the consent of the very states which are so magnificently over-represented.)

Brown v. Board of Education and the rest of the desegregation cases, although they marked a new era, cannot really be regarded as innovations of the Warren Court. By 1954 *Plessy v. Ferguson,* the original "separate-but-equal" case, was plainly on its last legs. It could not have survived reconsideration by even a conservative Court. Overt resentment of *Brown,* like its impact, has been largely confined to the states of the old Confederacy and is by no means universal even in them. Not many modern Americans would defend segregation by law; it is doubtful that even those brothers under the skin, George Wallace and Stokely Carmichael, would *openly* argue that it ought to be illegal for black and white to inter-marry or use the same swimming pool.

In any case, judicial efforts to frustrate the stalling tactics employed to preserve legal segregation (and those efforts have often been marked by more deliberation than speed) cannot cure the greater ill, which is *de facto* segregation. The courts cannot, for example, do much to keep middle-class parents from escaping to unbus-able suburbs or expensive private schools. They can do even less to abolish slums, segregated or integrated.

I take a very skeptical view of Justice Douglas's recent dictum that it is racial discrimination in the sale or rental of housing which "herds men into ghettos." The real-estate business is undoubtedly full of such discrimination, but no imaginable reform in the attitudes and practices of real-estate dealers, assuming that the courts could bring it about, would translate black slum dwellings (or white ones) into hygienic and more or less educated neighborhoods. That will require radical social and economic change, which only the executive and legislative branches have the means to accomplish. In the long run, the importance of *Brown* and the other desegregation cases may be seen to lie in their having put the law behind the Negro's claim to equality and reminded Congress of its constitutional power to outlaw private discrimination and do something to make the poor less poor.

The ordinary man's bitterest complaints about the Warren Court are based far less on the desegregation or reapportionment cases than on his notions of its attitude toward criminals. He sees it as a little clique of merciful asses, brimful of what Learned Hand once called the "watery sentiment that obstructs, delays and defeats the prosecution of crime." Not content with ordering a general jail delivery, it has instigated, in this view, a carnival of crime by making it virtually impossible for the police to obtain a conviction or even make an arrest. The criminals in "Dick Tracy" prate incessantly and arrogantly about their constitutional rights; even Dick is able to obtain convictions only by paralyzing them with moon rays and photographing them *flagrante delicto*. Sometimes he can protect the public only by shooting the criminal himself. The picture is frightening, but not entirely accurate.

If we actually look at the Court's best known decisions on due process in criminal cases, we find that *Gideon v. Wainwright* gave indigent defendants in all state felony trials what they already had in Federal courts and the courts of most of the states, a right to a free lawyer; *Escobedo v. Illinois* held that police interrogating a suspect in their custody must honor his request to consult with his lawyer; and *Miranda v. Arizona* added to this that prior to interrogation a person in police custody must be told that he is not required to say anything, that anything he does say may be used against him, and that he is entitled to a lawyer (free if he is broke) if he wants one—warnings reminiscent of the Judges' Rules which have long been in force in England and are familiar to all readers of detective stories.

None of these decisions seems revolutionary. In essence, they gave to poor, unskilled criminals what Mafiosi and the likes of Louis Wolfson had had all along—the means to exercise their constitutional rights to keep silent and talk to a lawyer. They took some of the sting out of Mr. Dooley's remark that "a poor man has a chanst in coort. . . . He has th' same chanst there that he has outside. He has a splendid poor man's chanst." Whatever merit there may be in the argument that society needs more protection and criminals less, there can be none in the proposition that rich, sophisticated criminals deserve a better chance than poor, ignorant criminals.

Moreover, such studies as have been made seem to suggest that Congress's attempt in the Crime Control Act of 1968 to overrule *Miranda* and similar cases is not only unconstitutional but unnecessary. Diligent students of the Yale Law School, manning around-the-clock shifts in New Haven police stations during the summer of 1966, concluded that *Miranda* had made very little difference to law enforcement in our fairly typical city—in part because the police rarely arrest suspects without substantial evidence and thus do not rely heavily on interrogation, and partly because compliance with *Miranda's* requirements does not seem to increase suspects' reluctance to answer questions. The decision's main visible effect was a certain sapping of police morale, resulting from its perfectly gratuitous strictures on police practice.

In short, the popular view that the Court has coddled criminals is simply not supported by the facts. Its holdings have not been revolutionary, and they have not crippled law enforcement. Some of them in fact, such as those which upheld the policeman's right to stop and frisk in circumstances which would not justify an arrest, or to conceal the identity of informers before trial, are regarded by some emotional liberals as evidences of a cop mentality. These decisions have received far less publicity than *Gideon* and *Miranda* —perhaps because they do not fit the Court's image.

There is no more rational basis for the opinion that the Court is determined to bulldoze down the temples of the gods and generally to eradicate religion from American life. *Engel v. Vitale,* which was widely mistaken for a holding that it is illegal for children to pray, held only that the use of public school time and teachers in the recitation of a blandly undenominational little prayer (addressed to "Almighty God" and seeking special favor for children, teachers, parents and the country at large) was an unconstitutional "establishment" of religion. Justice Black, who wrote the Court's opinion, did his best to soothe the sensibilities of the pious by inserting a little sermon in favor of both religion and prayer. He might have added that the effect of the decision on the quantity of genuine religion in the United States would be approximately nil; children (as I can testify from personal experience) do not become devout by gabbling 22 words once a day. The children and the teachers were left with perfect freedom to pray as much as they liked and in any form that appealed to them, at home or in church or, for that matter, in school. The real mystery is why the plaintiffs, the defendants or the 22 state attorneys general who filed briefs *amici curiae* urging that the prayer be upheld cared enough to litigate the case.

Similar observations may be made about *School District v. Schempp,* which came to the same conclusion about Bible reading in the public schools. I have long been made unhappy by the rising generation's almost total ignorance of the majestic literature of the Old and New Testaments, but I doubt very much that they would be better off for being exposed to a few verses at the beginning of the school day.

In areas of greater practical importance, the Court treated organized religion very kindly indeed. It held, for example, that the states could constitutionally supply textbooks to parochial schools; moreover, it did so by reasoning which has suggested to many state legislators that grants of public money to religious schools might also be constitutional. It held that a state cannot deny unemployment compensation to a Seventh Day Adventist who turns down a job which requires work on Saturday. And it refused to review state court decisions that property used for religious purposes could constitutionally be exempted from taxation. *That* enormous question will arise to plague the Burger Court.

In one treacherous area nearly everybody seems to agree that the Court has gone wrong, although there is no agreement among the Justices or anyone else as to the course it should have taken. I refer, of course, to the question of the extent to which the constitutional guarantee of freedom of speech stands as a shield between the police and "obscenity," whatever that word may mean. In half a dozen major cases the Court (and the individual Justices, for most of them filed separate and lengthy opinions) struggled with the monster, and in each one elaborated and augmented the confusion created by its predecessors.

The opinions are rich in touchstones by which censors and lower courts may tell "obscenity," which is not protected by the First and Fourteenth Amendments, from unconventional art and literature, which are. A book is obscene if "to the average person, applying contemporary community standards, the dominant theme of the material taken as a whole appeals to prurient interest." Fearing that this lucid explanation might be open to misunderstanding, the Court added that even material which did appeal to prurient interest and was, moreover, "patently offensive" could not be suppressed unless it was *"utterly* without redeeming social value." The lower courts, alas, continued to show signs of bewilderment. So the Court added yet another test: Does the publisher's advertising demonstrate an intent to "pander" to his customers' "erotic interest"? Peering through all this verbal murk, I sympathize, though I do not agree, with Justice Stewart, who equated obscenity with "hard-core pornography" and added that, although he would not and perhaps could not define that phrase, "I know it when I see it."

"Obscenity" remains triumphantly undefined. The upshot is that nine middle-aged or elderly (and, with one or two exceptions, sedate) lawyers have spent an inordinate amount of time reading books and watching movies which would bring a blush to the cheek of a mule or even of an editor of the Grove Press. The lower courts have wasted still more time in such pursuits. (This is, by the way, more than the sellers of dirty books have to do, for the Court mercifully held unconstitutional an ordinance which imposed strict criminal liability on a bookseller regardless of whether he had any knowledge of the book's contents.)

Oscar Wilde said, "There is no such thing as an immoral book. Books are well written or badly written." For some reason, pornography is with few exceptions badly written. It may be that the only alternative to the agonies of judicial boredom implicit in the present rule (if it can be called such) on obscenity is the straightforward and simple view of Justices Black and Douglas that *all* varieties of expression, "obscene" or no, are protected by the Constitution. Justice Douglas, indeed, cast a solitary vote in favor of reviewing the case of a couple of young ladies from Southern California who claimed that the Bill of Rights included a right to express themselves by wearing topless costumes. But the rest of the court, including Justice Black, had apparently had enough.

This summary of the Court and its doings in 16 turbulent years includes, of course, only those decisions on which the public image of the Court was based, and not all of them. Much could be, has been and will be written, for example, about the Court's antitrust decisions, remarkable chiefly for the violence of the arguments among lawyers and economists as to their meaning and the fact that from 1953 to 1967 the Government won 42 out of the 45 cases in which it was the plaintiff.

Something might be said about the nettles which the Court chose *not* to grasp—notably the question of the constitutionality of exempting from conscription people who object to war on religious grounds but not those who have philosophical reservations about it, and the problem of the President's power, without a declaration of war, to send the armed forces of the United States into combat overseas. These questions may—but probably will not—be tackled by the Burger Court, if it comes to be called that.

Despite the ritual garment-rending of the more excitable liberals, that Court is unlikely to reverse course and head back into the dark ages. True, Warren and Fortas, both mainstays of the "liberal" or "activist" wing of the Court, have already left the bench; Justices Black, Douglas and Harlan, all of them born in the 19th century, may well die or retire in the next four (or eight) years. A Court composed of five Nixon appointees, plus Stewart and White, with only Brennan and Marshall left to fly the old flag, would certainly be more inclined than the Warren Court to proceed slowly and with circumspection—in any direction.

It is likely that the sort of lawyer who inspires confidence in Mr. Nixon will be temperamentally cautious and responsive to the mood of the "forgotten Americans" who feel that criminals have received far too much solicitude and protection and their victims far too little. A Nixon Court could in strict theory undo everything the Warren Court has done since 1953, putting criminals, minorities and urban voters back where God and the Founding Fathers intended them to be. There is, of course, nothing but judicial etiquette to deter the Supreme Court from changing its mind and overruling its own earlier decisions; it has often done so, although usually only after a decent time had elapsed and circumstances and prevailing attitudes had changed. Indeed, many of the Warren Court's landmark decisions—*Brown v. Board of Education, Baker v. Carr* and *Gideon v. Wainwright,* for example—more or less frankly overruled earlier cases.

But this is very unlikely to happen. Few people today would want to kill *Brown, Baker* or *Gideon,* and in any event these cases have largely done their work. The vulnerable decisions are *Miranda* and the related cases on police interrogation, which are also the most unpopular among rank-and-file voters.

I do not think that even a Court with a law-and-order majority would overrule *Miranda.* There are, however, several ways in which it could narrowly circumscribe whatever effect the case might have if left in full vigor. It could, for instance, take a very strict view of what constitutes police "custody" and a very liberal view of what constitutes "waiver" by a suspect of his right to counsel. Congress has tried to dilute the *Miranda* rule by providing in the Crime Control and Safe Streets Act of 1968 that voluntary confessions shall be admissible in Federal trials and that a confession may be found voluntary despite the failure of the police to inform the suspect of his rights to remain silent and talk to a lawyer. By the same token, the provision of that act which requires the admission of eyewitness testimony seems to be intended to kill *United States v. Wade,* which extended the *Miranda* rule by holding that evidence of identification in a police lineup could be barred unless the suspect was represented by counsel. A Court so minded could retreat from *Miranda,* without actually overruling it, by holding (wrongly, in my opinion, but not altogether implausibly) that legislative approval and authorization (though unaccompanied by any legislative effort to insure that a suspect's constitutional rights are observed) confer on police practice a sufficient aura of legitimacy to make constitutional the admission of evidence so obtained. These provisions of the Crime Control Act apply only to Federal trials, but many state legislatures would not be hesitant about copying Congress.

At any rate, it is safe to predict that such a Court would not be quick to invent new protections for criminals, rich or poor. The right to a free lawyer would not be extended to persons accused of misdemeanor (though conviction of some misdemeanors can have serious consequences). When confronted with the argument that the death penalty, having become unusual, has thus become cruel as well, and so forbidden by the Eighth Amendment, a majority of such a Court might be swayed by the old-fashioned, perhaps reprehensible, but undoubtedly popular notion that in some criminals hanging effects a salutary improvement and ought to be more usual than it is—an attitude summed up in the well-known observations of a Scotch judge that the defendant "would be none the worse for a hanging."

Such a cautious Court would not borrow trouble. It would not, for example, go so far out of its way to kick Congress in the pants as did the Warren Court in the case of Adam Clayton Powell. (The Court was probably right in holding that the Constitution did not permit Congress to exclude—as distinct from expel—an elected representative who met its explicit requirements that he be 25 years of age, a citizen of the United States for seven years, and an inhabitant of the state in which he was elected; but the practical effect of that decision, like the Court's reason for making it, remains somewhat obscure.) It may likewise be surmised that such a Court would not be eager to wade deeper into the slough of obscenity; the lower courts would be left to make what they can of the existing ground rules.

But even if the Court comes to be dominated by Nixon appointees—which will not happen right away, if ever—it will not overrule the great decisions of the Warren Court, or even distinguish them out of existence. The Court has too much continuity for that. Moreover, as almost everyone knows, the records of its members before their appointment have rarely been reliable predictors of their conduct as Justices. After all, Earl Warren laid the foundation of his career as a tough prosecuting attorney.

Part 2

JUDICIAL ATTRIBUTES AND PHILOSOPHIES

Editor's Preface

THE IDEAL Supreme Court justice should have intellectual brilliance and rectitude; a self-conscious awareness of his own biases and an unswervable determination to be as impartial as human fallibility will allow; a confidence in majority rule tempered with a passion for personal freedom, equality, and fairness in procedure as well as substance; a vision of moral and national greatness combined with a respect for the federal system; a superior technical proficiency modified only by a sense of justice and philosophic breadth; ethical behavior beyond suspicion; and, if the gods will grant perfection, even a mastery of history, economic, literary skills, and, above all, statecraft and wisdom. Of the nearly one hundred men who have served on the Supreme Court, only Oliver Wendell Holmes and Benjamin N. Cardozo approached the ideal, and perhaps Louis O. Brandeis and Felix Frankfurter might be mentioned in the next breath. Such men are not, however, the type who tend to have the most lasting influence in the shaping of American constitutional law.

The justices who leave the most lasting marks on the Constitution are the powerful advocates, those in whom the judicial temperament flickers most weakly, whose deepest convictions cannot be bridled, and who believe unshakably not only that they are right but that they have a mission to impose their convictions upon the nation. Such men are the judicial activists, those in whom the capacity for self-doubt has atrophied. They do not appreciate, nor even understand, Holmes's dicta that the civilized jurist must be skeptical of his own first principles and must be able to make generalizations, always bearing in mind that no generalization is worth a damn. Many of our greatest—that is, most influential—jurists have been powerful advocates with a nearly limitless ability to persuade themselves that truth, history, wisdom, and the Constitution are on their side, governing their opinions which do little more than declare what the law is. Their position on the Supreme Court is a platform from which to preach to the nation and mold its public policy. They have the comforting assurance of knowing that what is best is what they believe, and that what they believe coincides with the text of the Constitution. Foremost among the powerful advocates in the history of the Court was John Marshall. Joseph Story, Stephen J. Field, and John Marshall Harlan were among other nineteenth-century examples of this judicial genre.

In our own time, Hugo L. Black, William O. Douglas, and Earl Warren are outstanding examples. They are liberal activists, but activism as a judicial philosophy has nothing to do with the liberalism or conservatism of its practitioners. Most activists in our judicial history have been conservatives. Yet Holmes, who in his personal belief was profoundly conservative, has the reputation of being a liberal because he was able, as a judge, to sustain liberal legislation despite his personal skepticism, even hostility, to it—a fact that "added cubits to his judicial stature," said Frankfurter, his apostle. Frankfurter himself, though personally a liberal, earned a reputation as a judicial conservative because he was able as a judge to vote in favor of positions which he privately abhorred. The fact is that judicial activism and its counterpart, judicial self-restraint or passivism, are less revelations of a judge's personal convictions—how he might vote if free to indulge his sympathies and preferences—than revelations of his concept of his role as a judge and that of the Supreme Court in a political democracy.

The most sophisticated of passivists on the Warren Court was Frankfurter, for whom judicial self-restraint expressed a democratic theory. He regarded the powers of the Court as "inherently oligarchic," the Court itself "the non-democratic organ of our government." Judicial review, he believed, restricts the electoral process which is at the center of democratic theory and practice; and it frustrates the policy-making power of the representative institutions which are the product of the electoral process. The Court may be responsive to the people, but it need not be, and it is not responsible in a political sense. Majorities make mistakes, but the Court is equally liable to error, and when it checks the majority it has sapped the capacity of the people to learn from experience and to correct their own mistakes. The real battles of liberalism, from this standpoint, are best won not in the Supreme Court but in legislatures and in the arena of public opinion. The liberal activists, by contrast, see the Court as one of democracy's institutions and the Constitution as a hedge against majoritarian excesses. With the Bill of Rights as their special armor, they are inclined to intervene as much as their judicial position will permit to make the country a better place and to redress wrongs against the poor, the unpopular, and the disadvantaged.

In the initial article in this section, Anthony Lewis, the Pulitzer Prize-winning reporter of the *New York Times* who covered the Supreme Court, examines the qualities needed by a member of the great tribunal. Then follow three articles, two by Lewis and a third by Fred Rodell, a Professor of Law at Yale, on the leading members of the Court during Warren's incumbency—Frankfurter, Black, and Warren himself. Interestingly, all three articles were written in celebration of their subject's seventy-fifth birthday. Lewis captured Frankfurter's ebullience, self-discipline, and, especially, his judicial philosophy. Frankfurter retired five years after the article was published, following a judicial career of twenty-four years of pre-eminent intellectual and technical distinction. While a justice, by sheer force of character, rigorous reasoning, and craftsmanship he led the wing of the Court that braked the activist proclivities of Black, Warren, Douglas, and Brennan.

With Arthur J. Goldberg in Frankfurter's seat, the activists were in command, and Frankfurter's old antagonist, Black, found that many of his dissenting opinions, especially in the area of the rights of the criminally accused, mustered a majority of the Court. Black's longevity (thirty-four years before his retirement in 1971) and his overpowering advocacy made him one of the most influential members in the history of the court. Incredibly, he served with one-fourth of all the members of the Court during the span of its history, and with five of its fifteen chief justices. And he served with extraordinary distinction and constructiveness. When Black was first appointed, the public was shocked by the news that he had briefly been a member of the Ku Klux Klan, but few knew the more revealing facts about his early life—that his first client was a Negro convict, that he was a civil rights lawyer in Alabama in the darkest days, that as a prosecutor he exposed third-degree tactics by the police against Negro suspects, and that when he first ran for the Senate the Klan opposed him while he proudly stood on a poor-man's platform: "I am not now, and never have been, a railroad, power company, or corporation lawyer." Unlike Frankfurter, Black changed little after he donned the black judicial robe. His judicial philosophy, so different from Frankfurter's, brings to mind the remark by Lincoln that two men may honestly differ about a question and both be right. Whether there is or is not a "right" side to the controversy between the activists and the anti-activists, the nation and the Court were served well by both Black and Frankfurter. Lewis, in his piece on Black, catches his zealousness and creativity.

Rodell's appreciation of Warren is also a highly partisan, misleading, and exasperating polemic against Frankfurter, and for that very reason makes provocative reading. A leading member of the school of legal realism which regards the judicial process as subjective and result-oriented, Rodell is completely uncritical of Warren, for the simple reason that he approves of his decisions. Lewis, whose article on Warren, "A Man Born to Act, Not Muse," was written two years later, is as appreciative as Rodell of Warren's achievements as a judicial statesman and equally perceptive in his understanding of Warren. But Lewis gives us a balanced portrait, complete with blemishes which he does not hesitate, though judiciously, to expose. Some of his criticisms, based on a comparison of Warren with Frankfurter and Black, seem overharsh. Warren's great colleagues may have revealed a more consistent adherence to their respective judicial philosophies, compared with the Chief Justice's presumed lack of a judicial philosophy other than reaching the just result and doing good; but however consistent their rhetorical adherence to a philosophy, Frankfurter and Black were as doctrinally inconsistent as Lewis claims Warren was. He judges Warren against perfectionist standards as if demanding that his results and statesmanship be combined with Frankfurter's superior craftsmanship and judicial temperament. The final selection in this section, an interview which Warren gave after his retirement from the Court, is a fascinating illumination of the mind and values of the man whom Lewis called "the closest thing the United States has had to a Platonic Guardian."

What Qualities
for the Court?

by Anthony Lewis

PRECISELY at noon tomorrow the nine justices of the Supreme Court of the United States will step through red velour hangings, take their seats at the bench and officially open a new term of court.

They are, at the moment, nine controversial men. The court has been through periodical storms of criticism in its 167 years, and it is in one now. The uproar began with the school segregation cases of 1954; it has grown since a series of decisions last June upholding individual rights against strongly asserted interests of Congress and the Executive.

Not since the court-packing fight of 1937 has the Supreme Court been so sharp a public issue. And as the liberal critics did then, so the chiefly conservative critics now focus much of their displeasure on the men rather than the institution. A major trouble with the court, they say, is that its members lack the proper qualifications. If only the justices were selected in a different way, we should have a court that would reach more satisfactory decisions.

The qualifications of an ideal justice can be measured only against the extraordinary scope of the job he has to do. The

From the *New York Times Magazine,* October 6, 1957, copyright © 1957 by The New York Times Company.

Supreme Court has the awful responsibility of final power in our system of government. When it finds in the Constitution some limitation on the power of the political branches, that interpretation can be reversed only by a constitutional amendment or through an over-ruling of the prior decision by the court itself. And the words of the Constitution offer only vague, often indeed conflicting guides for the solution of the great political questions which reach the court in the form of lawsuits.

Beyond the scope of the issues facing a justice, the volume of work is extremely heavy. Over a year the justices must pass on more than 1,000 petitions for review, hear hours of argument, write opinions in more than 100 cases—and still have time for the reflection which difficult issues demand. They must work collectively, accommodating themselves to each other's views, with all the intellectual and psychological obstacles that involves.

What, then, are the qualities needed for a seat on what Winston Churchill has called "the most esteemed judicial tribunal in the world"?

President Eisenhower has mentioned from time to time at press conferences some specific qualifications he seeks in Supreme Court appointees. Most significantly, he has said that he prefers to appoint men with prior judicial experience. Of his four nominees—Chief Justice Earl Warren and Associate Justices John M. Harlan, William J. Brennan and Charles E. Whittaker—the last three were judges when appointed, although their service on the bench had been comparatively brief.

The same theme of judicial experience has been sounded by Southern critics of the present court. Southern members of Congress have introduced bills which would require five or even ten years of prior judicial service for a Supreme Court nominee.

Justice Frankfurter, that most ardent student of the court's history, said in a speech recently that "the correlation between prior judicial experience and fitness for the functions of the Supreme Court is zero." Many of the leading analysts of the court's work, past and present, have agreed with this view.

The business of the Supreme Court today is entirely unlike the business of the average state court or lower Federal court. Their staple is private law—contractual disputes, suits for negligence.

Almost no such cases reach the Supreme Court. Its work is constitutional law and such special Federal problems as immigration law, taxation and administrative regulations.

Many of the justices regarded as the greatest in the court's history had no judicial experience before their appointment. Among this group are Marshall, Story, Taney, Miller, Bradley, Hughes, Brandeis.

Of course, there have been distinguished justices who were lower court judges. The pre-eminent examples are Holmes and Cardozo. But their merit was not that they had been judges but that they were Holmes and Cardozo. Holmes, when he was appointed, was known throughout the English-speaking world as a philosopher and historian of the common law. Cardozo was the leading judicial philosopher of his day.

In fact, sitting judges who have been named to the Supreme Court have often been without distinction. At the same time the most praised judges of lower courts have often been passed over for appointment to the Supreme Court. During his years as chief judge of the United States Court of Appeals for the Second Circuit, Learned Hand was certainly the most revered judge in the country. One of the most widely commended judges today is Calvert Magruder of the First Circuit Court of Appeals. No President of either party has promoted them to the Supreme Court.

President Eisenhower has, secondly, mentioned age as a factor— the need for youth on the court. That youth may be helpful cannot be disputed. But that it should not be a conclusive factor is indicated by the impact on history of Justice Holmes' thirty years on the court. He was 61 when appointed.

There has been a widespread assumption of the need for geographical distribution on the court. This has been a common practice, but not one without important exceptions. Between 1925 and 1932 Presidents Coolidge and Hoover made four appointments to the court. Three were New Yorkers—Stone, Hughes, Cardozo— and history surely does not regard their simultaneous service as a misfortune. President Eisenhower has said he "would never think of making an appointment to the Supreme Court merely on the basis of geographical distribution."

The President listed one other qualification: "We must never appoint a man who doesn't have the recognition of the American Bar Association." Names of prospective nominees are now in fact referred to the A.B.A. for its recommendation. This policy raises the question whether power over the appointment of Supreme Court justices should be ceded to a private organization—one, moreover, which represents just a little more than one-third of American lawyers and which has often spoken for a particular point of view.

These factors—judicial experience, age, geography and the opinion of the bar—may all be considerations in the choosing of a justice. But, should they be applied as rigid standards? Should such narrow and artificial qualifications limit the filling of a vacancy on the most powerful and intellectually demanding court in the world?

It would seem that the qualities to be sought in the ideal justice of the Supreme Court are of a broader kind. Foremost among them is largeness of view—an understanding of the political and social institutions which the court often helps to reshape. Understanding may come from experience in the world of affairs of the kind that Charles Evans Hughes brought to the court from his brilliant and creative years in New York politics. Or it may be the understanding of a philosopher like Holmes.

The need for the large view has been stated by Learned Hand. "I venture to believe," he wrote in 1930, "that it is as important to a judge called upon to pass on a question of constitutional law to have at least a bowing acquaintance with Acton and Maitland, with Thucydides, Gibbon and Carlyle, with Homer, Dante, Shakespeare and Milton, with Machiavelli, Montaigne and Rabelais, with Plato, Bacon, Hume and Kant as with the books which have been specifically written on the subject.

"For in such matters everything turns upon the spirit in which he approaches the questions before him. The words he must construe are empty vessels into which he can pour nearly anything he will. Men do not gather figs off thistles, nor supple institutions from judges whose outlook is limited by parish or class."

Most Presidents have sought appointees who shared their views on national policy, and of course that is a President's prerogative. But history shows that such efforts have not always worked out as intended. Jefferson and Madison, arch-opponents of Chief Justice Marshall, saw their own appointees concur in his Federalist views. Lincoln's appointees held his Legal Tender Act unconstitutional. Other examples abound. And it is today's irony that the justices named by President Eisenhower, whose election in 1952 marked a political shift to the Right, have helped set the court on what is generally regarded as a more liberal course.

High on the list of an ideal justice's qualities must be placed the ability of self-expression. The court's influence rests on the persuasiveness of its opinions. So an individual justice's place in history must depend, in part, on the clarity of his analysis and the power of his words.

The opinions of Holmes and Brandeis in dissent have had far greater influence on patterns of American thought in many cases than the holding of the majority. So it was when a bare majority found wiretapping constitutional. Holmes gave wiretapping the indelible label "dirty business." Brandeis wrote an eloquent essay on privacy:

"The makers of our Constitution . . . knew that only a part of the pain, pleasure and satisfaction of life are to be found in material things. They sought to protect Americans in their beliefs, their thoughts, their emotions and their sensations. They conferred, as against the Government, the right to be let alone—the most comprehensive of rights and the right most valued by civilized men."

The technical accomplishments of the lawyer also have a special place among the talents desirable in a justice. Subtle questions of Federal jurisdiction may underlie the broadest issues of policy—for example, the question of Federal power to override a state governor's opposition to school integration. Members of the court especially versed in the jurisdictional niceties have been relatively scarce in the past. One non-political complaint heard about the court today is that it does not deal adequately with technical legal problems.

Disinterestedness is another essential quality. No one can wholly put aside the prejudices of a lifetime, but it is a judge's duty to try. Closely related is what Professor Paul A. Freund of the Harvard Law School has called "the capacity to be reached by reason, the freedom from self-pride that without embarrassment permits a change of mind." Few have demonstrated this quality as gracefully as Justice Jackson, who once wrote an opinion disowning a view he had expressed as Attorney General and quoting Justice Story for a precedent: "My own error, however, can furnish no ground for its being adopted by this court."

A justice must also have, as Professor Herbert Wechsler of Columbia Law School has put it, "a sense for the importance of tradition—its special importance in a country with poor resources for developing and maintaining tradition." He must be able to work creatively within the confines of that tradition which is so much a part of the court's charter of legitimacy.

To do the work of the court—and it is hard, demanding work —a justice must be a man of intellect and of mental and physical stamina. He must be decisive when necessary; a judge has to make up his mind. At the same time he requires sensitivity to others, the ability to work in a group. He cannot be a prima donna.

Is there ever a candidate who can meet all these tests? The run of Supreme Court appointments in our history has not been particularly distinguished. Even with the best of intentions, it will never be easy to find the ideal justice. All the more reason, therefore, to eschew restrictive qualifications, to keep the ideal in view, to look for the qualities of a Supreme Court justice wherever they may be found—among men on the bench, at the bar, in the law school faculties, in public life.

The words of Learned Hand again sum up. The qualities which clear the path to truth, he once wrote, are "scepticism, tolerance, discrimination, urbanity, some—but not too much—reserve toward change, insistence upon proportion, and, above all, humility before the vast unknown."

An Appreciation
of Justice Frankfurter

by Anthony Lewis

IT IS HARD to believe that the Supreme Court justice who whistles "The Stars and Stripes Forever" in the marble corridors, the justice of the bright eye, the exuberantly curious mind, the energetic step—in short, that most youthful of men, Felix Frankfurter—is about to turn 75.

Mr. Justice Frankfurter celebrates his seventy-fifth birthday this Friday. He has been a member of the Court for almost nineteen years, and for three decades before he had been in or on the edge of public life. But despite this service he remains to the public, by all indications, a perplexing figure.

The puzzlement is not especially puzzling. For the justice is a man of contradictions. It would not be too inaccurate to characterize him as a passionate ascetic, a libertarian traditionalist, a worldly intellectual.

No better statement of the judicial philosophy of Justice Frankfurter can be found than that in one of his own opinions. A majority of the Supreme Court in 1943 held it unconstitutional for a state to require children whose religion forbade it to salute the flag. Justice Frankfurter, dissenting, began:

"One who belongs to the most vilified and persecuted minority

From the *New York Times Magazine,* November 10, 1957, copyright © 1957 by The New York Times Company.

in history is not likely to be insensible to the freedoms guaranteed by our Constitution. Were my purely personal attitude relevant I should wholeheartedly associate myself with the general libertarian views in the Court's opinion, representing as they do the thought and action of a lifetime.

"But as judges we are neither Jew nor Gentile, neither Catholic nor agnostic. . . . As a member of this Court I am not justified in writing my private notions of policy into the Constitution, no matter how deeply I may cherish them or how mischievous I may deem their disregard."

That, then, is the dominant theme—the need for judges to put aside their private views, to defer to legislative judgments, to exercise the self-restraint inherent in Justice Frankfurter's conception of the judge's function. It is a theme derived from, among other sources, the greatest of his heroes, Mr. Justice Holmes.

Of course, the Frankfurter view represents just one side of a continuing debate on the role of the Supreme Court. There are those, on the Court and off, who believe it should play a much more aggressive part in advancing civil liberties, and who regard Justice Frankfurter's philosophy as dangerously uncreative.

The reasons for judicial self-restraint in the Frankfurter canon are several. There is, first, the thesis that reliance on the courts to preserve our liberties drains responsibility from those who should exercise it—the legislature and the people themselves. The tendency is to say: Perhaps this legislation is unwise, but if it is too bad, the Supreme Court will knock it down.

A second reason is the belief that it is undemocratic and dangerous for nine men, appointed for life, to exercise their power to veto legislation, except in the narrowest, most evident and urgent cases. This belief was hardened in the crucible of the Nineteen Twenties and Thirties, when the private views of a slim majority on the Supreme Court overturned urgent economic measures of state and nation.

Finally, Justice Frankfurter believes that for the Court to attempt too much, to press its policy views, is to invite its own destruction. That was for him the lesson in the Nineteen Thirties, when a self-willed Court lost public confidence and brought itself to the brink of drastic reform.

Concern for the Supreme Court as an institution is perhaps first among Justice Frankfurter's motivations. It is this concern that has made him protest more than once against hasty decisions, and that made him, for example, read his colleagues last year a twenty-five-page lecture against taking on too many trivial cases for review.

Among the present justices he is the outstanding student of the Court's history. His institutional sense takes form also in a special respect for the Court's traditions.

The most significant aspect of his feeling for the institution of the Court is one inherited especially from another of his heroes, Mr. Justice Brandeis. That is Justice Frankfurter's insistence on confining the grounds of decision in any case to the minimum needed to settle it, avoiding constitutional decision whenever possible, and rigorously enforcing technical jurisdictional requirements. He is especially fitted for this job because he was, as a law school professor, an authority on jurisdictional rules.

These interwoven philosophical strands—self-restraint, the institutional sense, respect for tradition and technical rules—have brought on Justice Frankfurter the label "conservative." This comes as an unfriendly judgment from some who expected the new justice, when he was appointed in 1939, to be a judicial New Dealer. It comes as praise from, for example, a Boston bar which feared him in 1939 as a radical.

Both reactions are based on what Justice Frankfurter would consider the same misconception—the idea that a judicial decision has anything whatever to do with "liberalism" or "conservatism" in a political sense. Professor Louis L. Jaffe of Harvard Law School concluded in an authoritative study of Justice Frankfurter's opinions: "It is of the very essence of his judicial philosophy that his role as a judge precludes him from having a program couched in these terms of choice."

It would be a mistake, and a grave one, to believe that Justice Frankfurter's approach to his job limits his importance on the Supreme Court. A good case can be made—and is made, by his enemies as often as his friends—for the proposition that he has been a most influential member of the Court.

For one thing, he plays a paramount part in defining the issues. Because almost any case can be decided on many different grounds, the most important question may be what to decide. Again and again during oral argument before the Court Justice Frankfurter will raise the issue on which the decision is eventually rested. His role in conference is said to be similar. One of his loudest critics, Walton Hamilton, complained in 1947:

"The Court has no business allowing him to select, from all the issues the case holds, the question upon which it must turn."

Moreover, Justice Frankfurter has been a balance wheel, often casting the deciding vote in the Court's recurrent divisions. And he has helped to shape the course of decisions in ways that do not necessarily appear in the printed opinions.

Signs of his influence appear, for example, in the school segregation cases. Two especially notable factors contributed to the moral force of the 1954 decision. The first was the length of deliberation by the Court, the repeated orders for reargument of the cases. This calculated delay bore the Frankfurter trademark.

The second factor was the unanimity of the Court when it finally spoke through Chief Justice Warren. That unanimity may have been made possible by the formula devised to permit gradual desegregation—compliance "with all deliberate speed." There is a belief, that is, that one or more of the justices were reluctant even to decide the constitutional claim if a decision necessarily entailed immediate, drastic judicial enforcement. The gradual compliance formula is a concept that could have come from Justice Frankfurter, and the phrase "with all deliberate speed" is in fact a favorite of his that he had used in at least three opinions before the school cases.

Boston's misconception of Felix Frankfurter as a radical, and its subsequent mistrust of his appointment to the Court, derived in good part from his role in bringing the Sacco-Vanzetti case to world attention. He was a Professor of Law at Harvard then, and as a private citizen he wrote devastating attacks upon the murder convictions of the two anarchists. But the point was not their politics. It was that they had been deprived, in part because of their politics, of a fair trial.

A deep belief in the importance of fair procedure has been as evident in Frankfurter the judge as in Frankfurter the citizen commentator. His creed was expressed in a 1943 opinion: "The history of liberty has largely been the history of observance of procedural safeguards."

In this area the justice's philosophy does not emphasize deference to the political branches. As he sees it, the courts have special competence to pass on the requirements of fair procedure, and a special obligation not to be instruments of injustice. His particular interest has been the Fourth Amendment's prohibition against "unreasonable searches and seizures." Dissenting in 1947 from the Court's approval of a search without warrant, he wrote:

"What is involved far transcends the fate of some sordid offender. Nothing less is involved than that which makes for an atmosphere of freedom as against a feeling of fear and repression for society as a whole."

Closely related to his views on criminal procedure are his strong feelings on what he has called "the integrity of the prosecutorial system." One of the great experiences of his life was his service as assistant to Henry L. Stimson, then United States Attorney in New York, beginning in 1906. Mr. Stimson has been Justice Frankfurter's model of rectitude, integrity, selflessness. Very little distresses him so much as to see a Government officer fall below the Stimson standard.

To Justice Frankfurter, improper means can never be justified by the end of fighting crime. Thus, when Federal agents planted a recording device on an undercover man while he talked with a criminal, and so obtained the latter's conviction, the Justice dissented. He wrote:

"Of course, criminal prosecution is more than a game. But in any event it should not be deemed a dirty game in which 'the dirty business' of criminals is outwitted by 'the dirty business' of law officers. The contrast between morality professed by society and immorality practiced on its behalf makes for contempt of law. Respect for law cannot be turned on and off as though it were a hot-water faucet."

"Dirty business" had been Justice Holmes' phrase for wiretapping. Like him, Justice Frankfurter had wanted to hold wiretapping unconstitutional—and never quite had the votes on the Court to do so.

Underlying his views on wiretapping and illegal search—"the knock at the door," he has called it—is Justice Frankfurter's deep belief in the importance of privacy. For the same reason he has had relatively little sympathy for sound-truck operators and peddlers who invade the home to hawk their wares.

In 1948 he wrote:

"The men whose labors brought forth the Constitution of the United States had the street outside Independence Hall covered with earth so that their deliberations might not be disturbed by passing traffic. Our democracy presupposes the deliberative process as a condition of thought and of responsible choice by the electorate. To the Founding Fathers it would hardly seem a proof of progress . . . that the blare of sound trucks must be treated as a necessary medium in the deliberative process."

The phrase "the deliberative process" is one that comes naturally from Felix Frankfurter. He is that rare bird, the unashamed intellectual. In a softening civilization, he has retained the ability and the will to think problems through in a tough-minded way.

Perhaps one of his most important contributions to the Supreme Court has been his insistence on exposing the real difficulties in cases, refusing to ignore or evade them. No one has ever accused him of being mentally lazy. His effort—whatever his views on the merits of the case—is always to work out rational, not sentimental, solutions.

Nor is his intellectual life bounded by the Supreme Court. The world of ideas lives also in his home, thanks to a remarkable wife, the former Marion Denman. Friends—and the justice himself —ascribe much of the justice's success in life to Mrs. Frankfurter. She is described as a woman of unusual wisdom and conviction, his intellectual equal and not prepared to be bowled over by his brilliance, who has tested his ideas by making him define and explain and prove.

Justice Frankfurter is no ivory-tower intellectual. He is a cultivated man, an eighteenth-century man in the range of his interests. He reads everything—the most obscure newspaper stories, philosophy, science, complete reports of the high courts of Britain, Canada, Australia. He corresponds with people all over the world. Among his friends have been John Dewey, Thomas Mann, Al Smith, Alexander Woollcott, Albert Einstein, Alfred North Whitehead, Chaim Weizmann, Franklin Roosevelt.

One of his most important personal characteristics is his love of people as people—his interest, his joy in them. Without children himself, he loves children and they love him. The extraordinary affection which joins him to his former law clerks brings them from all over the country annually for a dinner, usually held near the anniversary of his appointment to the Court, which may be the high point of the justice's year.

He is a man who feels strongly about people and about ideas, a man of fierce loyalties and convictions. While he was a Harvard Law School professor he spent much of his time battling for causes. To meet him now is to sense an electric presence, to know the vigor of the views he can no longer publicly express.

The truth is that Felix Frankfurter, exponent of judicial restraint, is really a man of emotion. No one could fail to see this in the intensity with which he will argue any subject except Supreme Court business in private conversation, his small frame darting here and there, his hand now and then gripping his listener's elbow as he makes a point. This quality is evident in his teacher's love of provocation and contention, the unrestricted give-and-take with his law clerks, the heckling from the bench that distresses lawyers who are unprepared for it.

"A passionate person," one friend calls him, "who has given up the other passions of his life for this one—the institution of the Court."

That this passionate man finds it no easy job to be a judge, to put aside personal feelings, to suffer the disapproval of libertarian friends—all this is evident from the language of Justice Frankfurter's dissent in the flag salute case. The conflict of man and judge is a reason, too, for his need to explain himself in so many separate concurring and dissenting opinions.

He would not expect it to be said that he wholly succeeds in reaching his goal of judicial disinterestedness. But his effort does not slacken. Recently, during an oral argument, he got the impression that a lawyer was appealing to his personal view of a harsh deportation statute.

"Never mind what I think of it," he said sharply from the bench. "I think very ill of it."

Learned Hand, the revered retired chief judge of the United States Court of Appeals for the Second Circuit, was asked recently for comment on Justice Frankfurter's approaching birthday. His answer emphasized the justice's striving for disinterestedness.

"In consequence [of Justice Frankfurter's view of the judicial role]," Judge Hand wrote, "I regard him at the moment as the most important single figure in our whole judicial system.

"He has reached an age that in earlier times might have seemed too great for the severe public duties of his office. In his case a superabundant vitality that is apparent to all gives promise of a further long period during which he will sit in the Court, to whose work and standing he has contributed so much.

"It would be impossible for me to think of any other judge whose continuance in his duties I welcome more unreservedly."

Justice Black at 75: Still the Dissenter

by Anthony Lewis

ONE OF THE most remarkable figures in the history of the Supreme Court turns 75 tomorrow. Hugo La Fayette Black is in his twenty-fourth year on the Court; for fifteen years he has been the senior justice in point of service. He has been for years, and he remains, the leader of a new and important school of legal thought, locked in combat with an opposing school on the Supreme Court.

He marks, in a way, the beginning of the Court's modern history. He was the first of Franklin D. Roosevelt's appointees—named in 1937, just after the old Court had abandoned its attempt to turn back the tide of the New Deal.

It will be understandable if Justice Black thinks back, tomorrow, to his first days on the Court. Perhaps no other justice had so tumultuous, so unpleasant a beginning. Seldom has a man been so ironically misjudged.

He was a Senator from Alabama when F. D. R. nominated him to the Court. During the confirmation debate there was talk that he might have been a member of the Ku Klux Klan. His supporters denied it. He said nothing. Then, after he was confirmed,

From the *New York Times Magazine,* February 26, 1961, copyright © 1961 by The New York Times Company.

The Pittsburgh Post-Gazette brought forward proof that he had been in the Klan from 1923 to 1925.

"At every session of the Court," thundered an editorial in The New York Times, "the presence on the bench of a justice who has worn the white robe of the Ku Klux Klan will stand as a living symbol of the fact that here the cause of liberalism was unwittingly betrayed."

He had been on the bench only a few months when a newspaper man, evidently drawing on conversations with Justice Harlan F. Stone, suggested that there was concern among his fellow justices about Justice Black's competence. The articles questioned whether he could "carry his share" of the Court's work.

Can forecasts ever have been more grotesquely wrong?

In the history of the Supreme Court there has been no more zealous, no more single-minded advocate of individual liberty than Justice Black. No one would dream today of questioning his ability. Indeed, his skill, his dedication, his hard work and his tenacity are qualities equally admired by friends and feared by critics.

And there are admirers and critics in large numbers. It is difficult to be neutral about Hugo Black, for he is a man of strong and positive views. Before talking of Black the man, it is important to sketch the judicial philosophy which has provoked so much controversy and had so much influence.

The great conflict on the Court, the subject of endless discussion, is between those generally sharing the Black philosophy and an opposing school generally associated with Justice Felix Frankfurter. It is easy to exaggerate their differences; they agree on many fundamentals, from fair procedure to nondiscrimination on racial grounds. But there are deep differences.

The Frankfurter view emphasizes the importance of "judicial self-restraint," of permitting government to do things a judge may think even foolish, because the primary responsibility for government lies with legislators and executives. From this point of view those on the Black side are, in the late Justice Jackson's phrase, "libertarian judicial activists."

Justice Black would probably accept that characterization without shame. His view is that the Constitution commands the Supreme Court to enforce certain protections of the individual no matter what legislators may have thought, and no matter what the consequences. To do less, in his view, is to abandon the Constitution.

The justice set out his views a year ago in a rare address. It was a full-scale assault on the Frankfurter view that governmental needs—the reasons behind a challenged statute or order—must be weighed against individual interests in every case.

"I cannot accept this approach to the Bill of Rights," Justice Black said. "It is my belief that there *are* 'absolutes' in our Bill of Rights, and that they were put there on purpose by men who knew what words meant, and meant their prohibitions to be absolutes."

As an example of an "absolute," Justice Black mentioned the First Amendment's provision that "Congress shall make no law . . . abridging the freedom of speech." The phrase, he said, "is composed of plain words, easily understood." He understands it to mean, literally, "no law," no matter what justification may be offered.

Thus, Justice Black has resolutely—and so far unsuccessfully— argued that the First Amendment deprives the Federal Government of all power to punish the mailing of obscene material. Likewise, he dissented in passionate terms when the Court upheld the conviction of Communist leaders for conspiring to advocate overthrow of the Government. In his view, the Government simply has no power to keep a man from reading or saying what he wants, no matter how damaging a result the Government may be able to show.

Critics note that Justice Black himself has implicitly found some elastic in his absolutes when he saw a compelling governmental purpose. He wrote the opinion of the Court upholding the worst racist measure in this country's recent history—the removal of all persons of Japanese ancestry from the West Coast during World War II. It was a time of emergency, he said, when even martial law could have been imposed, and the military judgment had to be respected by the Court.

But Prof. Charles L. Black Jr. (no relation), of the Yale Law School, had made the point that even if there are no absolute absolutes, Justice Black's insistence that there are signifies an attitude that can make the difference in deciding cases.

A good example was a 1958 decision holding that Congress could deprive a native-born American of citizenship for voting in a foreign election. Justice Frankfurter, for the majority, said the statute rested on the Government's foreign-policy power. The only question, he said, was whether there was a "rational nexus" between that power and this specific statute. He found that there was, because voting by Americans abroad might embarrass our foreign relations.

Justice Black was one of four dissenters. He wrote:

"The notion that citizenship can be snatched away whenever such deprivation bears some 'rational nexus' to the implementation of a power granted Congress by the Constitution is a dangerous and frightening proposition. By this standard a citizen could be transformed into a stateless outcast for evading his taxes. . . ."

The debate, then, starts with different assumptions. The Frankfurter side looks first to the needs of government, Federal or local. Justice Black looks first to the individual. And to free the individual of governmental restraint he is more willing to break ground legally, to overrule precedent, to risk conflict with official and public opinion.

The most important expressions of the Black philosophy concern the First Amendment. Prof. Herbert Wechsler of the Columbia Law School has even suggested that the heart of the debate between the two judicial schools is really over the scope of the First Amendment.

In Justice Black's view, the First Amendment prohibits not only punishment for speech but punishment for not disclosing one's thought. He has argued that Congressional or state investigating committees may not, constitutionally, compel testimony on anything in the area of speech or belief—including Communist party membership.

The press, too, gets special protection in the Black view. One of his most important opinions, for a 5-4 majority, upset a contempt sentence imposed on The Los Angeles Times for running an article demanding severe prison sentences in a case still before the courts.

A number of other themes can be sensed in Justice Black's long record on the Supreme Court. One is sympathy for the little man, for the downtrodden—the alien, the criminal defendant, the injured worker.

He has fought for expansion of the Constitution's bars against double jeopardy and compelled self-incrimination. Only once in all his years on the Court has he voted to affirm a lower court which had upset a jury verdict for a plaintiff in a railroad injury case. Indeed, he loves the jury as an institution and has read the Constitution to compel its use in new areas.

He has been the foremost advocate of the proposition that free speech and other "individual rights" have a "preferred position" in the Constitution over economic rights. It might almost be said that for him governmental economic regulations are presumptively valid, restrictions on individual liberty presumptively invalid.

This is not to say that economic interests get no recognition in the Black philosophy. He wrote the principal opinion when the Court struck down President Truman's seizure of the nation's steel mills in 1952. But his point was not protection of an economic interest. It was that the President had attempted to legislate, a power confined to Congress by the Constitution.

A major theme has been what might be called Justice Black's search for certainty, for simplicity. He is uneasy about giving judges free rein to balance all the considerations and come up with what they consider a reasonable answer.

"The balancing approach to basic individual liberties," he said in his lecture a year ago, "assumes to legislators and judges more power than either the framers [of the Constitution] or I myself believe should be entrusted, without limitation, to any man or any group of men."

And so, in many areas of the law, Justice Black has looked for formulas that would avoid the necessity for nice judgments by judges. He has argued forcefully that the provisions of the Bill of Rights should be applied to the states exactly as to the Federal Government—not just those guarantees considered "fundamental" by the Court, as a majority has always held. Even in construing the Sherman Antitrust Law, he has favored an absolute standard, strict toward business.

This judicial philosophy has roots, as it must, in the life of Hugo Black.

He was born in Clay County, Ala., a backward rural area. His father was a poor farmer, then a general-store owner. It was the wrong side of the tracks.

The young man skipped college, spent two years at medical school, then switched to law. He was a trial lawyer, a police judge, a county prosecutor. After serving as an artillery captain in the war, he married a Birmingham girl from the right side of the tracks, Josephine Patterson Foster, and practiced law in Birmingham. It was during those years that he joined the Klan. He has never really said why, but the common assumption is that he wanted to get into politics and Klan membership was a help in those days. In 1926 he was elected to the Senate.

He may have been the most radical Senator the South ever produced. He led the fight for the Wage-Hour Bill and the Public Utility Holding Company Act. He mercilessly investigated the utility lobbyists, subpoenaing 5,000,000 telegrams to check their origins. The New York Times called him "a bitter and uncompromising advocate of extreme New Deal measures."

His nomination to the Supreme Court just after the defeat of Roosevelt's packing plan was a typical Roosevelt stroke. F. D. R. knew the Senate would not want such a radical on the Court— but would doubtless confirm him out of Senatorial courtesy. The vote to confirm was 63 to 16.

Justice Black has always believed that the storm that soon broke was really occasioned not by dislike of his past membership in the K. K. K. but by dislike of his radical economic views. A certain bitterness toward newspapers shows to this day, because of the part they played in what he considered a disingenuous attack. But his total commitment to freedom of the press as a doctrine has not been affected by this distaste for newspapers in real life.

From this personal history emerges the picture of a man who sympathizes with the underdog, who has no love for wealth or vested status, who is suspicious of unbridled power in either official or private hands. Hugo Black is a Jeffersonian, an old-fashioned agrarian radical.

All this may sound less human than Justice Black is as a person. He is no zealot who excludes from his life anything not connected with his cause. On the contrary, he enjoys small talk, he plays an avid game of bridge and he gets on easily with almost anyone. He is the only member of the Court who walks down the line in the public cafeteria joking with the waitresses.

He is fond of children—as is, interestingly, Justice Frankfurter. Justice William J. Brennan Jr. remarks that his 12-year-old daughter, Nancy, "has two special favorites—Felix and Hugo."

He is described as a particularly gracious and generous host—to, among others, colleagues whose judicial views he deplores. He will spend an evening with them discussing, not law, but world affairs and personalities and politics and books. Perhaps especially books, because Justice Black is an extraordinary reader. Lacking much formal education, he decided to make up for it by reading. He has read all of Jefferson, Plutarch, Locke, all the great original works of history and philosophy, classical and modern.

"What interests him," a friend says, "is what happened in other ages in the struggle for freedom. He can prove to you that what is happening today has happened before."

History is more than an avocation for Justice Black; it is part of his job. More than any other justice, he finds in history clues to the meaning of the Constitution. The clues become deep beliefs, even certainties. One admirer remarks:

"I don't believe there's another man in the country who has the love for the Bill of Rights that Justice Black has. It takes that sort of love to reach his degree of absolute certainty."

The depth of his feelings is often apparent in the courtroom. In 1959, the Court held that successive Federal and state trials of the same man for the same act do not constitute double jeopardy. Justice Frankfurter, in stating his opinion for the majority, made a passing reference to "the so-called Bill of Rights." When Justice Black read his dissent, his voice rang with passion as he said:

"This case concerns the Bill of Rights, not the so-called Bill of Rights."

The South remains very much a part of Hugo Black. One feels that he is troubled by the attacks made on him there because he has joined his colleagues in opposing racial discrimination. A son, Hugo Jr., practices law in Birmingham and pays some of the price for his father's views. (Another son, Sterling, is a lawyer in New Mexico and was elected a State Senator last fall; a daughter, Josephine, is married to a New Jersey doctor.)

Those who meet Justice Black now are struck by what one lawyer called "the great inner simplicity of the man." He shows no malice toward those with whom he disagrees—a factor important in his relationships with his colleagues. It has been said that in arguing over the decision of a case "he has a point of view, he urges it strenuously, vigorously, but no one ever feels bad when he's finished. He always indicates that the man on the other side has a point of view which he appreciates, even though he can't agree."

On the bench, Justice Black is gentle in manner, his voice soft and Southern. But no one should be fooled into thinking he is soft inside. Many who know him would agree with the one-time law clerk who called him "the most powerful man I have ever met."

During an argument he often waits to the end, then quietly asks a few questions that go to the heart of the case. If counsel is making a point he likes but making it badly—as often happens —he may begin, "As I understand your argument, . . ." and go on to restate it powerfully. If counsel is on the side Justice Black does not like, his few soft questions at the end will be steel inside. Unless counsel is careful, he will find his head severed painlessly.

A homely remark from Justice Black often will put a case in a new light. This term, for example, the Court heard argument on whether a defendant found guilty had a personal right to speak to the judge before sentencing. Another justice suggested that perhaps the defendant's lawyer could speak better for him, but Justice Black observed: "The lawyer's already done all the talking he could and got him convicted."

Frequently, in a Black dissent, there is an air of his standing alone against a hostile world—the despairing tone of one who has often fought against long odds.

Justice Black has frequently been in dissent, but he has no real ground for despair. For one thing he now has three colleagues who are quite regularly with him—Chief Justice Earl Warren and Justices Douglas and Brennan. They often pick up the one more vote needed for a majority. And, for another, Justice Black is a very determined fighter, who never gives up and who has won his share of protracted struggles.

Even on the issues he has lost, Hugo Black has been enormously influential. His constant push toward his philosophic goals has surely moved the Court nearer to them; his presence has played a most significant part in making this Court more concerned than any of its predecessors for individual liberty.

Justice Black's admirers regard him as the most courageous and creative of judges. His critics consider him "lawless," a judge who shapes the law to advance the interests he favors. But no one would question his influence. A Government lawyer put it this way recently:

"The test of his impact on the Supreme Court is to try to envisage it without him. Despite the great issues that have come before the Court, without him these would have been years of complacency."

It Is the
Earl Warren Court

by Fred Rodell

> *To the Birchers and churchers,*
> *Earl Warren*
> *Heads a Court only fit for*
> *abhorrin';*
> *As he hunches up there*
> *Like a big grizzly bear,*
> *They're convinced he's the bear that*
> *is foreign.*

NOR IS IT the Birchers and churchers alone who have, for some years now, been chucking brickbats at the big, bluff, friendly 14th Chief Justice of the United States and at the Court which he has finally come to lead toward the deeply democratic and libertarian ends he has long believed in. Thus, the Harvard Law School's Prof. Paul Freund, disciple of the late Felix Frankfurter, has accused the Warren Court of "a tendency to make broad principles do service for specific problems that demand differentiation, a tendency toward overbroadness that is not an augury of enduring work." Thus, Barry Goldwater recently intoned: "Of all three branches of Government, today's Supreme Court is the least

From the *New York Times Magazine,* March 13, 1966, copyright © 1966 by The New York Times Company.

faithful to the constitutional tradition of limited government and to the principle of legitimacy in the exercise of power." Thus, a former Frankfurter law clerk, now teaching at Yale, has wailed: "The Court seems to lack a sense of the limitations of the institution, a sense of what it can do single-handedly. If it tries to take on too much all at once, it will only undermine public confidence and damage its effectiveness." More bluntly, and certainly less evasively, a group that stretches from Southern racists to scared state legislators to little old ladies with Reds under their beds and tennis shoes at the ready, has been chanting for several years: "Impeach Earl Warren."

If that sturdy Californian—that one-time local prosecutor, District Attorney, state Attorney-General, three-term Governor and defeated candidate for the U.S. Vice-Presidency—is bothered by any of this hullabaloo, he does not show it. As he celebrates this week his 75th birthday, he seems more mellow, more gently sure of himself, more immune to sideline criticism than ever before.

Maybe he remembers that no less a critic than Thomas Jefferson once wrote of John Marshall and his Court: "An opinion is huddled up in conclave, perhaps by a majority of one, delivered as if unanimous, and with the silent acquiescence of lazy or timid associates, by a crafty chief judge, who sophisticates the law to his mind, by the turn of his own reasoning"—and that Marshall is known universally today as "the great Chief Justice." Surely Earl Warren knows that his own conduct of the Court is squarely in the boldly activist tradition of John Marshall—and that those bookish folk who purport to revere John Marshall, long dead, while reproaching a very live Earl Warren for not respecting their own anemic, academic and fast-fading philosophy of "judicial self-restraint" are contradicting and fooling none but themselves.

By contrast to his pretentiously professional detractors, such as one who bewailed that Warren "never had an abstract thought in all his life"—a comment intended as an insult but perhaps a tribute to Warren's realism—the Chief Justice is not one for self-delusion. He is well aware of his own strengths and disarming about what many might deem his weaknesses.

He has long conceded that he makes no claim to being an

intellectual in the look-it-up-in-the-library sense that characterizes many of his colleagues. Indeed, his first great and famous school-desegregation opinion, *Brown v. Board of Education,* was almost unique in its off-hand dismissal of mountains of legal and historical research from both sides and in its pragmatic dependence on the present-day results of separate schools.

When, as so often, Warren bends his bulk over the high bench to ask some prosecutor, defending an appealed conviction with citations and precedents and principles, "Yes, yes—but were you *fair?*" the fairness he refers to is no jurisprudential abstraction. It relates to such practical matters as methods of arrest, questioning of suspects, police conduct, trial tactics—matters which Warren understands as intimately as when he himself was doing the prosecuting back in Alameda County, California, 40-odd years ago.

In the course of a recent conversation with me, the Chief expanded on his nonintellectual, unabstract slant toward the job of judging and stressed some of the more positive facets of his philosophy. He does not consider himself, he said, much of a muchness as a writer; several brethren—unnamed—were more facile with words. What he cares about are results, and preferably unanimous or near-unanimous results, rather than fine or fancy phrases which may trigger dissents. It is not too hard to guess that both the first desegregation decision and the second ("with all deliberate speed"), a year later, were worked over and over in their wording by Warren in order not to lose a single vote—although Warren, of course, did not tell me this, nor did I ask him.

And it was neither Warren nor any of his colleagues, past or present, who told me some years ago (law clerks occasionally talk out of school) that a bare minimum of four votes brought the *Brown* case to the Court—by what lawyers call a grant of certiorari, after years of denying certiorari to similar school desegregation cases—and that in conference at least three Justices came close to dissenting until their new Chief put on all the pressure he could wield. I tell this tale—and let him who can prove it wrong deny it—to illustrate the result-minded pragmatism and power of Earl Warren.

It is precisely that sort of pragmatism that a Supreme Court Justice most needs today—when half the cases the Court hears deal with some new issue or new angle of individual rights and liberties, subjects which took up barely 2 per cent of the Court's calendar 30 years ago. Further, almost every case the Court now deals with is a public law case, involving, if not a constitutional question, the interpretation of a statute or the overseeing of an administrative agency.

That is why Justice Brennan, who spent seven years on various New Jersey courts, dealing with private litigation over wills and property rights and torts and trusts and such, laughs at the notion that prior judicial experience is worth 2 cents to a Supreme Court Justice, except in learning how to put on a robe. That is why such learned legal scholars as Holmes and Cardozo made their greatest contributions on state courts, not on the Supreme Court. And that is why such politically-minded realists as Marshall and Warren might have been failures as state—or even lower Federal—judges but can become giants as Supreme Court Justices.

Warren, like President Johnson, is no scholar. What both have working for them is the kind of devastating drive that less dedicated folk just plain succumb to. Warren, like Johnson, *uses* scholars. Black—and, to a slightly lesser extent, Douglas—along with bright young law clerks—have given Warren the precedents, the library references, the footnotes, when he wanted them. It is important to remember that if there were not legal learning on both sides no case would ever reach the Supreme Court. An honest judge—and Warren is one—passes over such matters lightly. He cares about results. Just as Marshall, no legal "scholar" either, sometimes depended on Justice Story to make him sound more learned, so Warren may depend on a colleague or a clerk. The one was—and the other is—more concerned with creating the stuff of future scholarship than borrowing book-learning ready-made from the past.

Going back to the Chief's own appraisal of his limitations and his virtues, I recall that he told me—quietly suggesting my question was moronic, which indeed it was to a confirmed judicial realist—that, of *course,* a man's early life and experiences could not but affect his views and votes on the Court. Thus, when a

Federal Employers' Liability Act case comes up for consideration, Warren still sees, mirrored in his mind, the tragic accidents in which railroad workers, of whom his father was one (though he escaped injury), were crippled or killed. "Safely city-bred judges can't envision such tragedies—or what they mean to a whole family," he exclaimed.

Not entirely irrelevantly, he granted that the city boys knew far more about money matters and financial stuff than he. Thus too, California's fear of—and discrimination against—Orientals, which offended even the adolescent pure-white Warren, laid the early background for his tough attitude toward Southern segregation. The fact that, as Attorney General of California, he pressed the uprooting and confinement of the state's Japanese residents can perhaps be explained by the emotional atmosphere of wartime. At the least, by contrast, it provides a measure of his subsequent growth.

But it is in the field of civil liberties as applied to criminal suspects that Chief Warren, for two decades a prosecutor, and so overseer of police activities, feels most at home, most confident of his own solid knowledge. As his Court, term by term, extends the protection of the Fourth, Fifth, Sixth and Eighth Amendments to the Constitution—as the guarantee against unreasonable searches and seizures, the privilege against self-incrimination, the right to counsel and other measures of fairness are given ever wider scope—Warren beams with a special pleasure and pride. For he will tell you that police and prosecutors, if they are at all efficient, do not have to cut corners or wink at rules—and that, when they do so, they are proclaiming their own laziness or stupidity.

He will tell you, too, that never once in his 20 years as a prosecutor did he have a conviction reversed for unfair treatment, in any form, of a criminal defendant. The charge against the current Supreme Court that Warren most deeply resents, because he knows from experience its falsity, is that of "coddling criminals."

Strangely—or perhaps not, in light of the man's result-oriented realism—his favorite decision during his tenure as Chief is none of the libertarian "criminal-coddling" extensions of the Bill of Rights, nor any of the equally libertarian First Amendment rulings on free speech, free press or free assembly that have led to charges that the Court is also coddling Communists. It is not even, as most people would probably assume, the first big desegregation case, *Brown,* in which Warren, less than a year on the Court, performed the near-miracle of achieving not only a unanimous vote but a unanimous opinion—and through which the Court took the lead over a reluctant executive (Eisenhower came close to disowning the decision) and a Dixie-dominated Congress (there would be no new Civil Rights Act if the "least dangerous branch" had not spoken out) in doing away with racial discrimination.

No, the Chief Justice did not hesitate a split second when I asked him to name his most important opinion. *"Reynolds v. Sims,* of course," he said. *Reynolds v. Sims* was the Court's second major voting-reapportionment ruling, built on *Baker v. Carr,* two years before. *Reynolds v. Sims* was technically not one case but six, all decided together, all applying the new constitutional cliché: "One man, one vote."

Expanding and expounding this principle so as to require every state legislature, in both houses, to be roughly proportionate to population, Warren wrote, though not this time for a unanimous Court: "Citizens, not history or economic interests, cast votes." And, again: "Legislators represent people, not trees or acres."

As in *Brown,* just a decade earlier, Warren was quite unworried that legislative history, dug from a library, might not support his reading of the "equal protection" clause of the Constitution on which the decision formally rested. Hence, he ignored rather than answered Justice Harlan's disturbed and scholarly dissent—much as John Marshall used to brush off pedantic impedimenta to the results he felt were right.

It is the new apportionment formula, out of *Reynolds v. Sims,* that Senator Dirksen is trying to reverse, in part, by constitutional amendment. Dirksen is well aware that throughout most of the nation the old disproportionate systems of electing legislators heavily favored rural rubes over city slickers—and that most rural rubes are Republicans. Senator Dirksen will, as he should, fail; too few people other than the rural representatives and their country constituents care. But the Senator might well consider for a second the man whose work he is trying to undo, the man who rates reapportionment and its equalizing of voting rights as his finest achievement.

It happens that Earl Warren is country-bred and a Republican. But Earl Warren's deep respect for the dignity and the equal rights of every human being—country-bred or city-bred, Republican or Democratic, black or white—is probably the top tool in his arsenal, the essence of his influence, the crux of his credo.

Three of the nouns most often used to describe the Chief are graciousness, warmth and strength. Thus, Judge Simon Sobeloff, a former U.S. Solicitor General, once remarked: "Few men in or out of government can equal the Chief Justice in human warmth. He will be distinguished in history as a great and gracious jurist."

No one who has ever watched as Warren, of a Monday morning, welcomes new members to the bar of the Court can discount the genuineness with which he performs this little gesture—pronouncing every name precisely, smiling as unaffectedly as if he were greeting an old friend.

But Warren, no wishy-washy charmer, is capable of anger even in public. On April 24, 1961, not half an hour after the welcome-to-the-bar-of-this-Court ceremony, Justice Black announced a 5-to-4 decision in the civil-liberties field and Justice Frankfurter, speaking in dissent, began to ridicule in open Court the decision which had not gone his way. Chief Warren, who had voted with Black, turned crimson, then almost purple, as he waited for Frankfurter to finish. Then, in quite unprecedented fashion, he turned on the second senior Justice:

"That was not the dissenting opinion that you filed. That was a lecture—a closing argument by a prosecutor to a jury. It might properly have been made in the conference room but not in this courtroom. As I understand it, the purpose of reporting an opinion here is to inform the public and not for the purpose of grading this Court."

Late that afternoon Warren was again his old, easy-going self as he took on questions—some sharp, some stupid, all politely parried or handled head-on—from a law-school class. He dismissed the morning's already front-paged incident with a reminder that even Supreme Court Justices are human and may lose their tempers from time to time.

What more is Earl Warren than—as already noted—big, friendly, bold, unbookish, libertarian, equalitarian, gracious, warm, strong—and human? With frank immodesty, let me quote here what I wrote of him 11 years ago, in the middle of his second term on the Court:

"Indeed, the most hopeful and happy omen of them all is the apparent judicial character of the new Chief Justice. Unblinded by the tweedledum-tweedledee twaddle of much that passes for learned legal argument, unblinkered into the narrow vision so often so typical of those with past judicial experience, he seems essentially a direct, plain-spoken politician who knows that his is primarily a political job. Of such, when they combine humanity with honesty, are judicial statesmen made. Not so wise as Holmes, not so intellectually daring as Black, not so dedicated as Brandeis or Douglas, not so independent as the 19th-century's Johnson or Miller or Harlan, and clearly not so liberal as any of these, he comes closer to resembling a might-be 20th-century Marshall. The same easy strength is there, and the same earthy approach to the esoterics of law. But where Marshall's achievement was to protect a weak nation, as a nation, from its people, Warren's opportunity is the precise opposite: it is to protect the people, as people, from their strong nation. Given the will and the goodwill to do it, he can succeed."

Eleven years after, still immodestly, I stick rather proudly to my prognosis, in which not one of my colleagues in constitutional law then joined. I stick, that is, with two minor amendments: "Clearly not so liberal as any of these" should go; Warren has proved more militantly liberal than about half of them, most notably than the above-the-battle Holmes. And I should not say today that "he can succeed"; I should say that he has spectacularly succeeded.

It cannot have been easy. When Warren came to the Court in the fall of 1953, so suddenly that he had to borrow a robe to be sworn in as Chief, the high tribunal was clearly at its lowest ebb since the Four Horsemen of Reaction were leading the Nine Old Men of the thirties into stubborn, antisocial economic decisions. Now the crusading zeal of the New Deal Justices, spent in over-turning old economic roadblocks to progress, had largely waned.

The Court had been encumbered in its work and in its vision by Truman's inept quartet of appointed cronies: Vinson (as C.J.), Burton, Minton and Clark.

After the deaths of Wiley Rutledge and Frank Murphy—both dedicated libertarians—in the summer of 1949, Hugo Black and William O. Douglas remained as a sort of rear guard for civil rights and liberties; for four years "Justices Black and Douglas dissenting" became as common in constitutional cases as "Justices Holmes and Brandeis dissenting" had been a generation before. I believe I violate no confidence when I report that both Black and Douglas talked to intimates—perhaps just to let off steam—of resigning from the Court in disgust and despair.

Into this sticky atmosphere (some of the Justices would not even lunch with some of their brethren) stepped the big, bland, blond Scandinavian (the family name was originally Varran) who had never sat on a court of any kind before. Uninformed rumor has long had it that Eisenhower appointed Warren to the nation's second most important post in gratitude—or even as a deal —for Warren's releasing the California delegation to Ike at the Chicago convention of 1952. Untrue. The most urgent backers of then-Governor Warren for the Chief Justiceship were Richard Nixon and William Knowland, both anxious to control California's Republican party and aware that they had no chance until Warren was out of the way. (Since Warren went to Washington, incidentally, the Democrats have controlled California.)

When Warren took the center seat on the bench and the end seat at the conference table, the intellectual leader of the Court was unquestionably that pseudoliberal lightning bug, the late Felix Frankfurter. Black—now followed, now led, by Douglas—had been able to challenge Frankfurter's widely conceded hard-core conservatism, especially in the field of individual liberties, until Murphy and Rutledge died, thus diluting most Bill of Rights dissents from four men to two.

Frankfurter, a disciple—as was his hero, Learned Hand—of the leave-it-all-to-the-legislature-and-don't-stick-your-judicial-neck-out philosophy of the 19th-century law professor James Bradley Thayer, favored an almost parliamentary form of government. (Douglas, in dissent, once chided him: "The philosophy of the opinion that sustains this statute . . . gives supremacy to the legislature in a way that is incompatible with the scheme of our written Constitution. . . . By proclaiming it we forsake much of our constitutional heritage and move closer to the British scheme.") So it was that, during the height of the McCarthy witch hunt, the Court, led by Frankfurter, upheld the whole nasty network of "loyalty" and "security" laws, over Black-Douglas dissents.

Not that Frankfurter approved of these laws; as a legislator he would have voted against them. But as a judge, weaned on the hands-off slant of Thayer and Hand plus a misreading of Holmes (to whom the freedoms of speech and press were matters of judicial moment), Frankfurter cornered himself into a crusade for logical consistency in constitutional law. If courts ought not to interfere with legislative judgments in the economic arena, why in the field of civil liberties?

Black's and Douglas's best dissents spell out the answer: Majority rule alone does not make a democracy; the other essential is the protection of primary rights of individuals and minorities *against* majority rule—and only the courts can provide this. Furthermore, Frankfurter was afraid that if the Court overused its power, it would, under Congress's knife, lose its power—a circular and self-defeating argument. Let's-not-use-it-lest-we-lose-it scarcely differs from let's-give-it-up. Pragmatists can catch this point while scholars scratch their heads; Warren, no scholar, caught it quickly.

It did not seem to matter much, in 1953, in which camp Warren would land. Technically, a Chief Justice is only the administrative head of a court of equals. Unless he is a personally powerful figure—a Marshall, a Taney, a Hughes—he wields no more influence than any eloquent associate. Thus, at best, libertarians ruminated, Warren might change unfortunate rulings from 7–2 to 6–3. That is precisely what Warren did— but not immediately.

Such is the prestige of the Chief Justice, in majority or dissent, that both Frankfurter and Black badly wanted him on their side and recruited him, from conference sessions to Court corridors to chats in chambers. But the more perceptive among the Court's personnel soon began to notice that, after argument or conference discussion of a tough constitutional twister, Frankfurter would be knocking at the Chief's door; the Chief would later be knocking at Black's. Statistics tell the story: During Warren's first term, he and Black were on opposite sides of split decisions 22 times; during Warren's second term, he and Black differed 12 times; in Warren's third term, his votes varied from Black's just twice.

Statistics do not, of course, tell the whole story. They do not tell, for instance, how Warren, at the spectacular school-desegregation end of his first term, managed to keep unanimous, in word as well as deed, eight associates of whom five had not wanted even to take on the issue, while three kept threatening to bolt into dissent. Was it perhaps by leaving the actual desegregation orders until the following term, and even then watering them down in the fatuous phrase "with all deliberate speed"—obviously inserted to satisfy some malcontent?

At any rate, in the anti-discrimination field, as it has spread from schools to buses and theaters and swimming pools and supermarkets and restaurants and all the rest, Warren has kept his Court well-nigh unanimous in case after case for close to 12 years. More than that, he has dragged both Presidents and Congresses along the desegregation trail—an astonishing feat of practical politics.

Progress in the two other fields where the Warren Court has made a major mark on the law of the land came more slowly. (The First Amendment separation-of-church-and-state cases, banning Bible reading and prayers in public schools, scarcely rate as major matters, despite the emotional to-do they caused.) For the two other big blows for liberty and democracy struck by the Warren Court—widespread extension of constitutional fairness to criminal suspects or defendants, and radical reapportionment of voting rights and representation—had to await further changes in the membership of the Court itself.

Warren's appointment had raised the libertarian minority from the despairing Black-and-Douglas duo to three. In 1956 William J. Brennan Jr., despite the fact that he had once studied under Frankfurter at Harvard, disappointed his former professor by joining, on most constitutional counts, the Black-Douglas-Warren bloc. Two years later, when Potter Stewart, as the most junior Justice, refused to align himself regularly with Frankfurter (or with Black), the stage was set for the Warren Court to go slowly to town.

The change began with the Bill-of-Rights cases, ranging from the First Amendment freedoms, to which the Vinson-Frankfurter Court had been almost stone deaf, through the Fourth to Eighth Amendment cases, calling for decency toward criminal defendants and dealing now with the extension of these decencies—the right to counsel, reversal of convictions based on illegally seized evidence and the like—to state, not only Federal, prosecutions. Justice Stewart, wetting his toes in the waters of constitutional controversy (although his record on the Federal Court of Appeals in Ohio had more than hinted that he would not be a blind follower of Justice Burton, also from Ohio, whom he replaced), started, a bit cautiously at first, to follow more often than not the Black-Douglas-Warren-Brennan line. That (date it around 1959) was the end of Frankfurter's dominance of the Court; it had lasted precisely a decade since, in 1949, Murphy and Rutledge died. This was also, the desegregation cases aside (and they were rather special, for who, once forced to vote with no procedural escape, would vote *for* segregation?), the time when Earl Warren took effective charge of the Court he had formally headed since 1953.

Yet it was not until three years after that (date it precisely March 26, 1962) that the big blow fell. Then was when the Court, in *Baker v. Carr,* handed down the first of its revolutionary reapportionment holdings, overruling an old Frankfurter hands-off decision, wading with eyes wide open into the "political thicket" against which Frankfurter and his ilk had long warned, forcing the ex-professor into an eloquently despairing swan song of dissent. There are those who believe that this case, in which Frankfurter's whole philosophy of government and law was discarded, contributed to the stroke which he suffered shortly thereafter—a stroke that led to his retirement and subsequently to his death.

There can be no doubt that the Court, in open hearing and in conference, has been a quieter, calmer place since Frankfurter left. Chief Warren, who never raises his voice, even in anger or annoyance, told me last fall that no voices had been raised in conference for the past three years. And I could not help remembering the two or three times when I had waited for Warren in his office just outside the inner sanctum of the conference room and had heard—though I caught no words—the shrilly rising decibels of a peeved and petulant Justice Frankfurter.

When Arthur Goldberg succeeded to the Frankfurter seat on the bench, that one sometimes crucial vote could not have changed more radically. By contrast to Frankfurter's insistence on self-restraint, Goldberg was so aggressively activist in his anxiousness to have the Court do good that the tale went around Washington that Black and Douglas were trying to hold Goldberg back. It is not just a tale but a fact that in Goldberg's first Court term the Court split 5-4 in 10 cases dealing with civil rights or liberties, and that, with Goldberg's vote, the libertarians carried all 10.

Justice Abe Fortas, who has now replaced Goldberg, is less of a whirlwind, but he has just as little sympathy with the keep-away credo of Frankfurter and his kind; it was Fortas who argued and won the celebrated *Gideon* case, in which the Court discarded an old Frankfurter ruling in extending to indigent state defendants the right to counsel in criminal cases.

At any rate—even without the support of Justices Harlan (Frankfurter's soft-spoken, gentlemanly but rarely effective follower toward a take-it-easy trend), Clark (far more articulate and able than when Truman named him, but still pogo-stick unpredictable), White (incredibly cautious for a Kennedy man, often a technical nit-picker) and Stewart (who fits no pattern save that of journalist turned judge, but still at heart a journalist) —even without these, the Court is now Earl Warren's Court and, without arrogance, he knows it. Some might call it Black's or Black's and Douglas's Court, as Vinson's Court belonged to Frankfurter. But I think I said it not too badly, again 11 years ago:

"Today it would be a tragedy if the Black and Douglas dissents—which are rather affirmations of a faith—should prove a dirge for the bravest dream of all. For under the inspiration of those two great Justices and the aegis of a potentially great Chief Justice, the American dream of freedom may be reborn."

There is no longer any question of *potentially* great. I doubt that any non-Bircher or non-churcher who knows the man and his work would fail to accord him—along with Marshall, Taney and Hughes—the accolade of greatness. Personally—and not just as a bauble for his 75th birthday—I happen to rate him the greatest Chief Justice in the nation's history.

His job has been tougher than Marshall's. Marshall had no Frankfurter, complete with followers, to try to hamstring him; only Jefferson's man, Johnson, so much as spoke up against Marshall. We should recognize, while he is still working for us, the rare strength and courage and wisdom of Earl Warren.

Exuding, as he does, quiet and confident power, the Chief feels no need to throw his weight around. Last fall I was chatting with the newly named Justice Abe Fortas in his Court chambers when his secretary suddenly announced, over the phone: "The Chief Justice is here, Justice Fortas." Warren had not summoned freshman Fortas, 20 years his junior, to his own office. He had done Fortas the courtesy of coming through the corridors to see Fortas. As he entered, he saw me also.

"Could I have a couple of minutes with you in private, Abe," he asked, "or would you rather I waited until Fred leaves?"

That, too, is the 14th Chief Justice of the United States.

A Man Born to Act, Not to Muse

by Anthony Lewis

NOT WITHIN memory, perhaps not since the days of John Marshall, have Americans sensed that a change in the Chief Justice of the United States could so profoundly affect their Government and their society. That much is clear from first reactions to the report that Earl Warren has decided to retire.

How far Congressional conservatives will get with their historically unsound claim that a President in his final year should not be able to appoint a Chief Justice, what effect a new Chief would really have on the present Supreme Court—all this remains to be seen. What the controversy and the speculation do show is that Earl Warren has made everyone aware of the power the Supreme Court may have to shape a nation.

The 15 years since he became Chief Justice have been years of legal revolution. In that time the Supreme Court has brought about more social change than most Congresses and most Presidents.

The Warren Court set the United States on a new path in race relations, wiping out the legal basis for discrimination. By imposing the rule that all citizens must be represented equally in state

From the *New York Times Magazine*, June 30, 1968, copyright © 1968 by The New York Times Company.

legislatures and the national House of Representatives, the Court eliminated the rural bias from American politics. It wrote what amounted to a new constitutional code of criminal justice, one restraining the whole process of law enforcement from investigation through arrest and trial, and applied the code rigorously to state and local activities formerly outside Federal standards. It greatly broadened the citizen's freedom to criticize public figures, and the artist's to express himself in unconventional and even shocking ways; it greatly restricted governmental authority to penalize the individual because of his beliefs or associations.

How much of this record can be attributed to the personal role of Chief Justice Warren? Not so much as his passionate critics and gushy admirers assume. The rantings of those who would "Impeach Earl Warren" overlook the fact the Chief Justice has only one vote among nine.

If various Presidents had not appointed justices of sympathetic temperament to sit with him, Earl Warren might be remembered as a great dissenter. No Chief Justice can command his associates' beliefs; the Court in recent years has not lacked for strong personalities and convictions.

But the legal revolution could not have taken place as and when it did without Chief Justice Warren.

He sensed the movement in American law—the growing concern about individual liberty as it faced the twin juggernauts of social conformity and governmental power. He put behind that movement his character and his public reputation, and they were vital in converting what might have been lost causes into accomplished change.

That he was a man of political experience rather than a scholar —an ordinary man, a rather simple man—all this was part of his contribution. At a time when the Supreme Court was undertaking to change so much so quickly in American life, and thus had inevitably become the subject of the most bitter controversy, the paternal, old-fashionedly patriotic figure of the Chief Justice was crucial to public acceptance of the change.

It is impossible to believe that without his leadership the Court would so boldly have taken what history may regard as the most far-reaching decisions of the period, the reapportionment cases.

The movement against racial discrimination was there before him, but his presence in 1954 undoubtedly made it possible for the Court to deal with school segregation resolutely and unanimously. In his absence, it is unlikely that the Court within a few years would have created such a host of new rights for state criminal defendants.

With one exception, on censorship of obscenity, the Chief Justice favored every major change in constitutional doctrine undertaken by the Court. That cannot be explained as coincidence.

The extent of the change in judicial attitudes over 15 years can be shown in a curious way by looking at two decisions from Chief Justice Warren's very first term. The curiosity is that he was part of the majority in each case.

A New York physician, Edward K. Barsky, had been convicted of contempt for failing to give the House Committee on Un-American Activities some records of the Joint Anti-Fascist Refugee Committee. Then the New York medical authorities suspended his license to practice. In Barsky v. Board of Regents the Supreme Court rejected a claim that by weighing matters unrelated to his fitness to practice, New York had unconstitutionally deprived Dr. Barsky of his profession. Justices Frankfurter, Black and Douglas dissented.

In Irvine v. California, the police had planted microphones in the bedroom of a gambler and used the records of his conversations as evidence in a gambling prosecution. The Supreme Court declined to rule out the bugged evidence and upheld the conviction, Justices Black, Frankfurter, Douglas and Burton dissenting.

Those decisions seem long ago and far away; it is highly doubtful that either would attract a single vote on the Court today.

Last December the Chief Justice for a majority found a Federal statute barring Communists from defense-plant jobs unconstitutional because it did not distinguish between active and passive Communists or between sensitive and nonsensitive jobs. That is a far cry from a day when small-minded state administrators could deprive a man of the right to practice a private, nondefense profession because of fears of his associations.

Again last December, over the sole dissent of Justice Black, the Court held that wiretapping was subject to the Fourth Amend-

ment's protections against illegal searches. Even without that decision, the accumulated cases barring evidence obtained from
defendants themselves by unworthy devices would have assured
reversal of Irvine's conviction.

As for the Chief Justice's part in those 1954 cases, his position
must have reflected a beginning uncertainty that led him to take
a conventional, restricted view of his role. But the change came
quickly. After Barsky, it is impossible to cite a case in which
he was unresponsive to a claim by someone suffering for his
political beliefs or associations. His record in the criminal-law
field after Irvine is one of overwhelming concern that suspects not
be overborne by unfair police tactics.

In part he must, after those early cases, have let a natural
humanitarianism flower. But there was something else. Most men
grow more conservative with age. When he was Governor of
California, experience made Warren increasingly more adven-
turous, more liberated from conventional views, and the same
thing happened on the Supreme Court.

He never attempted, like Justices Black or Frankfurter, to
propound a consistent theory of how a judge interpreting a constitution should approach his task. He was not a philosopher. But
the Supreme Court requires qualities of statesmanship as well as
scholarship, and Earl Warren surely has some of those: a sense
of history, an understanding of people, force, courage. For all his
political background, he recognized that a judge cannot court
popular favor: he never hesitated in the face of opposition from
Congress or the bar or public opinion.

The violence of the attacks upon him may, ironically, have
helped to liberate him from the habit of political compromise
and may have made him even more determinedly independent as
a judge. He is a proud man. It is possible that he saw his role
at first as one of moderation but that the obscene assaults after
the school-segregation case stiffened his resolve to be himself as
a judge.

It was the school-segregation cases that fixed him in the minds
of people abroad; Earl Warren represented to them the hope of
America, the promise of our society that it would raise up the
downtrodden without rebellion. At home, he became a convenient

symbol of hate for those who sought racial or political or con-
spiratorial explanations for their personal anxieties. For other
Americans, for the majority, he is a reminder of what sometimes
seem lost American virtues: openness, optimism, idealism without
ideology. In an age of character assassination, he saw good in
other human beings. In an age of governmental indecision, he
was decisive.

The personality that he projects to the outside world is friendly,
open-hearted but also a bit bland and remote—as if it were easier
for him to be kind in general than warm to a particular human
being. In fact, there are probably few people with whom Earl
Warren is really on intimate human terms. Nor is he quite the
easygoing outdoor type that his massive frame and unpretentious
California manners make him seem.

He is an intensely emotional man who burns at any sensed
lack of respect or lack of candor in others. The inner emotion
burst out infrequently in the courtroom. On three occasions he
took offense at Justice Frankfurter's oral version of a dissenting
opinion and answered back extemporaneously.

There was a revealing expression of his true feelings when
President Kennedy was assassinated; putting aside the official
prose that ordinarily marked his writing, the Chief Justice said:
"What moved some misguided wretch to do this horrible deed may
never be known to us, but we do know that such acts are commonly stimulated by forces of hatred and malevolence such as
today are eating their way into the bloodstream of American life.
What a price we pay for this fanaticism!"

His deep feelings, and his patriotism, led him to accept the job
of chairman of the commission to investigate the assassination
despite the tremendous physical burden and psychological strain
it imposed.

The critical question that history will ask is whether Chief
Justice Warren—and his Court—strained the role that judges
should play in a democracy, even in so legalized a democracy
as ours.

In the Warren years, attitudes toward law and the courts shifted
radically in the United States. Some of the qualities valued in the
judicial process—stability, intellectuality, craftsmanship—seemed

to be put aside. It was as an instrument of social change that the process came to be seen. Where once it had been an event for the Supreme Court to overrule one of its own prior decisions, that became common coin. The Court sat, many said, as a permanent constitutional convention—and accordingly, in the view of its critics, felt less obligated to justify its decisions in the language of the Constitution or the persuasiveness of precedent or the intellectual force of experience.

Even young teachers of law were surprised at how their students brushed aside all the nice questions about relationships between one decision and another. The important thing was the just result; the presumption was that any challenged governmental act was unconstitutional. That the Supreme Court should leave many questions to the discretion of the political branches of government—an idea once so treasured by liberal-minded legal thinkers—seemed forgotten.

For this shift in attitudes the Chief Justice bears considerable responsibility. For, far more than most other members of the Court, he has evidently felt unconfined by precedent or by a particular view of the judicial function.

The contrast with Justices Frankfurter and Black is instructive. Justice Frankfurter argued for "self-restraint" on the part of judges to let the elected leaders of government have more room for experiment. Justice Black scornfully rejects that position, but he has his own strictly defined view of the limits on judicial power. His limits are verbal—what he can find in the literal text of the Constitution. If the words are not there, it is beyond his power to hold a governmental action invalid, however unpleasant it might seem. Thus he cannot find any constitutional restraints on wiretapping or eavesdropping as such; they are simply not mentioned in the Fourth Amendment. Justice Harlan said in an appraisal of his great colleague that Justice Black "rejects the open-ended notion that the Court sits to do good in every circumstance where good is needed." The statement almost invites contrast to the Chief Justice's attitude.

In Warren opinions one does not find threads of the kind that run familiarly through the words of a Black or Frankfurter, arguing a legal theory year after year. The Chief Justice seldom troubled to quote his own losing arguments of the past. It is fair to say that he did not place a high value on doctrinal consistency.

Thus his opinions in the area of Communism and political speech seem to reflect a constitutional judgment that the values of free speech overwhelmingly outweigh the interest in social order asserted by government. But he did not follow that view when it came to the issue of obscenity.

The Chief Justice stood out from the trend of decisions that in his time turned the United States from one of the most puritan to one of the most permissive nations in the world in writing about sex—the one example of his resistance to a long-term judicial movement toward greater individual liberty. In a revealing case in 1964 the Court reversed the conviction of a theater manager in Cleveland Heights, Ohio, for showing a French film, *"Les Amants,"* that had been seen without incident all over the United States. Justice Brennan, in the principal opinion, said that the constitutional standard of obscenity must be a national one and that the film was unobjectionable by that standard. The Chief Justice, dissenting, thought different local standards were valid.

That was an astonishing judgment from a man who was prepared to impose rigorous new national standards for questioning of suspects on every local police force in the country. What seems an anomaly in that light, or in light of the Chief Justice's general views on free speech, must have a straightforward explanation. Earl Warren looked at the problem as a man with three daughters. Although he might in general be opposed to restrictions on expression, here was a social danger that government simply had to be allowed to attack.

Similarly this year, when the Court held that gamblers could invoke the Fifth Amendment's privilege against self-incrimination to avoid buying a Federal tax stamp, the Chief Justice alone dissented. The Court had only recently allowed Communist party members to invoke the privilege to keep from registering, but the Chief Justice said that case was different—it involved political activity, while this was only gambling. But the Fifth Amendment makes no distinction among those who may use it on the basis of what criminal charges they face. Evidently, the Chief Justice was just reluctant to inhibit Government control of gambling, no matter what he had agreed in other cases.

In short, there were areas in which he put the values of individual liberty aside because he felt government had to govern. And he did so without apology. It was a matter of common sense to him, not of consistency in judicial philosophy.

A Warren opinion, characteristically, is a world made new—a bland, square presentation of the particular problem in that case almost as if it were unencumbered by precedents or conflicting theories, as it inevitably must be. Often the framework of the argument seems ethical rather than legal, in the sense that one expects the law to be analytical. Chief Justice Warren's opinions are difficult to analyze because they are likely to be unanalytical.

An interesting insight into his views was given by a speech to the Jewish Theological Seminary in New York in 1962. The Chief Justice spoke of law as floating "in a sea of ethics" but indicated that law did not go ethically far enough. He suggested the development of a new profession, "counselor in ethics." By way of example, he said: "Our college campuses might look very different if such problems as the promotion of faculty members . . . were subject to deliberation on moral grounds. And our political campaigns, our nominations and elections might be different, if political parties included experts in ethics among those deciding policies."

To most lawyers the proposal must smack of astonishing naiveté. The point is that in the absence of other formal methods of weighing ethical considerations in life, the Chief Justice evidently felt that law and the courts must do so to a significant degree.

Even those sympathetic with his objectives have been critical of some opinions. The objection is that he would take too sweeping or too simple a view of problems that were complex and ambiguous.

Something of the sort was said by some critics of the monumental Warren opinion in *Miranda v. Arizona* in 1966. There, a 5-to-4 majority interpreted the Constitution's demand for "due process of law" to require an opportunity for every arrested person to see a lawyer before being questioned by the police—and to be given a lawyer if too poor to pay one. To some serious-minded critics, the Court in that case was trying to legislate a detailed criminal code for a continental country without the information or experience to do so, and without any sign of a moral vacuum on the issue that no one else was working to fill. The Court, in short, was trying to solve too much too broadly and too soon.

But if Chief Justice Warren occasionally appeared to put analysis aside because he found something outrageous, it must be remembered that there *were* outrages in American life—official racism, abuse of police authority, an unbalanced political system, intolerance of free expression—and that no other arm of government was doing anything about them. The willingness of the Supreme Court to deal with them bluntly and untechnically in the Warren era made a great difference. If the Chief Justice's approach was often generalized and moralistic, if simple answers were sometimes unsatisfyingly given to complicated questions, then at least American society was made to face some basic problems that it had ignored.

But appraising Chief Justice Warren's record in terms of the usefulness of particular results only raises the larger philosophical question: Is that the proper standard to apply to the work of a judge? And here we may get closer to the personal mystery—to the inner forces that motivated Earl Warren.

Generations of American law students have been taught that justice is a process. Chief Justice Warren, one must think, does not take that view. To him justice consists not of providing a fair mechanism of decision but of seeing that the right side, the good side, prevails in the particular case.

It is a delicious irony that a President who raised inactivity to a principle of government, Eisenhower, should have appointed a Chief Justice for whom action was all. President Eisenhower was obviously surprised and unhappy that the appointment turned out as it did. Could anyone have predicted the sort of judge that Earl Warren would be?

For 33 years before going on the bench he had been in public life in California—as District Attorney, State Attorney General and Governor. Through most of that career, he was regarded as a regular Republican, a favorite of the heavily right-wing group that ran the party. As Attorney General, he had attacked his election opponent for opposing a bill to make school children salute the flag, blocked the nomination of a liberal-minded law professor, Max Radin, to the State Supreme Court and opposed a pardon for that old radical figure Tom Mooney. As Governor he was a leading proponent of the wartime Federal order removing all persons of Japanese ancestry from the West Coast and putting them in concentration camps; opposing the return of the evacuees in 1943, he told a conference of Governors: "If the Japs are released, no one will be able to tell a saboteur from any other Jap."

Then, in 1945, he astounded his political friends—and enemies —by proposing a state program of prepaid medical insurance. Over the next eight years he became an apostle of liberal Republicanism, embittering many of his former conservative backers but achieving an extraordinary nonpartisan political grip on the state. A later Democratic Governor, Edmund G. (Pat) Brown, said of Earl Warren: "He was the best Governor California ever had. He faced the problems of growth and social responsibility and met them head on."

Ideologically, it was hard to categorize a man who had vigorously supported the Japanese relocation program and later fought the medical interests for a form of state-insured medicine. He was not a man who thought in ideological terms. He had advocated health insurance not because of some philosophical conversion but because he had fallen ill and suddenly realized how catastrophic serious illness would be for the man without resources.

But perhaps there is one unifying thread in his career—the commitment to action. Earl Warren was plainly a man born to act, not to muse, and very likely a man born to govern. Through all the apparent inconsistencies in his political life he exerted his powerful abilities in the way naturally open to him at any time. As District Attorney he was the enemy of crime and corruption. As wartime Attorney General and Governor he was a patriot, worrying about the flag and Japanese spies. When the war ended and the social and physical problems of an expanding California emerged, he applied his energy to them through the means available. It was crucial that his mind was never closed.

He learned from experience, and found new ways of applying to the problems of society his own strict morality and innate humanitarianism.

The difficulty, of course, was to know how such an instinct for action would be expressed in the narrow channels usually open to a judge. Now, after the event, it is possible to offer a theory: The great issues that came before the Warren Court called, in one sense, for a judicial choice between action and inaction—between exercising power for reform or allowing things to go on as they were.

It was Earl Warren's natural inclination to act: to break the long deadlock on reapportionment, to attack local police abuses long considered outside the scope of Federal restraints, to condemn official discrimination on account of race. Those were the opportunities open to the Supreme Court to make an impression on American life—that is to say, to govern. The instinct of government, and the sense of duty, did not depart Earl Warren when he put on a robe.

Learned Hand, that great skeptic among judges, said he would prefer not to be ruled "by a bevy of Platonic Guardians." Earl Warren is the closest thing the United States has had to a Platonic Guardian, dispensing law from a throne without any sensed limits of power except what is seen as the good of society.

Fortunately he is a decent, humane, honorable, democratic Guardian. But there are those—and not only niggling or illiberal spirits—who are troubled at the idea of a Supreme Court Justice, appointed for life and subject to no effective popular control, playing such a role in our system of government. Chief Justice Warren's great virtues, in an age of public cynicism and political sophistry, were his simplicity, his humanity, his courage; they are vital qualities on the most powerful of all courts, but without a philosophy of the law do they make a whole judge?

Judges of another day, filled with their own sense of natural justice, outlawed paper money and prevented a state from limiting bakers to a 10-hour working day and held unconstitutional a Federal law against shipment of goods made by child labor. In their revulsion against such decisions, the liberals of the nineteen-twenties and nineteen-thirties may have taken too constricted a view of what judges may properly do. But if we should applaud without undue historical uneasiness when the contemporary Supreme Court reaches a right-minded result, we may still feel it important that the Court arrive at that result by a process that inspires confidence and with an opinion that awakes the public conscience.

The philosophical problem was posed most acutely in the reapportionment cases. They were decided in opinions by the Chief Justice delivered on June 15, 1964. In the pillared courtroom that day, some listeners, as he spoke, felt as if they were present at a second American constitutional convention. The Court held that every house of every state legislature must be apportioned on the basis of population alone, with the districts as nearly equal as practicable. That meant that nearly all the 50 states would have to redistrict their legislatures, that political patterns fixed for decades would be destroyed.

The question asked by the Chief Justice in his opinion really determined the answer. He did not ask whether the Constitution applied to the whole issue of apportionment, or if so what theories of representation ought to be considered. He began with the premise that the democratic norm was equal treatment of individual voters and then asked what departures from absolute population equality the Constitution would countenance. He considered the demand for representation of geographical areas and dismissed it with disarming simplicity: "Legislators represent people, not acres or trees. Legislators are elected by voters, not farms or cities or economic interests. . . . The weight of a citizen's vote cannot be made to depend on where he lives."

In these cases even more was in question than the character of American legislatures, as Justice Harlan made plain in his dissent.

"These decisions," he said, "give support to a current mistaken view of the Constitution and the constitutional function of this Court. This view, in a nutshell, is that every major social ill in this country can find its cure in some constitutional 'principle,' and that this Court should 'take the lead' in promoting reform when other branches of government fail to act. The Constitution is not a panacea for every blot upon the public welfare, nor should this Court, ordained as a judicial body, be thought of as a general haven for reform movements."

The issue of the Court's function could not be framed more starkly than it was in the reapportionment cases. On the one hand, the precedents ran uniformly against judicial intervention, and history suggested that the apportionment question bristled with political difficulties. On the other, it was a situation crying for reform in which the political branches were almost by definition unable to act; unless the Supreme Court intervened, corrosion of confidence in state government would continue unchecked. Seen in those terms, the issue for the Supreme Court was not a legal one in any ordinary sense of the term: It was an issue of statesmanship. That assuredly is the standard by which Earl Warren would want to be judged as Chief Justice of the United States.

A Talk with Warren
on Crime, the Court,
the Country

by Anthony Lewis

SINCE HE retired last June as Chief Justice of the United States, Earl Warren has spent much of his time traveling with Mrs. Warren. Last month, shortly before the Supreme Court reconvened under his successor, Warren Burger, he was in London and agreed to an interview.

He naturally avoided comment on the record about politicians, past and present, and such partisan matters: The restraints on a Supreme Court Justice do not end with his retirement. But he gave his general views on a number of important subjects, and in the course of the conversation there were clues to the nature of the man who for 16 years was one of the most powerful influences on American life.

The most striking impression was what an old-fashioned American figure he is. He thinks people are essentially good; he believes in the genius of the American political system. His virtues are fairness, dedication to public service, courage. The baseball pennant races were still on, and he said he hoped the New York Mets

From the *New York Times Magazine,* October 19, 1969, copyright © 1969 by The New York Times Company.

would win just to show that Leo Durocher was wrong about nice guys.

His simplicity is a wonder in the year 1969. He thinks judges and other men are obligated only to do their best—and if in conscience they do, they need not lie awake at night. He believes in progress.

The interview follows.

CRIME

Mr. Chief Justice, what do you think are the reasons for the amount of crime that so deeply disturbs the United States today? Where do we look for solutions—to the courts, to the police, to general social reform?

WARREN: Well, of course there is no simple answer to that, but I believe that in the main it demonstrates that we have a disrupted society.

One thing that I think is really basic to our whole situation is that the people who are now, let's say, 30 years of age in the United States have never known anything but war conditions in our country and in the world. From the time they could learn to talk they have learned that we are in the war business, and young people are taught to kill and to recognize violence as a part of life.

Many hundreds of thousands, even millions of our young people have been thrust into actual warfare, have seen violence and all of the degradation that it brings about, and it has no horrors to them as it would to someone who had never been influenced by that kind of life. I think that that's had a great effect on our people.

Then also we have people in our big cities who are living in ghettos, without any employment of any kind. They are ignorant, they have had no schooling, they have no skills with which to compete in the economic market, they are easy prey to all kinds of bad influences in the community.

I think one of the things that must be done in order to eliminate much of that is to improve the condition of our cities. We must get rid of the ghettos, we must see that every youngster who comes into being in our country is afforded a decent education and is given some skill through which he can compete in the market.

Then, I think, he must not only have that skill but he must have the opportunity to get a job, he must be able to join a union. We must eliminate the discrimination that is so prevalent in many places if we are to have a society that in general will accommodate itself to the law.

You are saying in effect that the causes of crime are deep.

WARREN: Very deep, indeed.

Why do you think it is that the public and a number of politicians seem to blame crime rather on judges?

WARREN: Someone always has to be a scapegoat when there is crime, and the only people who cannot talk back, who cannot argue their case are the courts. The police can take their case to the public. The prosecutors can take their case to the public. The only people who cannot talk back but must do their job day by day are the courts. I don't mean by that, that the courts are faultless, but I mean that they are defenseless when it comes to entering into a debate as to who is the cause for crime.

What would you say were the most important criminal law decisions during the years of the Warren Court?

WARREN: I think one of the most important cases we had was the case about which you wrote your book, the *Gideon* case. That was the case which interpreted the Constitution to say that it meant just exactly what it said, that a man was entitled to counsel in a criminal proceeding.

Before that case in many places throughout the country a man was afforded counsel if he couldn't pay for it only if he was charged with a capital offense, and of course that means that hundreds of thousands of men every year were arrested and tried and perhaps had no legal advice at all. The *Gideon* case made it a living thing that every man charged with a serious offense was entitled to have counsel at his trial. That is basic, and I believe it was of tremendous importance.

Then also, I think, the case of *Escobedo* was a very important case, because in that case it was determined that when a man

was in jail and asked for his lawyer and
he was entitled to have him there.

There we had a case of a man who
and his lawyer was down the hall. He
lawyer called for him and the police told
could see each other only when they got thro
And then they went through him and against his p
his confession and convicted him on his confession.

Then we come to the *Miranda* case, and the question
If he's entitled to a lawyer when his lawyer is present, when is
first entitled to a lawyer? *Miranda* simply said that when the law
puts upon a man by putting him in restraint and taking him away
from his home and his family and his friends and starts to put
him behind bars, that he's then in the toils of the law in a criminal
case and is entitled to have representation of counsel.

That doesn't stop the prosecution of the case at all. But so far
as making him talk and convict himself by what he said is concerned, his right to a lawyer starts when he is put in durance vile.

*What do you say to the complaint widely heard from the police,
and even I think it is fair to say from the present Attorney General of the United States, that the* Miranda *rule—whatever its base
—just makes it too difficult to deal with criminals?*

WARREN: That same argument could of course be applied to
almost any rule that keeps the law enforcement agencies of the
state from excesses. It is always easier to obtain a conviction
if you are permitted to use excesses that are prohibited by the
Constitution, and thereby avoid the necessity of going out and
convicting a man on independent evidence.

It would be easy to let anyone come and crash into your home
at any time and search it and see if you possibly were committing
any crime, but the Constitution says that you can't do that. Of
course, that makes it more difficult to convict people; but there
are certain things that an ordered society must honor in the
rights of individuals—and things that cannot be countenanced in
a decent society.

*There is a more general concern about American criminal law,
I think expressed by your successor, namely that our criminal law
system has become too complicated, that the trial and appeal of*

goes on for years. There is a contrast, for example, with the ... ation in Britain, where ordinarily the whole conduct of the ... minal law is short and swift and therefore has more impact ... the potential criminal. What do you think about that?

WARREN: That's not new doctrine of any kind. That's been bruited around since long before I was a District Attorney 40-odd years ago. It is true in a sense that our whole society is more complex, our whole governmental system is complex. Here in England you have a small compact nation that in size is only half the size of my state of California, and as a consequence they can have a unitary system that will operate efficiently and smoothly and go right through to a quick conclusion.

They are not hampered by a Federal system such as we have, where for instance they can go through the state courts and then after that they have a right to come to the Federal system or to the Supreme Court on constitutional and Federal questions.

Now I wouldn't defend everything that exists in our Federal judicial system. We have great ills, and I think that many of them can be improved if not eliminated. I want to refer first to the great backlogs that we have in our courts today, whether it's in state courts or in Federal courts. I found recently that in Brooklyn, in the eastern district of New York, in the Federal court the average length of time between indictment and trial in a criminal case was 22 and 2/10ths months. Now you add to that the time between arrest and indictment and you'll find that you have a solid two years of delay there before a man has a jury trial. Now, if a man is innocent that is a practical destruction of his life, and if he is guilty and is out on bail during that period committing other crimes it's a great injustice to society.

Those things must be changed, they can be changed, and I think so far as the courts' responsibility is concerned it is largely one of administration. The answer to it isn't just putting on more new judges. When you have a bad system, even though new judges come in with great vigor and earnestness and a desire to make the system work properly, they find out that they cannot do what they had hoped to do, and they gradually fall into the same pattern as the others.

You wouldn't want to see us abandon our Federal system—the whole complicated relationship between the states and the Federal Government that you spoke of?

WARREN: No, in no sense. It is just one of those situations that does make our system more complicated and more time-consuming, but it does afford us certain protections against the centralization of power that, it seems to me, are just basic to our way of life.

That may strike some as ironic, since you and your Court were always accused of destroying states' rights and state powers.

WARREN: I could argue that, but I don't think there is any necessity. If anybody could show me anything that we have done in the time that I have been on the Court other than to insist that a man is entitled to counsel at all times after he has been put upon by the Government in a criminal case, and entitled to fair treatment, to due process in the trial of his case, I would concede that we had perhaps done something wrong. I can't think of any such thing.

Remembering your years as a District Attorney and State Attorney General, what do you think has changed about the problem of crime? Why does it seem to be growing so much worse?

WARREN: People are prone to forget that we have had enormous crime problems in other eras. I can refer particularly to the era in which I was a District Attorney, from 1925 until 1938. If you will remember, most of those years were years of the Prohibition era, and in it we had the bootlegging, the high-jacking, the rum-running and all the crimes that surrounded that liquor business, and particularly the gang murders that that involved.

To my mind, that was about as badly criminalized an era as we have had, and the public was contributing to it through their refusal to obey the Prohibition laws. We have situations that are comparable to that at the present time, but it is a different kind of crime that is dominating the situation. Now the things that people are terribly concerned about are the robberies and the burglaries and the muggings and the rapes and all these other individual crimes that largely emanate from the slums in our cities. The public is very much aroused about these, but even at the present time it is not aroused about organized crime. Where do we find the people crusading against organized crime, the

crime in which there is a big business, the narcotic business for
instance?

*Are you saying that the public on the whole disregards the big
crime, the organizations that rake in millions from narcotics and
gambling particularly?*

WARREN: I am. And furthermore I will say that that kind of
crime cannot exist and flourish in any community unless there is
corruption in some form, in some segment of law enforcement.
It might be the police, it might be the prosecutor, it might even
be contributed to by the courts.

*How do you feel about the use of wiretapping by law enforce-
ment officials on the ground that it is necessary to fight criminals
at their own level?*

WARREN: I think that any invasion of the privacy of the home
or of business that is not within the limitations of the Constitution is destructive of our security in this nation. While of course
there have to be searches and seizures under given circumstances,
they must under the Constitution be reasonable and the courts
must determine what are reasonable. The indiscriminate use of
wiretapping is an outrageous violation of the privacy of individuals and can lead to the grossest kind of abuse.

The prosecutor under our system is not paid to convict people.
He's there to protect the rights of people in our community and to
see that when there is a violation of the law, it is vindicated by
trial and prosecution under fair judicial standards.

THE COURT

*Mr. Chief Justice, you have said that the reapportionment cases
were the most important decided by the Court during your 16
years. It was predicted by some people that those decisions would
not be accepted by the country and would lead the Court into
great difficulties—the political thicket. Why do you think that
did not in fact happen?*

WARREN: I think it did not happen largely because almost
everyone recognizes that ours is a representative form of government, and if it is to be representative it must have fair representation, and by fair representation we mean that everyone should

have an equal voice. There had been such a departure from that standard for so many years, with no remedy of any kind available, that the nation was ready for the decision.

While those who were in office did not acquiesce, there was general recognition of the principle that your vote should be as good as mine and mine as good as anybody else's. It is consistent with our institutions and, I think, with the intention of the founding fathers, and I also believe that it will be conducive to better government. I say that because I believe in government by the people and I believe in the wisdom of the people when they are thoroughly informed and everyone participates.

As Governor of California, you defended that state's apportionment system, which gave grossly unequal representation to people in different parts of the state. Why did you take a different view as Chief Justice?

WARREN: Because on the Court I saw it in a different light. Politics has been said to be the art of the possible, and in it we accomplish what we can accomplish by compromise and by getting agreement with people. We look at a problem from that standpoint, not perhaps from a standpoint of exact principle, because politics is not an exact science.

But when we come to the Court and we face a similar problem where the question of constitutionality is raised, we then test it by constitutional principles; if it violates the constitutional principles, we no longer can compromise, we no longer can change to bring people into agreement, we have to decide the matter according to the principle as we see it.

Now in California, when I was Governor, we did have a malapportioned Legislature. Los Angeles County with 6 million people had one State Senator, and so did a mountain district with somewhere between 50,000 and 100,000 people.

That was not equal representation by any manner of means, but our system was getting along and the people were having an opportunity to vote upon it. There was no question of constitutionality raised. At that time I didn't reflect seriously on the constitutionality of it, and I went along with the thought that we were doing pretty well and we would leave well enough alone.

Now, when I got to the Court, I found what was happening

in some of these other states—Tennessee, for instance, where the matter first arose under *Baker v. Carr,* and other states where they had a constitutional provision that the representation must be equal. They had had terribly malapportioned legislatures for over 60 years, and those who were in office and had sole control of whether there should be a reapportionment absolutely refused to permit any change of any kind because it would affect their possibilities for election. When we ran across that and applied the constitutional provision, we found that it was not fair representation and we so held.

Also I think we'll find that when men go on the Supreme Court that the empirical views that they've had in certain fields do change. I don't see how a man could be on the Court and not change his views substantially over a period of years.

I think you said to me that he comes to realize that he has the last word.

WARREN: That's right. It is purely a matter of principle with him and not a question of accommodation.

Can you remember any specific area in which you felt your own views changing on the Court aside from reapportionment? I remember one case, Irvine v California, *that was decided soon after you came on the bench and that involved eavesdropping in a gambler's home in California. The conviction was upheld despite the use of this eavesdropping evidence, and you were with the majority. I would be fairly certain myself that in more recent years you would not have voted to sustain that conviction. Can you tell us anything about that?*

WARREN: Yes, I was shocked by the Irvine case. I thought it was a terrible abuse of power on the part of the police, a shocking invasion of privacy. If you will remember, I joined Justice Jackson in an opinion which suggested, because of that violation of privacy, that the Federal Government should investigate it as a violation of civil rights.

But just a few years before that we had had the case—not we, I wasn't on the Court at that time—the Court had had the case of *Wolf v. Colorado* in which it had held that an illegal search was a violation of the Constitution but that it was within the power of the states to remedy this situation. The Federal Government, the

Court, withheld its hand in that field. That having been a very recent case and a majority of the Court having agreed not to overrule it at that particular moment, and I being a new Justice on the Court still groping around in the field of due process, I went along with that opinion, shocked as I was at the conduct of the police.

That leads me to ask you something else. On reflection now, after the 16 years, how free should a Supreme Court Justice be to overrule a prior decision in a situation like that, where he is shocked? What are the pressures on you to stick with the past decision?

WARREN: I don't believe that there is any simple answer that I could give to it. I would say that I have been in dissent on a few constitutional cases in my career on the Court, and where I have been and the majority has held one way, normally I have gone along with it until and unless some flagrant thing developed to reaffirm my view that I was right in the first instance. If there was no new element in it, I would be inclined to go along and I've done that in a number of cases and I think that is the right approach.

But at the same time we have always had the view that in constitutional cases *stare decisis* is not absolute, that constitutional questions are always open for re-examination, and I believe that too. It's a combination of those two things that I've just talked about that I would say one must judge it by.

I suppose it is inevitably the case that the arrival of a new Justice or Justices on the Court may reopen a question because men have different views.

WARREN: Oh yes, oh yes, without doubt. In fact, even men of the same Court are entitled to change their minds when they are confronted by new conditions and have done so.

Do you think the constitutional decisions of the Warren Court in the three great areas of reapportionment, race and the criminal law—the sweep of those decisions, their general tendency—will last?

WARREN: In all three of those areas, of course, I believe that our decisions are consistent with the principles of the Constitution and that they were but implementations of those principles to be in accordance with the conditions of American life that confront us. I would, of course, believe that the decisions should stand, but I would not predict.

Different men see things in different ways, and it might be that others will see them differently. That is for those who are on the Court and have the keeping of the Court in their hands to determine in accordance with the Constitution. But I believe the decisions are wholesome, in the best interests of society according to constitutional principles, and in keeping with the life of our nation. Naturally I would hope that they would remain.

How much pressure does a Supreme Court Justice feel from the outside world? You came in as Governor of California, appointed by President Eisenhower, with certain relationships with the Republican party, although you were, of course, a very independent politician. Does all that drop off when you go on the Court? Do you still feel that you need the approval of people you have related to?

WARREN: To be on the Supreme Court is an entirely different kind of life, an entirely different responsibility. I think my change from being Governor of California to Chief Justice of the United States was almost a traumatic thing for me; but change you must if you are to do your duty on the Supreme Court.

In the first place I felt it necessary to divorce myself from every political activity of every kind and to try to bring myself to act in as non-partisan way as it is possible for a human being to do. I tried also to eliminate every influence from personal contacts that could be brought to bear upon me. As you know I secluded myself from the press.

I also adopted the practice of not reading my fan mail, whether it was good or bad, because I had the idea that if you were going to believe the good things that were said about you, you'd probably have to put some thought to the accuracy of those who were against you also.

In other words, I led pretty much of a monastic life on the Court, contrary to what I had been before—because I had visited with and exchanged views with people in every part of my state and I loved to discuss matters with newspaper people.

There is no pressure on the Court from individuals, because I think practically every American realizes that it would be improper for him to try to influence a member of the Supreme Court by any contact with him on a given case, and so the only pressure comes from the pressure of these problems that you are daily confronted with.

What about your relationships with your colleagues? It must be difficult at times living in that secluded way with just eight other people.

WARREN: There is no more intimate association, other than that of man and wife, I should say, than the association that we have on the Supreme Court of the United States. It can be a very agreeable and stimulating association, or it could be a bedlam and almost hell for a person.

But I want to say that during my term on the Court our relationships have been as fine as any that I could conceive of with eight other men.

It's true that we write differently and sometimes critically and sometimes with a little feeling, but that has not been carried over to our personal relationship. I can say, after 16 years and my association with—how many?—about 16 different Justices, that I have had nothing but admiration and affection for each one of them. I believe they were trying as hard as I was to be independent and to vote their convictions and their willingness to live with their convictions, and you can't ask more of people.

As you look back at the 16 years, is there a one day that stands out in your memory as a particularly happy day?

WARREN: I do not think at the moment of any day that was particularly joyful. Almost every day on the Court is a great day of responsibility. It doesn't lend itself to levity, and even when some very important cases are decided in conformity with one's views one must have a great feeling of responsibility and wonderment as to what the consequences may be. There is no exuberance, but there may be real satisfaction.

I didn't mean to suggest only exuberance; I think satisfaction is better. I remember the day that you delivered the opinions in Reynolds v. Simms, *for example, laying down the rule of one man one vote, and I had very much a feeling of history that particular day. I wonder whether you felt it.*

WARREN: Yes, I did. I think *Baker v. Carr* was the most important case that we decided in my time, because that gave to the courts the power to determine whether or not we were to have fair representation in our governmental system, and *Reynolds v. Simms* was merely the application of that principle.

It was a case in which I derived real satisfaction, although I was thoroughly cognizant of the controversy that it was going to start. As a matter of fact, people in California have said to me since, "Why on earth did you have to take that case of *Reynolds v. Simms?*" While I didn't respond to them in this manner, my real reason for it was because I had viewed the matter in a different way when I was Governor, and when I had to face it on the Court, I just thought that as long as I had to face it I would face it directly myself.

You mean you assigned the opinion to yourself.

WARREN: Yes.

How important do you think that function is—the function of assigning opinions? Does it give the Chief Justice a very different weight on the Court from his colleagues?

WARREN: No—I don't think it gives him any additional weight. But I do believe that if it wasn't done with regard to fairness, it could well lead to great disruption in the Court.

During all the years I was there I never had any of the Justices urge me to give them opinions to write, nor did I ever have anyone object to any opinion that I assigned to him or to anybody else. I did try very hard to see that we had an equal work load, that we weren't all writing in one field where one person would be considered the expert. Everybody, regardless of length of time they were on the Court, had a fair opportunity to write important cases.

There wasn't any of the back-biting that one senses in Mason's biography of Chief Justice Stone?

WARREN: Never one, never one shred of that—never have I had one indication of that in all the time I have been on the Court.

There were a lot of peppery exchanges between you and Justice Frankfurter over the decision of cases. Did that affect your relationship at all?

WARREN: No, no, no. I've been in dissent with Justice Black, too, recently where Black has been very, very incisive in his remarks, but that makes no difference at all.

No, Justice Frankfurter by nature was a very decisive fellow in his speech. Sometimes he could raise hackles, you know, but he was a delightful companion, and our relationships throughout the years I was there were always very friendly as they have been with all of the rest of the Justices.

Mr. Chief Justice, do you have thoughts about American lawyers and the American bar and how they have changed? Have the law schools been turning out better lawyers, or what do you think of our legal profession?

WARREN: I think the products of the law schools these days are infinitely better than they were in my day. I have a lot of contacts, as you can imagine, with youngsters out of law school, having had three or four law clerks each year. I deal with them on an intimate basis, and I come to know them almost like you would know a son, and when they leave me I feel almost like I used to feel when one of my boys would leave home to go to college. You just feel a sense of loss.

They are great people, and they couldn't have been as good as they were without having much better instruction, much more comprehensive instruction than we had when I was in law school. And you have to bear in mind also that the law now is infinitely more complex and voluminous than it was when I was admitted to practice in 1914.

Over the years various people have charged that the law clerks play a secret, powerful role on the Supreme Court. What do you think of that?

WARREN: I remember when President Eisenhower appointed Loyd Wright, the former president of the American Bar Association, to head up a commission on subversion, and he reported that great possibilities for subversion stemmed from these young law clerks who were just out of the law school. He referred to them as a group of young radicals and proposed in his commission report that all of them be given complete F.B.I. investigations and that they be confirmed by the Senate before they could be employed by the Supreme Court.

Now, the fact was that at that particular time our law clerks were more conservative than any young lawyers that I had ever seen. They were in that phase; at that time law schools were very, very conservative.

Since then, I want to say, the law clerks have become far more interested in public affairs, interested in the defense of people, interested in teaching and law schools, interested in constitutional questions.

Really they are a rare lot, and I think they are a great institution. The Court uses them normally only for one year, because it doesn't want to build up a bureaucracy. We bring new young men right out of the law school, and it's great for them, it's wonderful for the Court. We get great help from them, and I think that they can be a real force in our profession throughout the country.

If the law clerks have become less conservative, have the law schools also?

WARREN: You know now that the big law firms in New York, Chicago, San Francisco and Los Angeles are recruiting young men just like universities recruit football players. They go out and pay their way back to New York—you know, to visit with their office, show them the theaters and so forth, let them mix with their elders in their offices and invite them to come to the firm.

They tell me that in New York some firms are up to $17,000 a year now right out of the law.school, and the graduates are not beating a path to their door either. The firms are having difficulty in getting them because a lot of these boys work for the Peace Corps, they work in the Poverty Program, they go to work in district attorneys' offices, in public defenders' offices and in the Federal and state governments, and for Ralph Nader.

In other words, we'll put it they are interested in public causes where 15 years ago, or even 10 or 12 years ago, it was very difficult to get young lawyers to be interested in public causes.

I have only one real quarrel with the law schools—I don't know one in the country where they give an adequate course on the responsibilities of lawyers to the cause of justice, or where they give a comprehensive course on the reciprocal responsibilities of court and lawyers to the administration of justice, and I think that that has kept our bar from being alert to many of these problems that have confronted our courts.

The Court has suffered from that fact, too, because the great debate on important issues has never been developed as it should be. Take this proposal of Senator Dirksen's, that came through the Council of State Governments, for a new constitutional court of 50 members, the Chief Justices of every state of the Union to constitute a court above the Supreme Court of the United States—and then the other constitutional amendment on reapportionment. Those things went through Legislature after Legislature till almost two-thirds of them passed some kind of resolution on them, and there was no debate of any kind on the part of the bar in the country. To think of coming that close to a constitutional amendment on important subjects of that kind without the bar taking an interest is almost a frightening thing.

Perhaps you are saying that the organized bar in the United States has not improved quite so much as the law schools have improved?

WARREN: That is true. The American Bar Association for many years, particularly during the McCarthy era, never had a kind word to say for the Supreme Court. Everything was critical.

There have been some splendid men in recent years as president of the American bar. Last year Mr. William Gossett was the president, and he was a very enlightened person and has done a great deal to improve the situation, it seems to me. Mr. Bernard Segal, who's the new president of the American bar, is also a very enlightened, forward-looking man, and I'm sure he will make a real contribution to the work of the bar.

THE COUNTRY

Mr. Chief Justice, is there a day that you remember as the most unhappy of your years in Washington?

WARREN: That is not a difficult question to answer. The saddest day I remember, the saddest week I remember, the saddest year I remember all started one Friday afternoon when we were in conference and I received a note from my secretary, Mrs.

Margaret McHugh, to the effect that President Kennedy had been shot.

We immediately adjourned, and by the time I was back in my office Mrs. McHugh informed me that it had just come over the radio that the President was dead. And that and the following week were the saddest days I've ever seen not only during my 16 years but, I think, the saddest I've ever seen in any community in my life.

It was only a day or two after he was buried that President Johnson sent the Solicitor General [Archibald Cox] and the Deputy Attorney General [Nicholas deB. Katzenbach] to see me to ask if I would head a commission to investigate the facts of the Kennedy assassination. I told them that I wished they would tell the President I thought I could not do that, because the Court did not look with favor upon extracurricular commissions of that kind. I myself had expressed an aversion to it, and I thought it would be much better if he would get someone else, and I proposed a couple of names to them.

I thought that was the end of it. But in about an hour I received a message from the President asking if I could visit him at his office. I did so, and he told me of the wild stories that were going around the world and of what this might mean internally if there was not a thorough probe of the facts and some conclusion reached as to who was responsible for the assassination.

He told me that he had conferred with the leaders of both parties in the Congress and that he was going to set up a commission to explore the facts, and he said they would all serve if I would be the chairman of it. He thought that no less a personage than the Chief Justice of the United States, the chief judicial officer of the nation, should head it up. He told me it was of paramount importance; I remember him saying, "You served the country in uniform, and this will be a more important service than anything you could do in a uniform." And so I said, "Mr. President, in spite of my feelings about the matter, if you consider it of that importance, of course, I will do it."

I spent 10 months on that. I think that, too, was the unhappiest year of my life, because I spent at least half of each day and night on that—the rest on my Court work—and to review the terrible happenings of that assassination every day for 10 months is a traumatic experience.

Those days were the unhappiest days I have ever spent in the public service.

And you didn't get much in the way of applause for doing the job, did you?

WARREN: No, that is very true. But up to the present time no one has produced any facts that are contrary to the findings of that commission. A great many people have written to the effect that it might have been this, it might have been that, and some inferences could be drawn other than those that the commission drew. But there has been no confrontation of the facts at all to discredit anything that is in that report.

You are now in retirement, Mr. Chief Justice. How do you think you will like it, a person who's been as active and as engaged in issues as you have been?

WARREN: I'm not so sure how I will like it when I get back to Washington, in my new office in the Court, and the term opens and others all are working and I am not. I haven't felt the strain at all up to the present time because I remained on the Court until the end of the term, and I have been traveling since then.

I can say that I want to cure the problem by doing something that is worthwhile in three fields that I have been interested in. How much time I can or will give to each of them I don't know, but I hope in the aggregate that I will fill my days as I have in the past.

I am interested, of course, in peace, in our country being a leader in the movement for peace around the world. I am interested naturally in court administration; I think there is much to be done, and I have offered my services to the new Federal judicial center which I have worked to have established for many years. And then I am interested in the conservation of our environment, and there is so much to be done in that field that I may find some little niche where I can be of help.

In general, are you optimistic for the United States, or do you think that with all the troubles we've been having we are in a period of some kind of moral decay?

WARREN: I am optimistic, of course, about the United States.

For many years I have been at odds with those people who feel that we are living in a mature society, that the society is starting to disintegrate and that the institutions based on that society are themselves deteriorating and becoming degraded. I do not believe that.

I believe that this is a young nation, that we haven't yet reached our potential in any sense of the word. I believe that our forms of government are still on trial, that we are still going through the growing process, that we are learning from day to day.

And I think that many of the problems we have today are the result of more active conscience than they are of degradation or of decadence rather than degradation. I have been in the public service now for 52 years, and when I first went into the service of my state 50 years ago I found moral standards in government far below what they are today.

The standards of government today are head and shoulders over what they were in those days, and I am speaking now of local government, of state government and of Federal Government as well. There are a lot of things brought to light today that create real scandal, that in those days would never have been mentioned—they would just be overlooked.

So I think there is improvement. I think in spite of the travail we are going through now that we will emerge a better nation and a stronger nation, because I believe the things that we are learning will convince us that our system, being a pluralistic system, must also be a system of equality.

Do you take seriously the warning that President Eisenhower gave in his final speech, against what he termed the Military-Industrial Complex?

WARREN: Yes, I do, and I wish that General Eisenhower had said that before the day he left the White House. I think there is a great danger. One can find the industrial world linked with the military today in almost every request of the military.

I received something of a shock about six months ago when I read an article in one of the Sunday papers that was an interview with the top executives of the 10 largest defense contractors in the country, and each one of them said their companies were not expecting any decrease in their military contracts even if the war in Vietnam ended tomorrow.

It seems to me that the armed forces are always interested in improving their forces to the point of perfection as they see it, and with the alliance of the business world this becomes almost impossible to resist.

I also have some concern about bringing our universities and colleges into that same complex. You will find that a major portion of the budgets of our great universities these days is in the field of research for military purposes, and many have expanded to such an extent that it would be very undesirable from their standpoint to cut back to the size they were before.

I take it from what you said right at the beginning of this talk that you regard the ending of violence as vital for the future of the United States, and specifically the end of the war in Vietnam.

WARREN: I do indeed. I don't believe that we can continue to be in war, and continue to teach our young people that war is an essential part of their lives, and still expect our young people to grow up normal and quiescent.

Part 3

LEGAL SCHOLARS EVALUATE THE WARREN COURT

Editor's Preface

JUSTICE FRANKFURTER, it bears repeating, understood that the words of the Constitution are so unrestricted by their intrinsic meaning, or by history, or by tradition, or by prior decisions, "that they leave the individual justice free, if indeed they do not compel him, to gather meaning not from reading the Constitution but from reading life. . . . The process of constitutional interpretation compels the translation of policy into judgment, and the controlling conceptions of the justices are their 'idealized political picture' of the existing social order." This theme was reiterated in Frankfurter's writings over the length of his career as a law professor and as a jurist. That he was a realist who understood the subjective component of the judicial process cannot be denied even by his detractors. An even more insistent theme in his writings was expressed in the thought that, "If the function of this Court is to be essentially no different from that of a legislature, if the considerations governing constitutional construction are to be substantially those that underlie legislation, then indeed judges should not have life tenure and they should be made directly responsible to the people." Apart from his belief, reflected in this statement, that the Court in a political democracy has no warrant to govern, Frankfurter was also saying that a deliberately result-oriented constitutional adjudication is a corruption of the judicial process, leaving far behind the idea of the rule of law enforced by impersonal and objective judges.

In constitutional cases, as in any others, the judge who first chooses what the outcome should be and then reasons backwards to supply a rationalization replete with rules and precedents has betrayed his calling: he has decided on the basis of prejudice or prejudgment, and has made constitutional law little more than the embodiment of his policy preferences, reflecting his subjective predilections. From the standpoint of result-oriented jurisprudence, what was wrong with the opinions of the Court when it sustained state compulsion of racial segregation in 1896 or when it invalidated federal regulation of labor in 1936 was not that the justices decided on the basis of predilection, or made policy, or engaged in an act of arbitrary will, or legislated, or did any of the things that a realist might say was inevitable; what was wrong, rather, was that the Court's preferences were illiberal or its policy undemocratic or its legislation reactionary. This view of the matter is just a bit short of political and judicial monstrosity; it loses nothing of its monstrous character when the Court is praised simply for reaching the right or just result when it identifies with underdog litigants like radicals, aliens, Negroes, the poor, and criminal defendants who have been victimized by suppression, brutality, or discrimination. Justice Black, who presents the paradox of the powerful advocate who sees himself merely as a constitutional literalist and no more, concisely put the point when he asked why we have a written Constitution at all if its interpreters are left only to the admonitions of their own consciences.

The essays in this section present a debate among professional Court-watchers, legal scholars who are experts on the judicial process and constitutional law. Fred Rodell of Yale Law School, who wrote the scrappy defense of Warren and his Court reprinted in the preceding section, is here pitted against Louis L. Jaffe of Harvard Law School, Philip B. Kurland of the University of Chicago Law School, and Alexander M. Bickel, one of Rodell's colleagues at Yale. Rodell's first entry, "Crux of the Court Hullabaloo," was published in 1960, six years before his article in the preceding section. In 1960 the chorus of criticism against the Warren Court emanating from the law schools was scarcely more than a whisper. Rodell, confronted mainly by the irresponsible and uninformed froth of lay critics who disliked the Court simply because they disliked its results, could afford to be comparatively dispassionate when presenting an explanation of the "hullabaloo" about the Court wholly in terms of the divisions within it between the Frankfurter and Black factions. Rodell's bias is clearly on the side of the liberal activists, but he observes that the "intelligence and integrity of each side deserves the decent respect of the other," and that "no one supposes the Frankfurter faction does not believe in liberty, or the Black-Douglas bloc does not believe in order."

On the other hand, Rodell misrepresents Frankfurter's position and record in claiming that he believed in interfering in civil liberties cases no more than in cases where economic rights are claimed. In a 1949 case, *Kovacs v. Cooper,* Frankfurter explained why Holmes, whose views he approved, "was far more ready to find legislative invasion where free inquiry was involved than in the debatable area of economics." Frankfurter was in fact on the libertarian side in many cases dealing with church-and-state, desegregation, internal security, search and seizure, and coerced confessions, among others. Rodell's article also reflects his adherence to the Black position when Rodell refers to "the semantic absoluteness of most of the Bill of Rights' guarantees." But neither in the Bill of Rights proper nor, as Rodell has put it, in its Fourteenth Amendment supplement, is there any semantic absoluteness.

Notwithstanding Rodell's fairly balanced portrayal of the two wings of the Court in 1960, Jaffe, a former clerk of Justice Brandeis, felt compelled to explain, too subtly perhaps, why Frankfurter's position on the proper role of a judge distinctly limited his choice in any given case and why, indeed, he could not see a case simply in terms, as Rodell depicts it, of a choice between liberty and order. The trouble with Jaffe's position—and

Frankfurter's—is in the statement that a judge should enact into law not his own but the public's will. That leaves the injunctions of the Bill of Rights too flexible, destroys the idea of having constitutional limitations upon the majority will, and fails to explain how a judge can discern the public's will in any case not involving a statute which at least theoretically reflects that will. Even where it does, as in a statute compelling racial discrimination, the public cannot go unchecked.

When Rodell wrote the second article that is reprinted in this section, he unabashedly defended subjective, result-oriented constitutional adjudication. The other fellow's ox, not his, was being gored. His approach to a Supreme Court case—not unlike that of Warren, whom he celebrated—is *ad hoc* and anti-intellectual. After parodying the serious, academic critics of the Court, Rodell claimed: "The chief thing to remember about all this high-toned criticism, no matter how valid in the abstract, is that, translated, it really means: 'We don't like what the Warren Court has been doing.'" Rodell's translation simply is untrue, as the articles by Bickel and Kurland, both former Frankfurter clerks, show.

Bickel wrote, ". . . In addition to those who criticize the Warren Court, as is their right, because they do not like its results, there are professional observers of the Court who criticize it on other grounds, while as a matter of preference approving many if not most of the results it has reached." Similarly, Kurland wrote, ". . . The dissatisfaction [with the Warren Court] goes not merely to the results reached by the majority but also the manner in which those results are reached." Although Bickel and Kurland published their articles after Rodell's, the position they represented was well known among those whom Bickel calls "professional observers of the Court." Rodell's dismissal of that position as "high-toned criticism, no matter how valid in the abstract," calls to mind the point made by Kurland that the majority that controlled the Warren Court made little attempt to answer or solve the problems and arguments posed by their dissenting brethren.

Thus Rodell in his 1966 piece, "It Is the Earl Warren Court," emulated his hero by tersely stating, "He cares about results," and in another sentence acknowledges that he "ignored rather than answered Justice Harlan's disturbed and scholarly dissent—

much as John Marshall used to brush off pedantic impedimenta to the results he felt were right." Marshall may have been the "greatest," that is, the most influential justice in the history of the Court, but he was also one of the worst legal craftsmen. As Holmes once said to his Chief Justice, William Howard Taft, "Mr. Chief Justice, as Chief Justice of the Supreme Court I respect you. As former President of the United States I honor you. But as a lawyer you are no damned good." Rodell might ignore the views of Bickel and Kurland, as Warren did Harlan's, but ignorance is no blow for liberty and equality, nor an answer to the charge that Warren, Black, Douglas, Brennan, Goldberg, Fortas, and Thurgood Marshall did not offer adequately reasoned justifications or intellectually coherent explanations for their results.

That the Warren Court was usually on the side of the angels and full of good intentions is not the issue for Bickel and Kurland. Good intentions are not enough for the Supreme Court. As Kurland said, in a law review article, "If, as has been suggested, the road to hell is paved with good intentions, the Warren Court has been among the great roadbuilders of all time." Bickel did not argue that the Court should not be political or that it could avoid being political; on the contrary. His point was that it should not be political in the fashion of a legislature or an executive, and he demonstrated that the Warren Court was too political in that fashion. When he used the *Miranda* opinion to buttress his argument, he was not emulating the know-nothings who cursed the opinion because it supposedly handcuffed the cops or coddled criminals. His criticisms, he said and proved, were directed "at the manner of the Court's discharge of its function, not necessarily at the results it reaches." Similarly, Kurland, who acknowledged that the Court must in effect act as a "continuing constitutional convention," was concerned about its craftsmanship —the cogency with which its opinions convincingly explained its decisions or results, taking into careful consideration the arguments advanced by dissenters. Without facing, rather than facing away from, dissenting opinions, the Court too often offered merely its own fiat, rather than reasoned judgment, for its decisions.

Concern for the validity of the route by which the Court reached its decision is a major theme of Archibald Cox's book,

The Warren Court, the most sympathetic account yet published. Again and again he subjects to the scrutiny of a questing, analytical mind the opinions of the Court that Rodell applauded, and again and again Cox frets because the Court, though having reached the just result, may not convince a critic who may ask: Why respect a stump speech from a group of men who are not accountable to the electorate, who themselves have little respect for those seriously inquiring if there is something called the law and Constitution to which decision should conform whether or not it is best for the country in the minds of a majority of the justices who happen to be sitting at any particular moment? Rodell, like the Court he defended, ought to stir all good liberals to rollicking applause. Jaffe, Bickel, and Kurland, like Cox, still that applause by posing unanswered questions which cannot be avoided and will not go away by being overlooked. Scholars can, especially in their longer, technical works addressed to a professional audience, be carping, petulant, and pharisaical; they can give the impression that they have forgotten what they know better than most—that law is an instrument of society, existing not as art for art's sake but as a means for the sake of society's ends. But they cannot be ignored and cannot be gainsaid when they insist that any means to a justifiable end is, in a democratic society, a noxious doctrine.

Crux of the
Court Hullabaloo

by Fred Rodell

ITEM: ON A decision Monday a few weeks back, the Supreme
Court of the United States affirmed the conviction of Rudolf
Abel, a known and proved Russian spy, by a bare majority of five
to four, with Chief Justice Warren and Justices Black, Douglas
and Brennan dissenting.

Item: Bills to curb the Supreme Court's power in dozens of
different ways have been pouring into the Congressional hopper for
the past two years.

Item: The national debate subject which students throughout
the land have been arguing pro and con over the past school
term is, in substance: Resolved, that Congress be given the right
to reverse, by whatever vote, Supreme Court decisions.

Not since the Nine Old Men fought the New Deal in the mid–
Nineteen Thirties—a fight that ended in the capitulation of the
court and the consequent defeat of Franklin Roosevelt's court-
packing plan—has the court been so much and so long in controversy and in the news.

One reason, of course, is the famous desegregation decision of

From the *New York Times Magazine*, May 29, 1960, copyright © 1960
by The New York Times Company.

1954, plus its continuing aftermath. But here the court was, and remains, unanimous; the whole Federal Government backs its rulings; so does the whole nation outside the resistant hard-core South.

None of these facts is true about the chief crux of the current hullabaloo over the court. Here, much of the Federal Government, from members of Congress to the F. B. I., has been up in arms; much of the nation and the press views the court with suspicion or mistrust; and the court, as so often in its 170-year history, is divided against itself—witness the case of Rudolf Abel, Russian spy.

It was not, of course, that the four dissenters—who came just that close to upsetting Abel's conviction—approve of spies, are soft toward Russia, or want to set known criminals free. Rather, they felt that the evidence on which Abel was convicted had been grabbed in gross violation of the Fourth Amendment's guarantee against "unreasonable searches and seizures." And they further felt it their judicial duty to uphold the Constitution in the face of what they deemed its flagrant disregard—even on behalf of a Communist spy.

Here, in microcosm, is the major question that has impelled many Senators and Congressmen to try to clip the court's wings, that high school and college students have been debating all this spring, and that has split the court, not just of late but for almost twenty years: What is the proper role of the court, what should it do or not do, when the act of some other government body— state or Federal, legislative or executive—is challenged as plainly violating part of the Bill of Rights or its supplement, the Four-teenth Amendment?

On this key question, the court's division—the line-up of the justices—is not nearly so clear-cut as when Holmes and Brandeis and Stone and, later, Cardozo were regularly dissenting against the stubborn economic conservatism of their brethren earlier in the century. What is clear is only that Justice Frankfurter today captains one team, commonly if clumsily known as "advocates of judicial self-restraint," while Justices Black and Douglas co-captain the other team, dubbed" "judicial activists"; that Black and Douglas almost always have Warren and Brennan with them; and that Frankfurter usually signs up the other four. Despite the occasional shifting of sides by this justice or that, the Frankfurter team tends to win the close ones.

And despite the shifting, the basic battle can be bitter. When the venerable Judge Learned Hand—who, though not on the Supreme Court, has long been a coach and a comfort to the Frankfurter contingent—once dismissed the First Amendment's guarantees of freedom of speech and press as "no more than admonitions of moderation," Justice Douglas retorted: "The idea that they are no more than that has done more to undermine liberty in this country than any other single force."

Dissenting blasts against colleagues are often equally strong. A few recent examples may point up the problem—and a few quotes, the depth of the court's division.

A left-wing soap-box speaker in a political campaign was threatened by a couple of hoodlum hecklers. A cop ordered the speaker to stop before trouble started. The speaker refused—and got thirty days in jail. Should the Constitution's guarantee of freedom of speech or the state's police power prevail? The Supreme Court, in Feiner v. New York, upheld the jail sentence, six to three. Dissenting, Justice Black exclaimed: "I will have no part or parcel in this holding which I view as a long step toward totalitarian authority."

A Texas-born American citizen had voted in a Mexican town where he was then living. An Act of Congress says that any citizen who votes in a foreign election can thus lose his citizenship. The Department of Justice moved to denationalize this United States native. Should the Constitution's flat guarantee of citizenship to everyone born here (with no provision for taking citizenship away) or the Act of Congress predominate? The Supreme Court, in Perez v. Brownell, upheld Congress, five to four. Said Justice Douglas in dissent: "The philosophy of the opinion that sustains this statute . . . gives supremacy to the legislature in a way that is incompatible with the scheme of our written Constitution."

A college teacher, called before the House Un-American Activities Committee, refused to answer questions about his alleged past

Communist affiliations. He did not "take the Fifth" but claimed the right of silence under the First Amendment's guarantee of freedom of speech and assembly, plus the right to be tried, if at all, by a court, not a legislative committee. None of this kept him from being convicted for contempt of Congress. Should the relevant Constitution-based claims or the committee's power to punish recalcitrant witnesses take precedence? The Supreme Court, in Barenblatt v. U.S., backed the committee, five to four.

Concluded Justice Black in dissent: "Ultimately all the questions in this case boil down to one—whether we as a people will try fearfully and futilely to preserve democracy by adopting totalitarian methods, or whether in accordance with our traditions and our Constitution we will have the confidence and courage to be free."

What does it all add up to—this deep doctrinal division within the court—and whence did it arise? Though its philosophical sources stretch back through at least 2,000 years of political theory, its present explosiveness began to sputter soon after the clash between Old Court and New Deal twenty-odd years ago.

There is not a man on the court today, nor for many years past, who does not agree that the Nine Old Men were wrong to strike down social laws, in the name of the Constitution, and thus make themselves the country's economic overlords. But *why* was the Old Court wrong? Precisely how did the reigning justices abuse or stray from their proper judicial role? Here is the rub whose friction has split the current court—with results not unlike the splitting of an atom.

The Frankfurter faction feels that the Nine Old Men were wrong to substitute their collective judgment for that of other Government officers, especially for that of Congress, on any type of issue, under the aegis of any constitutional clause. This belief in judicial self-restraint, though all-inclusive, is not absolute; it will pay more deference to an Act of Congress—or a law passed by any legislature—than to the ruling of a regulatory agency or a local policeman's order.

But its strong slant is toward judicial hands-off whenever some other branch of government has acted—save when such action may create conflict within the Federal system; then the court should step in as a sort of impartial chairman or arbiter to keep order among our fifty-one separate sovereigns.

Most crucially, the Frankfurter view makes no distinction whatever between two different realms or reaches of Government action; with impeccable logic, it insists that the court should no more interfere where personal liberties may be infringed than where claimed economic rights are at stake.

The Black-Douglas view exalts this precise distinction. It sees the Old Court's error more narrowly—in the type of laws that were vetoed (all of them economic) and in the fuzzy imprecision of the Constitution's due-process and interstate-commerce clauses which the Old Court used to cut those laws down.

Unbothered by charges from the Frankfurter camp of illogic or inconsistency, the so-called judicial activists defend the distinction they make between personal liberties and economic rights on two major grounds: first, the semantic absoluteness of most of the Bill of Rights' guarantees, such as the First Amendment's flat and unqualified "Congress shall make no law . . ."; second, a deep conviction, born of both reason and emotion, that—regardless of syllogistic consistency about judicial review—this nation puts, or should put, a higher premium on individual dignities and freedoms than on material matters like the getting and keeping of money, and that the court should honor that preference under the Constitution.

To support this conviction, the Black-Douglas group rhetorically asks: Why have a written Constitution (save to set up the sheer mechanics of government) in a republic devoted to law by majority rule? Why have a written Bill of Rights—if not to protect *against* majority rule, and against executive excesses, too, the minimum democratic decencies that dictatorships view with scorn, from the First Amendment freedoms of speech and religion and press and assembly to the guarantees of fair treatment and trial for every accused person, be he charged with kidnapping or communism? And, most crucially, who better than the courts can be counted on to stand up against lynch-minded law-makers or over-eager officers or public pressures when the Bill of Rights is invoked on behalf of unpopular, or even despised, minority groups or nonconforming people?

In partial reply to this last question—and, of course, in support of their stand—the Black-Douglas group quotes James Madison, proposing the Bill of Rights to the first Congress:

"If they [the Bill of Rights amendments] are incorporated into the Constitution, independent tribunals of justice will consider themselves in a peculiar manner the guardians of those rights; they will be an impenetrable bulwark against every assumption of power in the legislative or executive; they will be naturally led to resist every encroachment upon rights expressly stipulated for in the Constitution by the declaration of rights."

The Frankfurter contingent also looks, but with a contrary slant, to constitutional theory and history. Their creed can be roughly summarized as: Leave law-making to legislatures and law-enforcing to executive officers, Bill of Rights or no; our job as judges is to interpret and apply laws, not to force any part of the Constitution down other governmental throats.

This attitude, while abstractly stressing a rather rigid separation of powers, in practice leaves the legislature supreme—as in constitutionless England. Indeed, an aura of Anglophilia—a leaning toward the parliamentary system and toward the views of British jurist John Austin—permeates the Frankfurter approach. As Douglas recently put it in dissent against a Frankfurter holding, "We [here] forsake much of our constitutional heritage and move closer to the British scheme."

Implicit, too, in the Frankfurter philosophy of judicial self-restraint is a strong reluctance maybe to embroil the court, even to uphold civil liberties, in the sort of trouble the Nine Old Men encountered by bucking the popular will in the name of the Constitution.

Thus, Justice Frankfurter, concurring in the Dennis decision which gave the green light of judicial approval to the Communist-controlling Smith act, said: "Civil liberties draw at best only limited strength from legal guaranties. . . . The ultimate reliance for the deepest needs of civilization must be found *outside* [emphasis added] their vindication in courts of law. . . ." And Frankfurter's long-time ally, the late Justice Jackson, wrote shortly before he died that "any court which undertakes by its legal processes to enforce civil liberties needs the support of an enlightened and vigorous public opinion. . . . I do not think the American public is enlightened on this subject."

Such statements are a far cry from the end of Black's dissent in the Dennis case: "There is hope, however, that in calmer times, when present pressures, passions and fears subside, this or some later *court* [emphasis added] will restore the First Amendment liberties to the high preferred place where they belong in a free society."

Given Frankfurter's scale of values, in which keeping the court out of trouble rates near the top, his fears have recently proved quite well founded. For during the 1957-58 term of court, the Black-Douglas drive for militant judicial defense of civil liberties prevailed in a number of cases, as other justices, including sometimes Frankfurter himself, shifted on occasion to the Black-Douglas camp. And it was these libertarian decisions which triggered the still rumbling *brouhaha* about the court in Congress, in the press, and throughout the country. Doubtless in consequence, the court majority quickly retreated to safer ground and, with rare exceptions, remains there today—though usually by a slim majority of one.

As with Frankfurter, so with every justice; what the whole debate boils down to is a question of scales of values—of conflicting choices between competing ends. Both positions are intellectually respectable positions; a thinking man, on or off the court, can with reason take either side and there are reasonable men on both.

Indeed, the recently published efforts of a few extreme Frankfurter partisans to ridicule as judicial automatism the Black-Douglas insistence on honoring the Bill of Rights to the letter are themselves the only rationally disreputable voices in the debate. The intelligence and integrity of each side deserves the decent respect of the other.

Justice Frankfurter often uses, in defense of his philosophy, the phrase "ordered liberty"—a phrase he borrowed from the late

Justice Cardozo. Self-contradictory on its face, the phrase is even more so when applied to a specific case or issue; for then the noun and the adjective must clash. And here perhaps is the very crux of the current Supreme Court split. For no one supposes the Frankfurter faction does not believe in liberty, or the Black-Douglas bloc does not believe in order. It is when a choice must be made between them that Frankfurter chooses order; Black and Douglas choose liberty.

The Court Debated —Another View

by Louis L. Jaffe

PROFESSOR FRED RODELL in an article last week in this magazine has persuasively defended the Supreme Court against the charge of usurping the powers of the people's legislatures and imposing its will on the nation. I am thoroughly in accord with him on this point.

The unanimous decision holding that school segregation denied Negroes the constitutionally guaranteed "equal protection of the laws" was absolutely sound. And in other cases where the Court, though divided, has upheld civil liberty claims, the decisions have been well within the area of legitimate difference of opinion. There has been no usurpation. And all those who look upon the Court as the single most powerful support of the rule of law should be rushing to its defense.

But to Mr. Rodell's characterizations of the opposed Frankfurter "team" and Black-Douglas "team," I must take strong objection. Frankfurter, he argues, feels that it is wrong for the Nine Old Men "to substitute their collective judgment for that of other Government officers, especially for that of Congress, on any

From the *New York Times Magazine,* June 5, 1960, copyright © 1960 by The New York Times Company.

type of issue under the aegis of any constitutional clause"; the Court's "job is to interpret and apply laws, not to force any part of the Constitution down other governmental throats."

To put Rodell's characterization more baldly: Frankfurter refuses to uphold against legislative encroachment the constitutional guarantees of civil liberty. Black and Douglas, on the other hand, proceed on the basis that the purpose of the Bill of Rights is "to protect *against* majority rule and . . . executive excesses, too." Rodell concludes that when a choice must be made, "Frankfurter chooses order; Black and Douglas choose liberty."

Rodell's formulas are no doubt easier to understand than my more complicated exposition of what I conceive to be the true situation; and they contain an important germ of proof which I shall discuss later. But his reduction of the actual complexities—not less true for being subtle—to simple slogans produces a distorted and misleading conception of constitutional adjudication.

There are indeed distinguished judges (Learned Hand is one) and lawyers (the late Charles P. Curtis was one) who believe, as Rodell charges of Frankfurter, that the judicial defense of civil liberties against the legislature is undemocratic and futile. They do not set a high value on liberty which does not arise out of the conscience of the people and its elected representatives.

I would not deny that Justice Frankfurter shares to some extent Judge Hand's skepticism of the value of judicial protection of civil liberties, and that it affects his judgment. But what Mr. Rodell distorts is the character of the questions presented to the Court and the area in which judgment or choice, if you will, operates.

In each of the examples cited by him in which the Court has split, he manages, by characterizing the issues in terms of the constitutional phrases or by quoting stirring pronouncements about "free societies," "totalitarian methods," etc., to convey the impression that the majority has chosen to condone a clear and obvious violation of the constitutional guarantee. "Why," he asks, "have a written Bill of Rights—if not to protect against the majority violation of the constitutional guarantees of fair trial whether for kidnapping or communism, the guarantee of free speech, the press, religion and assembly?" Why indeed? I agree with him and so does every last justice on the Court.

But in the cases put by Mr. Rodell, the question was whether the claim *was* guaranteed by the Constitution, and, in every case, there was a reasonable argument that it was not. Mr. Rodell and Justice Black would not, perhaps, agree with this assertion. Rodell speaks of the "semantic absoluteness of most of the Bill of Rights' guarantees, such as the First Amendment's flat and unqualified 'Congress shall make no law' . . . [abridging the freedom of speech, etc.].

Now it is one of the most difficult things in the world to persuade a layman that there has never yet been formulated a rule of law so clear that legitimate disagreement will not arise as to its meaning and application. But a *lawyer* who denies this will be regarded by his fellows as either stupid or disingenuous. My colleague, Professor Lon Fuller, is fond of putting the case of a statute that prohibits "vehicles" in the public parks. He then asks: Does it apply to a baby carriage? As to many, probably most, cases arising under this statute, we would all agree; automobiles clearly are covered.

And it is so with these constitutional guarantees. A law which punished The New York Times for criticizing the President's foreign policy would be instantly struck down. Critics focusing on the controversial cases are apt to overlook or belittle the enormous value of this great solid, assured area of protection.

The controversial free-speech cases provide a good example of the misleading character of the Rodell-Black analysis. I shall speak of three of them, the Roth, the Dennis and the Barenblatt cases, the last two of which Rodell discussed.

First the Roth case. This posed the question whether the Federal Government and the states can prohibit obscenity. Yes, said the Court; no, said Black and Douglas. Why not? Justice Black has given as his reason that the First Amendment of the Constitution says Congress shall make "no law abridging" free speech and that means *"no law abridging"* (italics original).

What is wrong with his argument? Simply this. A law must be put in its historic context. It must be interpreted in the light of the objectives, expectations and general understanding of the law-giver. This, at least, is the beginning of interpretation, though, as we shall see in a moment, it is not the end, for as time changes and new problems emerge, the meaning of the law changes, too.

Now, to return to our free-speech guarantee. It has never even been suggested (until recently by Black) that the Founders meant by enacting the First Amendment to supersede the law against defamation. Yet a law forbidding defamation on pain of paying damages comes close, if you take the guarantee literally, to being a law "abridging free speech." There is dispute as to how many states at the time of the Constitution had laws against obscenity. But some states did, and all of them have since enacted them.

Almost no one is prepared to argue that the Founding Fathers intended the First Amendment to protect against dismissal of a teacher who preaches racial hatred in his class or a Cabinet officer who announces to the press that the President is a fool. However absolute in terms may be the First Amendment, to insist or to pretend that it must for that reason—and that reason alone—be read without qualification is contrary to the conditions of the processes of legal interpretation.

If obscenity is to be protected as "free speech," it must be because it serves the underlying *purpose* of the guarantee to do so. That is a very different thing from the argument based on literal absoluteness. If the argument is put in terms of purpose, reasonable men can differ, to say the least, as to the outcome. There is a legitimate choice as to the outcome.

I shall have something to say concerning the proper judicial approach to this task of making a choice where reasonable men could differ. But first I would like to repeat that in all of the cases put by Mr. Rodell, there *was* an open choice as to the applicable meaning of the Constitution.

Perhaps the most important and most arguable of all of them is the Dennis case. This was a prosecution against eleven Communist leaders for willfully advocating the destruction of the United States Government by force and violence. Justice Black in his dissent said, "There is hope, however, that in calmer times, when present pressures, passions and fears subside, this or some later court will restore the First Amendment liberties to the high preferred place where they belong in a free society."

The majority rested its judgment on evidence that the Communist party was the agent of a hostile foreign government in readiness "to initiate a violent revolution whenever the propitious occasion appeared." This, they argued, was more than an exercise of free speech. Justice Holmes, one of the great exponents of free speech protection, once said that it would not protect a man "in falsely shouting fire in a theatre." In other words, there comes a point where words become action which, as such, the state is entitled to forbid.

The Court in the Dennis case may have drawn the line between word and action improperly. It is no doubt true that hysteria has influenced Congressional and Executive action in this area. But somewhere the line will have to be drawn and in consequence there will be some limit on speech. The drawing of that line will reflect the judge's judicial philosophy and, in my opinion, it is proper that it should.

In the Barenblatt case, a college teacher called before the House Un-American Activities Committee refused to answer questions about his alleged past Communist affiliations. The majority of the Court denied that the question infringed his constitutional rights of free speech and assembly. This, said Black dissenting, permitted the people to "try fearfully and futilely to preserve democracy by adopting totalitarian methods."

The majority relied on what it regarded as Congress' legitimate concern to unearth a revolutionary conspiracy. This the Court believed overbalanced Barenblatt's claim to silence. A claim to silence concerning one's political associations is not in a strictly literal sense an abridgement of free speech. It does, however, serve some of the same purposes of promoting free political action.

In this case, then, as in Roth and Dennis, there were conflicting considerations concerning the application of the constitutional guarantee, and fairness to both majority and dissent compels the conclusion that the difference among the judges was a reasonable one.

Which brings us to the really difficult problem in this whole matter. It is this: where the question is precisely one concerning which men can differ, what principle, what attitude should the judge bring to its solution?

I have said that the judge should first seek the historic meaning and purpose of the constitutional provision. This meaning may emerge so clearly for reasonable-minded judges that the answer is felt to be inescapable. All the judges agree, for example, that the guarantee of a jury trial means a jury of twelve men and a unanimous verdict, though the Constitution says nothing on either point. But it is felt that in this case "jury" must be understood in its historic character.

On the other hand, there are clauses of the Constitution, less precise or less technical, which will be read against the continuing stream of historic experience. This has been particularly true of the great and venerable guarantee that a person shall not be deprived of life, liberty or property without "due process of law." Justice Frankfurter has said that due process "expresses a demand for civilized standards of law. It is thus not a stagnant formulation of what has been achieved in the past but a standard for judgment in the progressive evolution of the institutions of society."

The law of torture is an excellent illustration. Due process is as old as Magna Charta; yet even 300 years later, in the time of Elizabeth, men were, by common consent, put on the rack to extort confessions. In 1952, California convicted a man of possessing dope; the evidence was dope which he had swallowed to evade detection and which the police had recovered by a forced emetic. The Supreme Court held that this was not due process.

But how does the judge know or find what are the "civilized standards of law"? Justice Frankfurter has said that judgment "must move within the limits of *accepted* notions of justice. . . ." If this is so, the judge is the mere medium of the community's conscience, and so may be compelled to reject a claim that he himself favors.

It is just here that there emerges the sharpest difference between the Frankfurter wing and the Black-Douglas wing, which will more often than not include Warren and Brennan (in that order). Black himself at times denies that he expresses anybody's conscience, the public's or his own. It is not for a judge, he says, but for legislators, and they alone, to enact into law the public's conscience. If a judge tries to do it, he will usually, Black believes, end up by foisting his own notions on the law. No, says Black, it is the Constitution which speaks, and for him it speaks with crystal clarity.

But at times he will be found appealing to "our traditions," to the ideals of a "free society," etc. And however he may reach the result, he for the most part upholds the claim to constitutional protection. This is true even though it is overwhelmingly the case that the "public conscience" does not support the claim. That was the situation in the obscenity matter where the Legislature, Federal and state, had openly and universally for upward of 100 years seen fit to condemn obscenity.

A recent case involved an attack on the practice of performing a blood test for alcohol on an unconscious defendant, the results of which were used to prosecute him for manslaughter by automobile. The practice was approved by statute and custom in forty-seven states. The Court upheld it, but Warren, Black and Douglas thought that it violated the privilege against self-incrimination and was as bad as the forced emetic in the narcotic case.

The Black group, then, might be said to consult their own consciences rather than the public's. Frankfurter would argue that this is contrary to the judge's warrant of authority. A judge is to enact into law not his but the public's will—indeed, Black himself is the first to insist on this. But it must be admitted that the Frankfurtian formulation is somewhat deceptive as a guide to practice. In a number of cases it is of the essence of the problem that the public has been unable to clarify its conscience or formulate a position.

This is particularly true, for example, concerning police methods of interrogating suspected criminals. The third degree flourishes. The public is uneasy but afraid at the same time to hamper the police. In such a case, is there "an accepted notion of justice"? If the law is to break new ground, if it is to give concrete expression to the half-formed purposes of mankind, must not the judges seek out, if not precisely their own view, at least the view that is coming to be, the view, let us say, of those whose moral judgment is respected?

I think that if it be accepted that the Constitution is not static, the judges must perforce go somewhat beyond *"accepted* notions of justice." Furthermore, judges who seek out the "accepted notions of justice" will seldom innovate. For that we may have to look to judges whose notions of their rightful area of choice is a little less strict.

Some judges and lawyers, as I have said, do not think that judicial leadership is consistent with democracy. They point to England, where parliamentary supremacy appears to have insured a greater popular regard for civil liberty than is true with us. But we do have a Constitution which the judges are sworn to uphold. And we are not England. We are a motley people riven by cultural, sectional and racial strains. Because of that we have had to fight a civil war to put into the Constitution a guarantee against official discrimination on racial grounds.

Congress has power to enforce this constitutional provision but, because of continuing sectional conflicts, its record of achievement has been meager. Any society needs leaders to help overcome its fears and clarify its better impulses. If leadership is stymied in the legislature, it is appropriate that it work in some measure through the courts.

I arrive, then, at this conclusion concerning the present division on the Court: Each wing and each of the judges within these wings, every one of whom has his own special attitude, is making an appropriate contribution to the course of constitutional litigation.

The Court should be thought of in this connection as a small, selected group of elders, representative of a range (though relatively narrow) of attitudes toward the constitutional process. Teams, cliques, alliances will form and reform. Innovations will prevail on one day; retreats on another. An overwhelming number of positions will at any one time be more or less fixed. There may be certain persistent trends. Growing protection of Negro rights and of rights of accused persons are two such, whatever the halts and starts within the large movement.

Such a schema does, to my mind, represent a conception of the law as a stable, objective regime not subject to the naked will of the judges but at the same time responsive, as the law must be if it is to fit a dynamic people, to society's ever-emerging conscience.

The "Warren Court" Stands Its Ground

by Fred Rodell

A LITTLE old shawl-bedecked, rocking-chair lady in a recent New Yorker cartoon pricked out on a circular sampler "IMPEACH EARL WARREN." At about the same time, a real-life group of Protestant, Catholic and Jewish clergymen united in charging that two Supreme Court anticensorship rulings—one allowing the sale of Henry Miller's "Tropic of Cancer," the other permitting the release of a French film, "The Lovers"—"virtually promulgated degeneracy as the American way of life."

This past summer, the House of Representatives actually passed a bill denying all Federal courts—the Supreme Court, of course, included—the right to rule on any voting-reapportionment case (this bill was fast buried in the Senate); and only a few weeks ago, Barry Goldwater charged that "of all three branches of Government, today's Supreme Court is the least faithful to the constitutional tradition of a limited government and to the principle of legitimacy in the exercise of power." And this, despite the fact that Earl Warren and three of his colleagues were named to the Court by a well-known Republican.

The list of attacks could go on and on—and doubtless it will in

From the *New York Times Magazine*, September 27, 1964, copyright © 1964 by The New York Times Company.

the weeks ahead. As the Court comes back to Washington to start a new fall term, it faces a barrage of criticism and disquiet, considerably more substantial than previous outbursts from the Birchers, the pro-school-prayer churchers and the still-sullen segregationists of the South.

Not since the Nine Old Men of unhallowed memory struck down the first New Deal almost 30 years ago—perhaps not since John Marshall's Court put the separate states in their places in order to strengthen an adolescent nation—has any Supreme Court used its politico-legal power so broadly and boldly as did Earl Warren's in the term that ended last June. Small wonder, then, that its display of judicial force and authority, coming as the culmination of a decade of constitutional change that began with the school-desegregation decision of 1954, should have caused many to conclude that, and others to wonder whether, the Court had gone too far.

What, then, did the Court do last term to kick up all this fuss? High, though not alone, on the priority gripe-and-growl list stands the "one man, one vote" rule for the apportionment of voting districts. Two years earlier the Court had given fair warning that something like this might be in the offing when it held that unfair apportionment could be a denial of "equal protection of the laws" and was therefore a proper subject for scrutiny by Federal courts. But few expected a follow-up decision so mandatory and so sweeping as to require roughly equal representation in both houses of all state legislatures—in obvious contrast to the two houses of Congress.

Also on the hate list were decisions in the racial-discrimination field, where the Court plowed steadily and almost unanimously ahead. The original 1954 school-desegregation ruling was extended a little further when it held that Virginia's Prince Edward County could no longer keep its public schools closed to escape integration. A batch of sit-in convictions was reversed, though on the narrowest possible grounds, leaving still to be faced the crucial question of the possible right of property owners to discriminate against would-be Negro customers. The overturning of a murder conviction against a Negro because of the systematic exclusion of Negroes from the jury was standard and almost routine.

But neither standard nor routine—not, at least, since the days when the Nine Old Men made a habit of it—were two decisions branding parts of acts of Congress unconstitutional. One of these, to the dismay of the John Birch Society and other jingoists, declared void Section 6 of the Subversive Activities Control Act, under which U.S. passports were denied to citizens with Communist ties. The other, more publicized and less deplored, threw out Section 352(a) of the Immigration and Naturalization Act, whereby naturalized U.S. citizens could lose their citizenship by simply staying abroad for a period of years—a penalty never imposed on the native-born. In both instances the Court exercised its ultimate power by overriding, in the name of the Constitution, the will of an equal branch of the Federal Government.

Again, in a whole series of precedent-shattering decisions, the Court extended the protection of parts of the Bill of Rights well beyond old-established limits and set aside several past Court rulings to do so. The Fifth Amendment's guarantee against self-incrimination, for instance, was applied whole-hog to state prosecutions; the Sixth Amendment's right to counsel was widened to cover preliminary police questioning; the Fourth Amendment's safeguards against unreasonable searches and seizures were expanded, as in holding state officers to Federal standards in getting search warrants, and so on.

Then there was the appeal of Governor Barnett of Mississippi against his conviction for contempt of court. The four dissenting justices thought that a jury should be required in the trial of a criminal-contempt charge, while the five majority justices strongly hinted, in a footnote, that they might agree if it were more than a "petty offense." All in all, whether one approved or disapproved of this well-nigh unprecedented display of judicial power, it was a memorable term.

In a sense, Earl Warren's Court has been building toward this climax since his appointment 11 years ago. But the building has been slow and mainly below the surface—in the gradually increasing number of dissenters and the increasing vigor of their dissents against those supporting the philosophy of judicial self-restraint (the "take-it-easy boys") who, except in the desegregation cases, have generally prevailed. The major turning-point came with the retirement in 1962 of Justice Felix Frankfurter, for more than 20 years the Court's most articulate and insistent advocate of self-restraint, and his replacement by free-swinging, libertarian, activist Arthur Goldberg.

The Frankfurter influence waned as first Warren, then William Brennan (both Eisenhower appointees) regularly joined those two old New Deal warhorses, Hugo Black and William O. Douglas, in liberal dissent. The occasional addition to this quartet of Potter Stewart (again Eisenhower's choice) now and then turned potential dissent into majority doctrine. Frankfurter could carry only faithful John Harlan with him in his bitter judicial swansong protesting the Court's first entry into the "political thicket" of reapportionment in 1962.

Today the close civil-liberties cases (as opposed, in legal parlance, to those involving Negroes' civil *rights*), which used to come down predictably, while Frankfurter still sat, five to four against the liberty claimed, have for the past two terms come down just as predictably five to four the other way. On other matters, too, the conference room no longer echoes with the now eloquent, now shrill voice that so long urged his colleagues to keep "hands off." Quiet John Harlan, to whom passed the torch of self-restraint, cannot match his mentor in powers of persuasion.

For the first time in the Court's 175-year history, therefore, a consistent—if bare—majority of the justices, scorning self-restraint where individual liberties are at issue, are determined to enforce the Bill of Rights (plus the 14th Amendment) against any Government action, state or Federal, that disregards or infringes its guarantees. From the protection of equal voting rights to the protection even of obscene literature from censorship, it is this determination which has brought down on the Court's head the current storm of protest.

Whoever the protesters, their complaints are commonly couched in abstract phrases familiar to students of political theory and campaign oratory. There is talk of "judicial usurpation of legislative functions so as to dislocate the tripartite separation of Government powers." There is talk of upsetting the constitutional system of checks and balances. There is talk, of course, of improper and unwarranted interference with states' rights. There is talk of an unelected, lifetime-appointed autocracy, bending the law and the Constitution to its will—or its whim.

The chief thing to remember about all this high-toned criticism, no matter how valid in the abstract, is that, translated, it really means: "We don't like what the Warren Court has been doing." That, of course, is the protesters' privilege, and no one would defend it more militantly than the Warren Court, but it does not become the critics to conceal their real motives—which are usually self-interested and often more emotional than rational— behind convenient, conventional and essentially meaningless shibboleths like "states' rights." (How can a political abstraction like a state, as distinct from the people and the government officials of that state, have rights?)

The ancestors of the very same white-supremacist Southerners who today damn the desegregation decisions as usurpation, as unconstitutional and as violations of states' rights raised not a peep when the 19th-century Supreme Court legalized the separation of the races in Plessy vs. Ferguson—a judicial fiat no more demanded by the words of the Constitution than the 1954 desegregation case and its progeny. Even more to the point, it is usually forgotten that during the years before the Civil War, when the Supreme Court of Dred Scott notoriety was Southern-oriented, the South was all for national judicial supremacy, while the abolitionist North, flouting the Fugitive Slave Act, adopted states' rights as *its* slogan. By the eighteen-sixties the slogans—but not the underlying beliefs—had been exchanged.

Accusations of too-much-Court-power have also reversed polarity. In the nineteen-thirties it was the liberals who cursed the Court for killing progressive legislation and the conservatives who praised it as a bulwark in defense of property rights. Today it is, by and large, conservative elements who accuse the Court of usurping power and upsetting the Federal balance in its equalitarian, libertarian drive—and most liberals applaud. Similarly, most people realize that the outraged opposition to voting reapportionment comes from rural state legislators who may lose their jobs, from their Congressional counterparts and from rural voters who will lose their long-held comfortable control over city and suburban slickers as they lose their loaded votes. They may all mouth the familiar accusations against the Court, but what they really mean is: "This will hurt me."

Throughout the nation's history, any branch of the Federal Government that used its power to the full has been criticized for doing so—and the criticism has largely stemmed from those against whose interests the power was, or seemed to be, used. Strong Presidents—notably Lincoln, with his suspension of the constitutional writ of *habeas corpus* and his Emancipation Proclamation, and Franklin Roosevelt, with his revolutionary First Hundred Days and his near-miss with the Court-packing plan—were regularly charged by opponents with usurpation and disregard of the separation of powers. So were strong or stubborn Congresses —like the Reconstruction Congress, that rode rough-shod over the Supreme Court and impeached the President, and the Wilson Congress whose "little group of willful men" blocked the arming of American merchant ships in 1917 and later kept us out of the League of Nations.

At the judicial level, the hostility directed by New Dealers at the Nine Old Men of the nineteen-thirties was as nothing compared to the fury of the then-Republicans under Thomas Jefferson over what they saw as the arrogant assumption of top government power for the judiciary by Federalist John Marshall and his Court. Yet today those power-usurping decisions are revered by the legal clan and Marshall is known as "the great Chief Justice." What the Marshall Court did—what every Court has to do, though none since has done it so boldly—was to read new and specific meanings, in order to decide specific cases, into the often imprecise words of the Constitution. And the Warren Court is doing just that today.

What, then, of sober legal scholars like Frankfurter who have questioned what the Court is doing and called for self-restraint? It is important to remember that they do not question the Court's *power* to do what it has done of late, nor are they suggesting that the Court relinquish the right which Marshall first fully asserted to hold other branches of government, even Congress, to the Constitution. What they do question is the *wisdom* of some recent uses of that power.

Justice Frankfurter was afraid—and his followers share his

fear—that if the Court should play its supervisory role too often and too eagerly, especially in such unpopular causes as protecting the civil liberties of Communists or criminals, then wide public protest might lead to restricting the Court's powers. The Constitution gives Congress complete control of the Court's appellate jurisdiction, under which almost all the cases the Court hears come before it. Congress could, as it has in the past, take any type of case it might please out of the Court's hands.

Further, the whole Federal judiciary depends on Congress for its appropriations, and it may also depend, as in Little Rock, on the executive to enforce its decrees. Without power of purse or sword, as it is commonly put, the Court is uniquely vulnerable to the other two branches of government. This vulnerability, plus the fear of reprisals, is one of the main reasons behind the Frankfurterian philosophy of self-saving self-restraint.

Beyond this, Justice Frankfurter, an unabashed Anglophile, had unbounded admiration for the British Government, where Parliament reigns supreme. In case after case he would implore his colleagues to leave even constitutional issues to Congress or to state legislatures, partly on the theory that it was healthy in a democracy to let the people, through their elected representatives, correct their own mistakes. But his optimism was highly unrealistic when applied to laws which violated the constitutional rights of unpopular or despised individuals or minority groups. And it became absurd—as all the justices but Frankfurter and Harlan realized—when applied to the reapportionment issue, where favored and entrenched voters and legislators had already blithely ignored constitutional commands for countless years.

More significantly, the argument for judicial self-restraint on the grounds of vulnerability is, in essence, circular and self-defeating. What it adds up to is: Let us not use our power lest we lose our power. But power let go by default might as well be lost. What the argument neglects to take into account—and what Franklin Roosevelt overlooked when he proposed his Court-packing plan—is the immense prestige of the Court as an institution. Regardless of popular, and passing, indignation at this or that decision, its prestige is bound to protect it from any but minor incursions on its authority.

At any rate, it is clear that the new majority of the Warren Court will have none of this timidity. They see nothing to be gained and much to be lost in declining to use the power which no one—save a few crackpots—denies is theirs. Even in the unlikely event that a constitutional amendment or Congressional action should reverse or temper the more extreme parts of the recent reapportionment rulings, there would still remain a substantial achievement in bringing about a more truly representative government—something that would never have happened if the advice of the self-restrainers had been heeded.

The Warren majority sees its highest duty in militantly upholding, against legislative or executive encroachment, the individual rights and liberties guaranteed by the Constitution. From freedom of speech to fair trials to equal protection of law and all the others, it is these rights that mainly distinguish our Government from dictatorships, right or left.

A century and a half ago the Marshall Court, buffeted by bitter criticism, stood its ground, in the name of the Constitution, for what it believed. History has vindicated it. The Warren Court, equally sturdy, will take its chances with history, too.

Is the Warren Court
Too "Political"?

by Alexander M. Bickel

EARL WARREN became Chief Justice of the United States on Oct. 5, 1953, by appointment of President Eisenhower. It was a sudden succession. Chief Justice Warren's predecessor, Fred M. Vinson of Kentucky, had died unexpectedly that summer, after seven years of service. They were not years of outstanding achievement. All too often a majority of the Court supported, in a tone of avuncular patriotism, the loyalty-security mania and the xenophobia of the day. In criminal cases, the same majority frequently spoke with the one-sided zeal of the prosecutor. This is, of course, not a comprehensive, and hence not an entirely fair, characterization of the Vinson Court's discharge of its function. For example, the Court also carried forward the process, begun under Chief Justice Hughes in the nineteen-thirties, of desegregating state institutions of higher learning; it declared the white primary unconstitutional, and it forbade enforcement of racial covenants. But these were not the dominant features of the Vinson Court's record.

Earl Warren's tenure as Chief Justice has already exceeded in length that of any of his predecessors appointed in this century.

From the *New York Times Magazine*, September 25, 1966, copyright © 1966 by The New York Times Company.

This is, however, the least of the reasons (it is merely symbolic of the fact) that when Chief Justice Warren took his seat in October 13 years ago, a new era opened in the history of the Court. Not every decade and not every two decades in the life of that institution constitute an era. And no new era necessarily begins when an old one closes, as one did after the Court-packing fight in 1937. At such a time, it often takes the Court some years to rearrange itself and its doctrines. It takes, Brandeis once said, some years for a new Justice to find himself in the movements of the Court, and it may take the Court some years to find itself in the movements of its time. The current era in the history of the Court dates from Oct. 5, 1953.

As Chief Justice Warren took office, unquestionably the prime business facing him and his colleagues was the school segregation cases. The Court—which then still included Justices Reed, Frankfurter, Jackson, Burton and Minton; in addition to Justices Black, Douglas and Clark, who continue to serve—had heard argument on these cases during the prior term. It had heard the venerable leader of the American Bar, the late John W. Davis, urge that the separate-but-equal rule of *Plessy v. Ferguson* not be reversed. "Sometime to every principle," Mr. Davis had argued, "comes a moment of repose when it has been so often announced, so confidently relied upon, so long continued, that it passes the limits of judicial discretion and disturbance." The Court, before Chief Justice Vinson's death, had then set the cases down for reargument. Mr. Davis's plea had struck a chord, and it is not unlikely that it had struck it in the mind and heart of Chief Justice Vinson, among others.

In no circumstances could a majority of the Court have been found to reaffirm the separate-but-equal rule. But there is reason to believe that had Chief Justice Vinson lived, something very different from the opinion read by Earl Warren on May 17, 1954, would have come down, and something by no means unanimous. The might-have-beens of history are incalculable, and most of them are not significant; the civil rights revolution was coming, in this year or another, by this means and by others, in this institution and in other ones, and it has in any event not been wholly or even mainly the product of Chief Justice Warren's Court. But it would be a foolish determinism which depreciated the importance of the decision of May 17, 1954, and of the shape and manner of that decision.

That was the beginning—and what a beginning: the most consequential judicial event, very probably, in a century—but it was only the beginning. Since then, the Court has declared religious prayer and Bible-reading in public schools unconstitutional; it has ordered the reapportionment of the national House of Representatives and of both houses of state legislatures on an approximate one-man, one-vote basis; it has enlarged the rights of the accused in criminal trials; and in decisions culminating just this past term in *Miranda v. Arizona,* it has laid down a whole set of new rules to govern the conduct of police throughout the country toward persons arrested on suspicion of crime.

The Court has also—needless to say, this listing is not comprehensive—severely limited the power of government to forbid the use of birth-control devices, to restrict travel, to deny employment to persons whose associations are deemed subversive and to discourage newspapers, through application of the law of libel, from vigorously adverse comment on the actions of public officials. Finally, without reaching major constitutional issues, the Court has been most niggardly with affirmances of convictions for contempt supposedly committed by witnesses before Congressional committees.

This record is, in all, quite a departure from the records of the Vinson Court, and of its predecessor, the Court presided over by Harlan F. Stone for five years. It is, moreover, in absolute as well as relative terms, a record remarkable for the vigorous exercise of the judicial power, for bringing that power actively and imaginatively to bear on numerous vital issues of the day.

How, then, does one assess such a record? Everything else being equal, it is well for institutions of government to act. But everything else is never equal in a free society, especially in one organized on the principle of federalism. Even in the political organs of the Federal Government, action is not always preferable to forbearance, since there are other institutions, smaller and closer to the people, whose competence should sometimes be respected. And even in those other institutions, action is not always the preferred course, since there ought at times to be a presumption in favor of private ordering.

In the Supreme Court, which is the remotest, the most insulated and least responsive of our institutions of government, a rash of decisive action is something of an ominous symptom. It is no sign of healthy progress in our society that so many of its supposed ills should have remained to be cured by the Supreme Court. And yet the Court has a function, which is not to be performed merely on the periphery of American life. A Court that operates on the periphery, and is otherwise content simply to join a chorus, to speak in the conventional, and as was the case with the Vinson Court, sometimes in the vulgar, tones of a majority of the moment —such a Court does not do its part to make workable the infinite paradoxes of the American system of separation of powers. Such a Court is not the Warren Court. But that is to say very little. It is merely to withhold condemnation.

There are values and interests in play, of course, and it is inevitable that one should judge the Court's actions on segregation, on reapportionment, on school prayers, on criminal procedure and so on in accordance with one's system of values and with one's interest. So might one judge the actions of a philosopher king, deeming some good and some bad, and all to be lived with from necessity. But that is clearly unsatisfactory in a democracy, for unlike the subjects of a philosopher king the people of the United States are not the passive observers of their government, but its masters. They are entitled to know, especially those who do not themselves approve of the Court's actions, why it should have been this particular institution of their government, this particularly remote institution, which they are powerless to control, that took these actions.

No one possesses a systematic and universal prescription for the proper exercise of the Court's role. No one has a self-consistent set of rules that will automatically label one intervention by the Court proper, and another improper. It is a matter of attitudes, of caution and of courage, of vision and of prudence. And it is a matter of history and of tradition, which are certainly not static, and which do not speak with precision to present problems, but which do sanction some and exclude other lines of approach. The

Court, like other institutions, is in part the maker of the history and the tradition that bind it, and other institutions are also constrained by the history and the tradition they have made. Unlike the other institutions, however, the Court has no mandate; it is nobody's voice but its own. It is called upon, therefore, to justify its actions in ways not required of the other institutions.

The Court does not discharge its office simply by doing what even most people may think is right or necessary. The Court must be able to demonstrate by reasoned argument why it thought the action right or necessary. It must try to persuade even those whom it may be unable to convince, and to persuade them at least of its own honest and detached effort to apply reason to the problems of society, and to solve them in a manner that is harmonious with a relevant tradition. For if the Court's decisions carry only the authority of its will, what claim have they to control the electoral institutions, and the constituencies of those institutions? If the function of the Court cannot be differentiated from that of Congress and the other political organs, it cannot be justified. The Court is, therefore, not the place for the clean break with the past, not the place for the half-loaf that is better than none, for the split difference and other arbitrary choices, or for the action supported by nothing but rhetoric, sentiment, anger or prejudice.

No one knows how to tell the Court all that it should do and how to do it. It is not so difficult, however, to see what the Court might better not have done, or how it should not have done it. Hence, in addition to those who criticize the Warren Court, as is their right, because they do not like its results, there are professional observers of the Court who criticize it on other grounds, while as a matter of political preference approving many if not most of the results it has reached.

The criticism of the Court that is, perhaps, most frequently heard and that pretty well encompasses all other ones is that the Court is too political. This criticism is misguided or well-taken, depending on what is meant by it. If it means that the Court should make no decisions that can in any sense be deemed political, but should follow some certain body of rules called Constitutional Law, the answer is that The Law as so conceived is a myth, it does not exist, and hence the Court, in order to function at all, must make law rather than simply follow it. Therefore, it must make what are bound to be, in a sense, political decisions.

But if the criticism means that the Court's occasions and modes of policymaking should be different from those of the elected organs of government, then the criticism is well-taken. It means, then, not that this has been a political court but that it has in some instances been wrongly political, that it has been political after the fashion of a legislature or an executive rather than a court.

Illustration of this charge against the Warren Court may begin with the case of *Miranda v. Arizona,* decided this past spring, in which the Court held that police interrogation of a suspect to whom a lawyer has not been made available is in most circumstances unconstitutional. Two years earlier, in *Escobedo v. Illinois,* the Court had foreshadowed this decision. The *Escobedo* case evoked a truly remarkable response. For the first time since the Court had begun to reform criminal procedures, law-enforcement officials themselves set about taking a serious look at what they were doing, and thinking of ways to reform themselves. In addition, the American Law Institute, a private but very prestigious organization of lawyers, judges and law professors, began work on a proposed model code of police procedures.

Had the Court waited another year or two for the fruition of some of these efforts, it could then have decided the final constitutional issues in light of such new procedures as had been worked out. And it might then not have found it necessary to promulgate on its own hook, as in fact it did, a detailed set of rules—a veritable police manual—governing practices of interrogation. The Court might have been in a position, instead, to review rules formulated by others.

Given its insulation, and the inevitably episodic nature of its approach to most problems, the Court is not the suitable agency to make administrative decisions, not the agency to *run* anything. The Court consists of only nine men, each of whom independently considers each case. It must wait for a case before it can act, and in the cases it gets the records and briefs often do not contain all the information and all the ideas that they might. There is little staff, and if there were much more, something would be lost of independent and personal attention to problems by the justices themselves. The jurisdiction is nationwide.

For these and additional reasons, the Court works best not as a front-line administrator, executive or legislator, not as an initial decision-maker, but as a reviewing agency. There can be, of course, no assurance that other institutions will respond to judicial invitations to take the initiative—*vide* the aftermath as well as the background of the school segregation cases. Yet it makes a difference whether the invitation is issued at all, and whether the Court shows some patience when, as in this instance, the invitation appears to have been taken up.

The Court seemed to know that it was laying itself open to this criticism—to the charge that it was acting more like an administrator or a legislature than a court—since it emphasized in its opinion in the *Miranda* case that the very detailed rules it was laying down for police conduct need not be taken as the final command of the Constitution in every detail. "We encourage Congress and the states," said the Court, "to continue their laudable search for increasingly effective ways of protecting the rights of the individual while promoting efficient enforcement of our criminal laws."

And the Court declared its readiness to be "shown other procedures which are at least as effective" as the ones it was laying down. It remains to be seen, however, whether the Court will in fact be receptive to such other procedures. And it is certain, at any rate, that by seizing the initiative in the *Miranda* case it will have discouraged efforts to work them out.

The *Miranda* case is thus an instance when the Court took on a job that legislatures and other agencies might better have been allowed to do first—though this is not to suggest that the job the Court did is altogether a bad one. It is an instance, in another aspect as well, of a decision that was political in the wrong sense. A week after it handed down its opinion in the *Miranda* case the Court decided that its new rules concerning interrogation of suspects were not to be applied retroactively to convicts now serving sentences. In the past the Court had applied some of its decisions in matters of criminal procedure retroactively, and some not. And it had worked out certain reasonably satisfactory distinctions to explain the difference, although of late it had begun to blur these. But the striking thing about the Court's handling of the problem in the *Miranda* situation was its decision not to apply the new rules even in cases quite like the *Miranda* case itself—and there were a few dozen of these pending—in which defendants were appealing convictions that had not yet become final.

Now, the Court may have been justified in declining to risk the general jail delivery that might have resulted from full retroactive application of the *Miranda* rules. A decision to announce those rules exclusively for prospective application, and thus not to apply them even to Ernesto Miranda himself, might also have been supportable. But the rules were applied to Miranda (convicted of kidnapping and rape in Phoenix) and to three additional defendants, and yet not applied to dozens of others in precisely the same situation.

This was arbitrary. It is difficult to think of a rational explanation for it that is consonant with the *Miranda* rules or with rules concerning retroactivity, and the Court really attempted none. And it is in this sense that one may call this action by the Court improperly political, as opposed to judicial. An action for which there is no intellectually coherent explanation may be tolerable, and it may be necessary (it may, for example, be a rough-and-ready compromise that makes possible any action at all), but it is for the political institutions to take, not for the Court.

There are, unfortunately, other illustrations of the sort of decision by arbitrary assertion that in the political institutions is usually the upshot of a series of compromises—or that passes, if you will, for the voice of the sovereign people—but for which there is no excuse in a Court speaking in the name of the Constitution. One such illustration may be found in the famous reapportionment cases of 1964. For in those cases the Court shied away from full adherence to the principle to which its reasoning led—whether that reasoning be thought right or wrong—namely, one man, one vote. The Court has allowed variations from the principle by this or that number of percentage points. The labeling of one variation as constitutional and of another as not is a purely arbitrary exercise, as is the allowance of variations at all.

Again, in the *Ginzburg* obscenity case of last term, finding it all too difficult to articulate a meaningful definition of obscenity, the Court held a book obscene partly for the reason that the way it was advertised "stimulated the reader to accept [the material] as prurient; he looks for titillation, not for saving intellectual content." The implications of this criterion are far-reaching, and they are staggering. It is highly improbable that the Court intends to pursue these implications and, for example, permit the banning of Boccaccio or Kinsey if improperly advertised. Yet the Court's struggles with the problem have produced no definition of obscenity that would clearly sanction works such as these, while at the same time proscribing Mr. Ginzburg's publications.

But then, what is the basis of the decision? If the Court could find no self-consistent standard to guide it, if, though it groped for a balance between contending interests and ideologies, it found none that it could explain or even seriously promise to apply to other cases in the future, then why should we accept its decision, whatever it may mean? Would we not be much better advised to let the politically responsible institutions strike such balances from time to time without interference from the Court?

Two more examples may be of interest, in which, far from making a principled decision, the Court seems simply to have settled on that solution of a problem which a majority felt instinctively was about right, even if it was not one that could be justified in terms of previously accepted, and as yet unrepudiated, premises. In *Harper v. Virginia Board of Elections* the Court declared the poll tax unconstitutional, holding that it is not plausibly related to "any legitimate state interest in the conduct of elections."

But, complained Justice Black in dissent, "the Court gives no reason. . . ." And it did not. Also dissenting, Justice Harlan argued that payment of a minimal poll tax might plausibly be thought to promote "civic responsibility, weeding out those who do not care enough about public affairs to pay $1.50 or thereabouts a year for the exercise of the franchise." The Court failed even to address itself to this point. And it thus left the impression that it outlawed the poll tax because it does not like it, although as in the rhyme about Dr. Fell, the reason why it could not tell; that is, it could not tell a reason which was persuasive on the premise that, good or bad, qualifications for voting are the business of the states unless they are capricious or based on race.

In *Katzenbach v. Morgan* the Court upheld Section 4(e) of the Voting Rights Act of 1965, which overrides the New York requirement of literacy in English and enfranchises Puerto Ricans literate only in Spanish. The Court supported its decision in part by contending that even if, in the absence of a showing that the vote is denied on the basis of race, Congress has no direct power to change the electoral law of New York, it does have power under the Fourteenth Amendment to cure or forestall other discriminations practiced by the state. Therefore, the Court argued, if Congress thought that Puerto Ricans were otherwise discriminated against by law or administrative action in New York, it had the power to enfranchise them as a means of preventing such discrimination in the future, on the theory that the vote would enable them to protect themselves against discrimination.

But the Court could adduce not a shred of evidence that Puerto Ricans are in fact discriminated against by state action in New York. Furthermore, as in the obscenity cases, the implications of the Court's argument are staggering, and it is not to be assumed that the Court would be willing to pursue them. Yet it simply disregarded them.

The implications are these: presumably, any group which does not have the vote—aliens, commuters from New Jersey, 16-year-olds—may be thought to be in danger of being discriminated against by New York in other ways as well; certainly there is at least as much evidence that New York discriminates against aliens and against New Jersey commuters as there is that it discriminates against Puerto Ricans. Consequently, under the Court's reasoning, Congress could bestow the vote on these groups, and on any group which it fears may be discriminated against, even though its fears are grounded solely in the fact that the group in question is deprived of the vote. There is then nothing left of state autonomy in setting qualifications for voting.

The Court, however, did not purport to abolish that autonomy. The opinion, again, is just not intellectually coherent. It upholds the power of Congress to enfranchise Spanish-speaking Puerto Ricans not because on principle Congress ought to have this power but, one must suppose, simply because, like Congress, the Court thought that it was a good thing to enfranchise Spanish-speaking Puerto Ricans, while it would not think it a good thing, perhaps, to enfranchise citizens of New Jersey or aliens.

These criticisms are directed at the manner of the Court's discharge of its function, not necessarily at the results it reaches. They are institutional rather than substantive criticisms, and many people who like the Court's results—and would like them whoever had produced them—have little patience with such criticisms. They want to get on with the business of government and of reform, not theorize about it. But it must be said, with deference, that such an attitude is very much like being satisfied with Mussolini because he made the trains run on time, or like the late Senator Taft's reported remark that Joseph R. McCarthy, whatever his methods, was good for the Republican party.

An entirely authoritarian government, on the one hand, and on the other hand a government in which all power rests in one or even in a few institutions that are all equally close to the people —either form of government faces few, if any, important institutional problems. It will always be true that some one institution can do some things better than another, and that a wise allocation of competences will take this into account. But the serious problems arise when, as in our system, we distribute some but not all powers to popularly responsive institutions, giving other powers to an authoritarian one, not responsible to the electorate, and when even among the popular institutions some are closer to the people and more readily responsive than others. Then problems of the allocation of competences become serious, because in the end what is in question is democratic responsibility. And so with us the constantly recurring institutional problems are the division of powers between the Federal Government and the states, and the division of powers between the Supreme Court and everybody else.

It is to these problems that the Warren Court, in its spectacular career, has paid less attention than it should. Our system confides to the Supreme Court great power, greater than that of any other judicial body in the world. It is the power to render reasoned, principled decisions. There—in the process by which these decisions are reached, not in the results, however good, humane or politic —is the justification of a power that needs justification in a democratic society, and there also is its limit. And the limit is transgressed—again, regardless of the result—and has on occasion been transgressed by the Warren Court, when a decision is rendered that amounts, after all, to nothing but an arbitrary choice.

The Court Should Decide Less and Explain More

by Philip B. Kurland

NONE OF THE newspaper columnists and politicians who speak of the credibility gap that afflicts the executive branch seem to be concerned with the deeper and wider credibility gap created by the Supreme Court. The inadequate reasons put forth by the Court in support of its judgments are the cause of this second gap, or gulch.

The defenders of the executive and the defenders of the Court give the same excuse: many of the actions of these two branches of government cannot be explained in terms that would be acceptable to or understood by the public. A better argument probably is that the failure of these two branches to justify their actions is attributable, at least in part, to a lack of the time that deliberate and truthful explanations demand. Perhaps in the case of the Presidency that time cannot be made available. In the case of the Court, however, it should be possible to restrict its duties in such a way as to allow it to eliminate or at least to reduce its credibility gap.

From the *New York Times Magazine,* June 9, 1968, copyright © 1968 by The New York Times Company.

The tasks that have been assigned to or assumed by the Supreme Court of the United States are awesome. Any one of them would tax the capacities of nine Platonic guardians, no less those of nine mere lawyers. The duties are to: (1) Allocate power between the nation and the states and among the executive, the legislative and the judicial branches of the national Government; (2) protect individuals against the encroachments of the leviathan of government; (3) supervise the administration of justice—especially criminal justice—in the Federal and state courts; (4) oversee the proper execution of the law by the fourth branch of Government, the administrative agencies; (5) give meaning to legislation that is frequently ambiguous and occasionally meaningless; (6) act "as the conscience of the nation."

Too little time and too many such burdens are the main (although not the sole) reasons why the Court has often erred in the direction of (Prof. Milton Handler ticks off the list) "overgeneralization, disrespect for precedent, needless obscurity of opinions, discouraging lack of candor, disdain of the fact-finding of lower courts, tortured reading of statutes, and seeming absence of neutrality and objectivity."

The time has come to consider whether some change in the Court's obligations could not result in a better work-product: carefully reasoned, candid opinions, recognizing the proper roles of the legislatures and the lower courts, and explaining why precedents, however hoary or recent, should be rejected or amended.

The Court is not now, if ever it was, capable of performing all of its duties well. It should, therefore, be limited to those duties that are most important—it should deal only with constitutional cases. So long as it acts as a "continuing constitutional convention," that ought to be its only function.

In other words, with such a limitation, the Court would be left only with its powers of judicial review of the constitutional validity of state and Federal action. It would be relieved of the many less important decisions it is now called upon to make each year—decisions which deprive it of the time to perform properly its duties of explication and application of the Constitution.

The kinds of cases that the Court now hears but which would be removed from its ken under the proposal may be seen on the list of cases argued before it during a recent two-week period. These cases dealt with such questions as: May a lawyer be disbarred for advancing money to plaintiffs suing to recover for the "wrongful deaths" of their husbands? Can a corporation recover damages for the negligence of a Federal bankruptcy receiver? Can a suit in a state court to enforce a "no-strike" clause be removed to a Federal court? What is the proper basis for fixing counsel fees in a case arising under the Social Security laws? Can a Federal court enforce a state law authorizing stockholders to inspect corporate records?

These cases are not unimportant. But it is hardly appropriate that they should compete for the Court's attention with such fundamental problems as the validity of Federal aid to parochial education, or the scope of the Fourteenth Amendment's ban on private discrimination in the sale or lease of housing.

There are many ways of evaluating the work of the Court. Most of the Court's critics choose to do so in terms of their personal predilections for or against the conclusions that the Court reaches. This makes irrelevancies of the Court's opinions. These critics would treat the Court as they treat the other two branches of the Government—as a political body to be used to reach political objectives. Thus, those who were in the vanguard of the Court's attackers when its judgments supported the vested property interests against the claims for social justice of the less well-to-do are now among the staunchest defenders of a Court that they see as the protector of the underprivileged against the rapacity of their would-be oppressors.

So, too, the onetime defenders of the Court have shifted from a faith in the Court as the last bastion of freedom against creeping Socialism and the Communist menace to a belief that the Court is leading the destruction of that individualism that was once the essence of American democracy and is anathema to the welfare state.

Thus, to the result-oriented, the work of the present Court is to be approved or disapproved depending on whether they are for or against the extension and centralization of governmental authority, for or against the spreading egalitarianism, for or against the creation of special privileges for minorities as compensation for the deprivations that have long been part of their minority status, for or against the increase of power of an appointed judiciary to resolve problems apparently too difficult for solution by the elected representatives of the people.

It might be pointed out to those who appraise the Court in this way, whether they applaud or deplore its conclusions, that the Court is not now, and never has been, an originator of social, economic or political policy. Essentially, it is a moon rather than a sun. It reflects, if at times it distorts, changes already immanent in our society. Its function is more to justify than to initiate, to choose among proffered contending social values rather than to create them.

Indeed, its judgments are put into effect only to the extent that the society is prepared to receive and accept them. It can decree school desegregation, but it cannot establish it. It can command the abolition of prayers in public schools, but it cannot accomplish it. It can punish the state for the brutalities and improprieties of its prosecutorial systems by freeing the convicts, but it cannot eliminate the barbarities.

And so, even for the pragmatists who would measure the Court's function in terms of its judgments rather than its opinions, the Court's opinions assume an importance. For, to some degree, the acceptance of the Court's rulings is dependent on a belief that the Court is not the same kind of political mechanism as the legislature and the executive.

This is one reason why the supporters of the Court at any given time in American history are called upon to defend it—whatever the truth might be—as a nonpolitical, reasoning, objective, judicial body. For the establishment of the mystique of the robe is not only necessary to an acceptance of its judgments; it is necessary as a defense against the far greater political power that the other branches of Government are capable of wielding against a judiciary that cannot wrap itself in its magic robes. The history of the Supreme Court reveals that in every period of crisis, the contest over the destruction of the Court's powers has been resolved each time by two factors. First, a defense based on the judicial nature of the Court's functions. Second, a hasty, or not so hasty, withdrawal by the Court from positions that have endangered its public support. With regard to both factors, the Court's opinions have proved important.

Therefore, whether one accepts the Court's opinions at face value, that is, as reasoned explanations of the Court's judgments, or solely as materials from which the myth of judicial independence is to be fashioned, the Court ought to be given ample opportunity to fashion opinions that are persuasive justifications of its exercise of power. That the Court's opinions do not now have this quality is debated by its defenders and assailants. But there is certainly, at least, a *prima facie* case to be made that the deficiencies of the opinions are approaching the danger point.

The confrontation between the Court and the Congress may easily develop from the controversy over the present bill directed to "crime in the streets." The issue may well be framed in terms of whether the Court or Congress is to be supreme in giving meaning to the Fourteenth Amendment. The Court would be surer of success if its opinions more cogently justified its conclusions.

The case against the adequacy of the Court's opinions—that is, the majority opinions—may be drawn entirely from the Justices of the Court themselves, as those Justices express themselves in dissenting opinions. (It should be emphasized that dissension in the Court is not in itself evidence of malfunction. Indeed, additional time to resolve the important constitutional questions that come before the Court may result in more rather than fewer opinions in each case. The defect stressed here is that the writers of the Court's majority opinions do not now attempt to solve or answer the problems or arguments with which they are faced either by their brethren or counsel. When the opinions themselves are examined to discover the reasons for the multitude of opinions that are now used to dispatch so many cases, it becomes clear that the dissatisfaction goes not merely to the results reached by the majority but also the manner in which those results are reached.) Samples from recent dissenting opinions make the point:

In rejecting the distinctions drawn by the Court in affirming the conviction of Ralph Ginzburg for the publication of Eros and "The Housewife's Handbook of Promiscuity" and exonerating G. P. Putnam's Sons for publishing "Fanny Hill," Justice Stewart wrote:

"The Court today appears to concede that the materials Ginzburg mailed were themselves protected by the First Amendment. But, the Court says, Ginzburg can still be sentenced to five years in prison for mailing them. Why? Because, says the Court, he was guilty of 'commercial exploitation,' of 'pandering' and of 'titillation.' But Ginzburg was not charged with 'commercial exploitation'; he was not charged with 'pandering'; he was not charged with 'titillation.' Therefore, to affirm his conviction now on any of those grounds, even if otherwise valid, is to deny him due process of law. . . . But those grounds are *not,* of course, otherwise valid. Neither the statute under which Ginzburg was convicted nor any other Federal statutes I know of makes 'commercial exploitation' or 'pandering' or 'titillation' a criminal offense. And any criminal law that sought to do so in the terms so elusively defined by the Court would, of course, be unconstitutionally vague and therefore void."

One will search the majority opinion in vain for an adequate answer to these charges.

In a case in which the Court struck down the Virginia poll tax as unconstitutional, although two earlier decisions of the Court had sustained such a tax, Justice Black took exception:

"Although I join the Court in disliking the policy of the poll tax, this is not in my judgment a justifiable reason for holding this poll tax unconstitutional. Such a holding on my part would, in my judgment, be an exercise of power which the Constitution does not confer upon me.

"If basic changes as to the respective power of the state and National Government are needed, I prefer to let those changes be made by amendment as Article V of the Constitution provides. For a majority of this Court to undertake to do so under the Due Process or Equal Protection Clause amounts, in my judgment, to an exercise of power the Constitution-makers with foresight and wisdom refused to give the judicial branch of the Government."

What are the troubles with the opinions of the Court according to outsiders who study the institution? The words of Professors Bickel and Wellington of the Yale Law School written a decade ago are still apposite: "The Court's product has shown an increasing incidence of the sweeping dogmatic statement, of the formulation of results accompanied by little or no effort to support them in reason, in sum, of opinions that do not opine and of per curiam orders that quite frankly fail to build the bridge between the authorities they cite and the results they decree."

One need not, of course, turn to critics so unfriendly to the Supreme Court as those at the Yale Law School. Listen to some of the Court's best friends on the subject. Prof. Harry Kalven Jr. of the University of Chicago, for example: "I think that part of the current grievance is the momentum, the haste with which the Court changes: The failure to connect up its current decision with something it has inherited from the past."

Every specialist group will report on the ignorance of the Court as displayed by its opinion in the particular area of that group's expertise. Tax lawyers deplore the Court's deficiencies in the field of taxation; admiralty lawyers, labor lawyers, patent and copyright lawyers agree on one subject, that the Court is inadequately informed or is unable adequately to use the information it has in disposing of the cases in their fields.

Nor is it the lawyers alone who complain in this way. The Court, especially in recent years, has taken to history as a guide to decision. This is what a friendly historian, Prof. Alfred A. Kelly of Wayne State University, said about its efforts:

"The present use of history by the Court is a Marxist-type perversion of the relation between truth and utility. It assumes that history can be written to serve the interests of libertarian idealism. The whole process calls to mind the manipulation of scientific truth by the Soviet Government in the Lysenko controversy. The Court's purposes may be more laudable and the politics involved less spectacular, but the assumptions about the nature of reality are the same."

Economists speak in much the same way of the Court's economic edicts.

But what hope is there that a reduction in the Court's burden will make its opinions more logical, informed and well-founded?

That it is only a hope must be conceded. For it is possible that the Justices would use such additional time as was made available to them further to barnstorm the country making speeches in support of decisions that the Court has already made or those it is about to make. Or the time might be used for such exploits as mountain-climbing or visiting foreign countries as guests of the State Department. Or in entering more into the social life of which Washington offers such an abundance. If the hope were to be realized, however, the Justices might well undertake to follow a procedure long since established in the United States Court of Appeals for the Second Circuit in which *each* judge prepares a written memorandum of his view of the case and distributes it to his colleagues *after* oral argument, *after* a chance to study the brief, and *before* casting his ballot. This could make for a greater opportunity for study of the problem, for dialogue among the Justices, for an attempt to meet rather than bypass the points made in opposition to the conclusions stated by the majority. Such a reduction in the Court's burdens might even give the Court the time to read and, perhaps, to master the extralegal authorities that the Justices are now so prone to quote. If the Court were only given the time to recognize that in rewriting the Constitution of the United States it is committed to one of the most important and formidable tasks that government affords, it might be prepared to give that task the attention that it deserves.

Any discussion of precisely how the Court's workload is to be cut would benefit by a look at how it grew. The total number of cases offered to the Court for disposition has increased by 250 per cent in the three decades since Franklin D. Roosevelt urged an increase in the number of justices on the ground that the amount of business was too great for the nine members of the Court to handle. A major factor in this increase is that a large number of subjects have been brought into the Federal realm that heretofore had been left to state dispositions. Thus, despite the fact that the Court has eschewed disposition of cases concerned solely with matters of state law since 1938, the essential nationalization of the law, not only through judicial decisions but by Congressional action as well, has multiplied the heavy burdens on the Court. Moreover, thanks to the Court itself, many subjects are now to be disposed of by constitutional standards that were once left to development by the common law and by legislative action. Thus, much of the law of libel and criminal procedure, once almost entirely in the domain of the states, must now be determined by tests that the Court has purported to derive from the amorphous language of the Constitution.

How then to retrench so that the Court's docket once again is a manageable size, and time is made available to the Court for extended consideration of fundamental issues? Several possibilities exist. One is the elimination of nonconstitutional cases coming to the Court directly from the Federal courts rather than going through the intermediate courts of appeals. Senator Joseph D. Tydings of Maryland has introduced a bill to bring this about, and that is certainly a minimal step which must be taken. But this will not significantly reduce the Court's heavy docket.

A second suggestion is for the creation of a series of specialized courts to remove such business from the Court's purview. Solicitor General Erwin N. Griswold has been urging for many years, for example, that a Court of Tax Appeals be created to provide the necessary centralized review of tax cases that are now so badly handled by the Court. A Court of Patent Appeals has also been suggested. Opposition to the creation of specialized courts derives largely from arguments such as those of Judge Learned Hand that specialized courts suffer from narrowness of outlook and other defects which would outweigh the benefits to be expected from their use.

A few years ago, Col. Frederick Beryans Wiener, a veteran student of and practitioner before the Supreme Court, spoke of the need for a fourth tier of Federal courts. He would interpose between the Courts of Appeals and the Supreme Court another set of appellate courts to screen the cases that come to the High Court through the Federal system. The major drawback in such a proposal is that the appellate processes are already unduly extended and costly. But again, a balance of values will have to be made. Indeed, the proposal I offer is a modification of the Wiener idea.

As things stand now, every case that is begun in the Federal judicial system is a possible candidate for Supreme Court adjudication. There are about 70,000 civil cases begun in the United States district courts each year and an additional 35,000 criminal cases, not to mention 180,000 bankruptcy proceedings and an untold number of administrative proceedings. Of these, about

6,000 cases are processed through the 10 Courts of Appeals. Moreover, every state court case that involves the construction of a Federal statute or the constitutionality of state action is also appropriate for Supreme Court consideration. In each term, about 2,750 or so petitioners or appellants seek leave to have the Court undertake to decide their cases and these requests are in the form of full-blown briefs.

The Court generally decides to accept for review those cases that present important constitutional questions which are ripe for adjudication, cases that present important issues of statutory construction, and cases that reveal that different appellate courts have interpreted statutes or Supreme Court decisions differently, so that there is an absence of uniformity in the application of important Federal law. Thus, much of the Court's time is concerned with winnowing the wheat from the chaff. At the moment, in part because of the absence of a specialized Supreme Court bar, there is nothing to deter a lawyer from asking the Court to review any case that has been lost in the next highest court below. Any proposed statute must relieve the Court of much of this winnowing and reviewing if it is to be meaningful.

The statute I propose would establish a new court in the Federal system. To that court would be assigned the power to review, at its discretion, all cases involving the interpretation and application of Federal statutes and common law, whether arising in state or Federal courts. The court should be made up of from seven to nine members who should be of sufficient stature and capacity to perform the very difficult tasks that it will encounter. To the Supreme Court a litigant would be permitted to offer for adjudication only cases involving a constitutional question.

The Supreme Court's jurisdiction should be entirely discretionary, so that it need take only those cases that present serious and important constitutional controversies. It is expected that the number of such cases would be no greater than the constitutional cases that it now decides.

Similar bifurcation of jurisdiction exists in other constitutional systems, notably the French and the German. Certainly there are details to be worked out by the appropriate Congressional committees before such a general scheme can be put into effect. It would be desirable if those committees were to receive the kind of cooperation and guidance from the current members of the Supreme Court that the Justices made available when the last major overhaul of the Court's jurisdiction was legislated in 1925.

At that time the Court was, with some exceptions, given the power to exercise discretion over which cases it would pass on. Since 1925, the chore of choosing the cases has threatened to become so time-consuming as to be the primary rather than the secondary commitment of the Justices' efforts. Certainly, we need a more pragmatic response to today's problems than the one that answered the difficulties more than four decades ago.

Editor's Epilogue

by Leonard W. Levy

ON JULY 4, 1971, some two years after his appointment as Chief Justice, the *New York Times* published excerpts from an exclusive interview with Warren E. Burger, headlining the story that accompanied the interview, "Burger Asserts Reform Is Not Role of Courts." Unlike the interventionism that permeated Earl Warren's philosophy, Burger in his statements embraced the philosophy of judicial self-restraint. Moreover, he was constantly unimaginative, conservative, and even a bit crabbed. Immediately he de-emphasized the influence that the Supreme Court might have for changes in the law. "And changes in the law made by judicial decisions," he added, "ought to be approached with considerable caution. It was never contemplated in our system that judges would make drastic changes by judicial decision. That is what the legislative function and the rule making function is all about." The Court sat, Burger declared, merely to decide cases. From its decisions, he acknowledged, "some changes develop, but to try to create or substantially change civil or criminal procedure, for example, by judicial decision is the worst possible way to do it."

When asked whether youthful hopes might be justified by "the prospects of accomplishing a change in the system through law," Burger replied: "I sincerely trust that some of their hopes may be justified, but I am beginning to have an uneasy feeling that this may be another one of the situations in this era that we are living in of creating expectations that are beyond fulfillment." He added that young people entering the legal profession "on the theory that they can change the world by litigation in the courts" were bound to be disappointed. They were entering the profession for the wrong reason, because the law "is not the route by which basic changes in a country like ours should be made. That is a legislative and policy process, part of the political process. And there is a very limited role for the courts in this respect." When asked what he saw as the greatest challenge to the Supreme Court in the next few years, he did not discourse on the Bill of Rights nor on reform of any sort; he replied, "I would say that the greatest challenge is to try to keep up with the volume of work and maintain the kind of quality that ought to come from this Court." At the end of the interview, Burger summed up his judicial philosophy: "Inherently, the Supreme Court function is one in which nothing ought to happen very rapidly except the disposition of specific cases. In the evolution of legal doctrine, legal principle can't be sound if its growth is too fast." He might have added, though he did not, that legal principle cannot be sound if its growth is too quickly stunted, or if recent decisions were overruled merely because new members of the Court disliked them. This is what has happened since President Nixon's appointees have shifted the balance of power within the Court.

Warren concluded his career as Chief Justice only a few weeks after the resignation of Justice Abe Fortas, who had been a steadfast and influential member of the group that composed the majority of the Court in cases on civil rights, reapportionment, criminal justice, the rights of the poor, and freedom of association. Nixon therefore had two vacancies to fill. Following Burger's appointment, he nominated Clement F. Haynsworth, Jr., a conservative, "strict constructionist" Southern jurist whom the Senate refused to confirm because his judicial career was tainted with racism and conflict of interest. Nixon then appointed a carbon copy of

Haynsworth, George Harrold Carswell of Florida, who added mediocrity to his other infirmities, and the Senate rejected him as well. Consequently the Court consisted of only eight men during the first year of Burger's incumbency. Near the close of that term, too late to participate in the Court's decisions, Harry A. Blackmun, an able jurist who was a near duplicate of Burger, was confirmed as Fortas' successor.

During that 1969–1970 term of the Court there was a perceptible change in the tone and trend of its decisions. In Warren's final year the Court had voted in favor of a civil liberties or a civil rights claim in 81 per cent of the cases it decided. In Burger's first year that figure fell to less than 56 per cent, while the Chief Justice himself voted against the government and in favor of the right claimed by the individual in less than 31 per cent of the cases. Burger's opinions and the recent tendency toward blunting, even subverting, the opinions of the Warren Court illuminate by contrast the achievements and values of the latter. Two of the opinions delivered by the new Chief Justice during his first term may serve to illustrate that fact.

In *Ashe v. Swenson* the question was raised whether a state may try a person more than once for a single robbery in which there were several simultaneous victims. Ashe, having been acquitted for robbing one of the victims, was tried again and convicted for robbing another. The double jeopardy clause of the Fifth Amendment provides, "nor shall any person be subject to the same offence to be twice put in jeopardy of life or limb. . . ." For more than half a century the Court had followed a rule of the federal criminal law that when an issue of fact, such as guilt or innocence, had been determined by a final and valid judgment such as a jury verdict, that issue cannot again be litigated in a subsequent suit between the same parties. The Court found that this rule applied in Ashe's case, because the double-jeopardy clause incorporated it as a constitutional requirement against the states through the Fourteenth Amendment. Apart from this rule, several of the justices were of the opinion that Ashe's acquittal at the first trial brought double-jeopardy standards into play, thus barring the second prosecution. Burger alone dissented from the decision that his conviction should be reversed. In an ascerbic opinion, revealing his tough line on the rights of the criminally accused, he condemned the members of his Court for trying to "improve on the Constitution." Ashe had committed not one robbery but several and could be tried for each separately without violation of the double-jeopardy clause. Burger's proposition was an eccentric one which would have opened the route to multiple jeopardy.

In *Coleman v. Alabama* the Court split 6 to 2, holding in favor of the right to counsel at a preliminary hearing, prior to indictment, even if that hearing is not a required step in a state's criminal process. In 1932 the Court had held that a person accused of crime "requires the guiding hand of counsel at every step in the proceedings against him." In *Coleman,* Justice Brennan for the majority enumerated the various reasons that counsel must be provided at a preliminary hearing, if there is one, in order to protect "the indigent accused against an erroneous or improper prosecution." Justice Black, who was from Alabama, in a concurring opinion explained why the preliminary hearing was a definite part or stage of a criminal prosecution in that state, and he observed that the "plain language" of the Sixth Amendment requires that in "all criminal prosecutions, the accused shall enjoy the right . . . to have the assistance of counsel for his defense." Justice Douglas, also concurring, made Black's point explicit when he declared that "a strict construction of the Constitution requires the result reached." Justices White and Harlan agreed that recent decisions by the Court furnished ample ground for holding that the preliminary hearing was a critical event in the progress of a criminal prosecution, warranting the right to counsel. Harlan asserted that had he been free to consider the case "upon a clean slate," he would have voted to affirm the convictions, but that was not a course open to him given his "due regard for the way in which the adjudicatory process of this Court, as I conceive it, should work." Justice Stewart, who wrote the opinion of the Court in the *Ashe* case, dissented here because the record did not show that evidence of what occurred at the preliminary hearing was used against the accused at their trial.

Given this posture of the Court, Burger's dissenting opinion was extravagantly distempered. He accused the majority of making new law on the basis of their views on "sound policy"; he also displayed an egregious contempt for precedents. "I do not acquiesce in prior holdings that purportedly, but nonetheless erroneously, are based on the Constitution," he asserted. "That approach simply is an acknowledgment that the Court having previously amended the Sixth Amendment now feels bound by its action. . . . I am bound to reject categorically Mr. Justice Harlan's and Mr. Justice White's thesis that what the Court said lately controls the Constitution. While our holdings are entitled to deference I will not join in employing recent cases rather than the Constitution, to bootstrap ourselves into a result, even though I agree with the objective of having counsel at preliminary hearings. By placing a premium on 'recent cases' rather than the language of the Constitution, the Court makes it dangerously simple for future Courts, using the technique of interpretation, to operate as a 'continuing Constitutional convention.' " Reading the Sixth Amendment literally, Burger found that it did not create a right to counsel at a preliminary hearing. He then accused the majority of seeking to "reshape the Constitution in accordance with predilections of what is deemed desirable."

Burger's dissenting opinion had a Lockean quality. The great John Locke, a dreadfully inept constitution-maker, believed that written statements of fundamental law must, like the laws of the universe, be immutable in order to be eternal. He once framed for Carolina a constitution expressly providing that "every part thereof, shall be and remain the sacred and unalterable form and rule of government for Carolina forever." As insurance he added that "all manner of comments and expositions on any part of these fundamental constitutions, or on any part of the common or statute laws of Carolina, are absolutely prohibited." By contrast, the framers of the United States Constitution recognized the inevitability of change and the need for plasticity. They therefore provided for an orderly amendment procedure and for a Supreme Court whose duties—"the judicial power shall extend to all cases . . . arising under the Constitution, the Laws of the United States, and treaties"—required it to engage in "all manner of comments and expositions." Burger's literalism, had it prevailed, would have enshrined Locke's approach, wiped the slate clean of precedents, and put the Constitution into an eighteenth-century deep-freeze.

When Justice Blackmun joined the Court for its 1970–1971 term, Burger's views began to prevail. The two men rarely differed. That fact plus the coincidence that they were from the same state and were old friends gave rise to the gibe that they were the "Minnesota Twins." The Twins were contenders for the Court's pennant during that term, when the tribunal once again functioned with a full compliment of nine justices. A new majority emerged as the Court decided many of its cases by close votes. "Damn the precedents and full speed astern" might have been the motto of the Burger Court. "Change without continuity," President Nixon had said on the day the new Chief Justice took his office, "can be anarchy. Change with continuity can mean progress." For a Court led by "strict constructionists," though not of Douglas' kind, there was a remarkable degree of change. But the continuity was frequently absent, making, if not for a sort of legal anarchy, at least for a lack of stability, as the following cases suggest. They are not representative cases. One might choose an equal number in which continuity did in fact exist, with the support of Burger and Blackmun; so too one might choose an equal number of cases in which continuity existed, as in *Ashe* and *Coleman,* despite the opposition of the newest appointees. The cases here chosen are those in which their side dominated, with the support of justices who had dissented when Warren and Fortas were on the Court. Now the dissenters, formerly members of the majority, represented continuity with the Warren Court.

All members of the Court know, as Max Lerner once quipped, that "judicial decisions are not babies brought by constitutional storks," but some of the justices do not think that the facts of judicial life are fit knowledge for public consumption. Justice Douglas, rarely a supporter of illusions or proprieties, made a candid admission that he watched with an expression of wonderment in a case involving a longshoreman's damage suit for injuries sustained aboard ship. Finding himself on the short end of a 5 to 4 decision, Douglas said: "Changes in membership do change decisions; and those changes are expected at the level of constitutional law. But when private rights not rooted in the Constitution are at issue, it is surprising to find law made by new judges taking the place of law made by prior judges." In the cases that follow, from the 1970–1971 term of the Court, the new judges made new constitutional law. The cases show distinctive patterns. In every one involving a decision by a lower federal court which had been following precedents, the Supreme Court reversed; in those cases going directly to the Supreme Court from the highest court of a state, the decision below, with one exception, was affirmed. Moreover, in every one of these cases, the Court decided against some claim of a civil liberty or civil right. In all these cases the Court divided closely, either 5 to 4 or 6 to 3, and the differences of opinion were intense and vinegary in expression. With one exception, Justices Douglas, Brennan, and Marshall were together, dissenting in every case.

In a 5 to 4 decision in *Dutton v. Evans,* the Court held that the right of an accused under the Sixth Amendment to confront the witnesses against him did not preclude the use of hearsay evidence against him. The dissenters complained that "the majority reaches a result completely inconsistent with recent opinions of this Court. . . ." In *Wyman v. James,* the administration by New York of the program for Aid to Families with Dependent Children (AFDC) raised a Fourth Amendment question of unreasonable search. AFDC is a welfare program supported by federal grants-in-aid but administered by the states supposedly under regulations of the Secretary of Health, Education, and Welfare. HEW prohibited state welfare agencies from entering a home without permission, but New York's law prescribed periodic home visits as a condition for continuance of welfare assistance under AFDC. Mrs. James, having refused a visitation from a social worker on grounds that it was a warrantless search of her home, was cut from the welfare rolls. Justice Blackmun for the Court ruled that the visit, though possessing "some of the characteristics of a search in the traditional sense," did not fall within the Fourth Amendment's proscription. Justice Marshall, dissenting, concluded: "In deciding that the homes of AFDC recipients are not entitled to protection from warrantless searches by welfare caseworkers, the Court declines to follow prior caselaw and employs a rationale that, if applied to the claims of all citizens, would threaten the vitality of the Fourth Amendment. . . . I find no little irony in the fact that the burden of today's departure from principled adjudication is placed upon the lowly poor." In *Richardson v. Perales,* a case similar in substance though not in its constitutional issue, the Court held, also 6 to 3, that there had been no violation of due process of law when a social security claimant was denied a disability claim on the basis of uncorroborated hearsay medical evidence untested by cross examination and contradicted by direct medical testimony. Blackmun was again the Court's spokesman.

In *Harris v. New York,* the "illegal confession" case, Chief Justice Burger for a Court divided 5 to 4 terminated one of the most notable but controversial trends of the Warren Court on the rights of the criminally accused. The new ruling was that a confession admittedly illegal, because it had been obtained during an interrogation conducted without apprising the accused of his constitutional rights to counsel and to remain silent, might be introduced against him at his trial for the purpose of attacking his credibility if he took the stand in his own behalf to deny his guilt. The police had unquestionably violated the rule of *Miranda v. Arizona.* By distinguishing away *Miranda,* the Court left it a no longer distinguished case—sapped of its vitality and thrust. Justice Brennan for the dissenters declared, "It is monstrous that courts should aid or abet the law-breaking police officer." Burger's opinion, in effect, provided an incentive to the police to ignore *Miranda* in the expectation that the Court would develop more permissive rules sanctioning clearly illegal police practices. "Thus," said Brennan, "even to the extent that *Miranda* was aimed at deterring police practices in disregard of the Constitution, I fear that today's holding will seriously undermine the achievement of that objective. The Court today tells the police that they may freely interrogate an accused incommunicado and without counsel and know that although any statement they obtain in violation of *Miranda* can't be used on the State's direct case, it may be introduced if the defendant has the temerity to testify in his own defense. This goes far toward undoing much of the progress made in conforming police methods to the Constitution."

In a related 5 to 4 decision in which the Chief Justice again gave the opinion of the Court, the holding was that the constitutional right against compulsory self-incrimination had not been violated by a state statute requiring a motorist involved in an accident to stop and identify himself, even though by so doing he might be providing evidence that could be used against him in a criminal prosecution. The dissenters protested, "One need only read with care the past cases cited in today's opinions to understand the shrinking process to which the Court today subjects a vital safeguard of our Bill of Rights." *Piccirillo v. New York* was another case on the Fifth Amendment's self-incrimination clause decided against the claim by a 5 to 4 majority. The prisoner had been compelled, under a grant of immunity from subsequent prosecution, to answer incriminating questions; his evidence provided the basis for a police officer's charge that the prisoner offered him a bribe, which the prisoner admitted. The Court sustained his conviction for bribery on a highly technical distinction which the dissenters regarded as "not in keeping with the generous interpretations which the Fifth Amendment has heretofore received by this Court."

Labine v. Vincent was another 5 to 4 decision in which the majority, through Justice Black, held that a state statute which precluded duly acknowledged illegitimate children from sharing an inheritance with legitimate children, when the parent dies without a will, did not violate the equal-protection clause of the Fourteenth Amendment. To reach this result the Court distinguished an analogous 1968 case. Justice Brennan, for the dissenters, asserted with some heat that the Court had reached its result of excluding illegitimate children from the protection of the constitutional clause by upholding "the untenable and discredited moral prejudice of bygone centuries which vindictively punished not only the illegitimates' parents, but also the hapless, and innocent, children. Based upon such a premise, today's decision cannot even pretend to be a principled decision. This is surprising from Justices who have heretofore so vigorously decried decision-making resting upon personal predilections" of the members of the majority. Brennan declared that the 1968 decision of the Court held squarely against the present decision specifically in the context of discrimination against illegitimate children in the same state.

Rogers v. Bellei, decided 5 to 4 in an opinion by Justice Blackmun, made it impossible to believe that a strict construction of the Constitution rather than the presuppositions and prejudices of the majority controlled the decision. The citizenship clause of the Fourteenth Amendment makes no distinction between persons whose citizenship derives from birth or naturalization. In 1964, ruling that the rights of citizenship of the native born and of the naturalized person were the same, the Court voided a provision of the Immigration and Nationality Act which divested the citizenship of anyone continuously residing for three years in a foreign country of which he was formerly a national. In that case, Mrs. Schneider's citizenship, which derived from that of her mother, was restored. In the 1967 *Afroyim* case, the Court voided another provision of the same act which forfeited the citizenship of a naturalized citizen who voted in a foreign election. On that occasion the Court ruled that Congress had no power to take away an American's citizenship without his express consent. Against these cases the Court in 1971 upheld the constitutionality of a provision of the same act forfeiting the citizenship of anyone who, having been born abroad and deriving his citizenship from an American parent, does not return to the United States for a five-year continuous residence between the ages of fourteen and twenty-eight. The Court in fact made a tenuous distinction between its new ruling and the precedents, but Justice Black, for the dissenters, angrily alleged that by the narrowest vote, made possible by "a simple change in its composition," the Court had overruled the precedents. "This precious Fourteenth Amendment American citizenship," he added, "should not be blown around by every passing political wind that changes the composition of this Court." Justice Brennan, in his dissenting opinion, damned the majority opinion as completely lacking a rational basis. Summing up a trend, he observed tartly: "Since the Court this Term has already downgraded citizens receiving public welfare, Wyman v. James . . . and citizens having the misfortune to be illegitimate, Lavine v. Vincent . . . , I suppose today's decision downgrading citizens born outside the United States should have been expected. Once again, as in *James* and *Labine,* the Court's opinion makes evident that its holding is contrary to earlier decisions."

James v. Valtierra, the "low-income housing" case, resulted in a 5 to 3 decision in which Justice Douglas took no part and Justices

Blackmun and Black switched positions; Blackmun voted with the dissenters against a majority that included Black and Burger. The majority sustained the constitutionality of a state requirement that a publicly financed low-rent housing project must be approved by a majority of voters in a local election. That requirement survived a claim that it violated the equal-protection clause of the Fourteenth Amendment. The Court's opinion was a depressing contrast not only to analogous precedents but to another opinion delivered a week earlier in the "school busing" cases. There the Court unanimously held unconstitutional a state act which forbade the busing of pupils for the purpose of creating a racial balance in the public schools of a Southern city; in addition the Court explicitly empowered the lower federal courts to order a busing system where it appeared that the assignment of children to the schools nearest their homes would not result in an effective dismantling of a dual school system based, for all practical purposes, on race. Yet in the "low-income housing" case the Court vitiated the impact of these busing decisions. Referendums on publicly assisted housing projects for low-income groups often prevent construction, as in the case arising from San Jose, California, in *James v. Valtierra,* with the result that racial ghettos remain unbroken because of residential segregation. That is, in the cities of the North, where de facto segregation exists, as compared with segregation resulting from state action as in the South, racial ghettos spawn racial schools. Burger, speaking for the Court in the busing cases, exempted the de facto segregation situation. Thus the effect of the decision in the *James* case meant a continuance of those racial ghettos. In that case the Court found that California's requirement of a referendum made no reference to race. In reality, however, many of the poor who would have benefited from publicly assisted housing were Negroes. The decision reversed a lower federal court decision which rested on a 1969 precedent that voided an act of Akron, Ohio, which provided that an open-housing law could not take effect until approved by a city referendum. As Justice Marshall declared on behalf of the dissenters in the *James* case, "It is far too late in the day to contend that the Fourteenth Amendment prohibits only racial discrimination; and to me, singling out the poor," who include most Negroes, "to bear a burden not placed on any other class of citizens tramples the values that the Fourteenth Amendment was designed to protect."

In *Whitcomb v. Chavis* the Burger Court gave its first fully considered judgment in a reapportionment case, a subject on which the Warren Court had made numerous celebrated decisions revitalizing the system of representative government in the United States. In consonance with those precedents, a lower federal court found unconstitutional the apportionment scheme of Indiana which prohibited the division of any county into state senatorial districts. Marion County, the state's most populous, included Indianapolis, whose Negro voters in the inner-city ghetto were grossly underrepresented because of the provision that there must be multi-member representatives elected at large by the whole county. The Supreme Court, reversing the lower federal court, held that the multi-member legislative district in this case did not result in invidious discrimination against Negroes, because there was no evidence that the apportionment scheme was designed to dilute the vote of any minority. The three dissenters saw only a racial gerrymander, and, through Justice Douglas, declared: "It is said that if we prevent racial gerrymandering today, we must prevent gerrymandering of any special interest group tomorrow, whether it be social, economic, or ideological. I do not agree. Our Constitution has a very special thrust when it comes to voting; the Fifteenth Amendment says the right of citizens to vote may not be 'abridged' on account of 'race, color, or previous condition of servitude.' "

In *Palmer v. Thompson* the five-man majority held that the act of the city of Jackson, Mississippi, in closing its public swimming pools rather than operate them on a desegregated basis, did not deny Negroes the equal protection of the laws, because whites were affected by the closing in the same way as blacks. The dissenters, with Justice White as their spokesman, rejected that reasoning because, "The fact is that closing the pools is an expression of official policy that Negroes are unfit to associate with whites." The dissenters also joined Justice Marshall's opinion which concluded that by removing public swimming pools from the protection of the Fourteenth Amendment, the majority "turn the clock back 17 years."

McKeiver v. Pennsylvania was a case in which the Court, divided 6 to 3, ruled that a juvenile court proceeding is not a criminal prosecution within the meaning of the Sixth Amendment, making unnecessary a trial by jury as long as fundamental fairness in procedure is followed. Justice Blackmun, giving the opinion of the Court, ruled that recent precedents had not determined decision. In 1967 the Court, in one of its reformative opinions, based on the premise that the Bill of Rights is not for adults only, made available to juveniles the rights to appropriate notice, counsel, confrontation and cross-examination, and freedom from compulsory self-incrimination. A year later the Court ruled that trial by jury in criminal cases was fundamental to the American scheme of justice, and consequently must be provided by state courts. The dissenters, led by Justice Douglas, believed that these precedents established for juveniles a right to trial by jury at least in a case, such as that before the Court, in which the juvenile offenders faced long incarceration.

In all these cases, which illuminate by contrast the views of the Warren Court, the Burger Court no less than the Warren Court displayed an audacious disregard for and circumvention of precedents, clearly revealing its own values and policy choices. Despite pretenses to the contrary, it could do no other, for as beauty exists in the eye of the beholder, so American constitutional law exists in the collective eye of those who happen at any moment of time to dominate the Supreme Court.

Suggested Reading

Henry J. Abraham, *Freedom and the Court,* New York, Oxford University Press, 1967 (paperback).

Alexander M. Bickel, *Politics and the Warren Court,* New York, Harper and Row, 1965.

Alexander M. Bickel, *The Supreme Court and the Idea of Progress,* New York, Harper and Row, 1970 (paperback).

Ramsay Clark, *Crime in America,* New York, Simon and Schuster, 1970 (Pocket Books paperback).

Richard Claude, *The Supreme Court and the Electoral Process,* Baltimore, Johns Hopkins University Press, 1970.

Harry M. Clor, *Obscenity and Public Morality: Censorship in a Liberal Society,* Chicago, University of Chicago Press, 1969 (paperback).

Archibald Cox, *The Warren Court,* Cambridge, Mass., Harvard University Press, 1968.

Robert Dixon, *Democratic Representation: Reapportionment in Law and Politics,* New York, Oxford University Press, 1968.

Norman Dorsen, ed., *The Rights of Americans: What They Are— What They Should Be,* New York, Pantheon Books, 1971.

Thomas I. Emerson, *The System of Freedom of Expression,* New York, Random House, 1970.

Leon Friedman and Fred L. Israel, eds., *The Justices of the United States Supreme Court, 1789–1969,* New York, Chelsea

House, 1969, 4 vols. Consult vols. 3 and 4 for biographical sketches of members of the Warren Court.

Fred P. Graham, *The Self-Inflicted Wound,* New York, Macmillan, 1970.

Alfred H. Kelly and Winfred A. Harbison, *The American Constitution: Origins and Development,* 4th ed., New York, W. W. Norton, 1970.

Milton R. Konvitz, *Expanding Liberties,* New York, Viking Press, 1966 (paperback).

Samuel Krislov, *The Supreme Court and Political Freedom,* New York, Free Press, 1968 (paperback).

Philip B. Kurland, *Politics, the Constitution, and the Warren Court,* Chicago, University of Chicago Press, 1970.

Philip B. Kurland, ed., *The Supreme Court Review* (issued annually, 1960–1970), Chicago, University of Chicago Press.

Leonard W. Levy, ed., *Judicial Review and the Supreme Court: Selected Essays,* New York, Harper Torchbooks, 1967 (paperback).

Anthony Lewis, *Gideon's Trumpet,* New York, Random House, 1964 (Vintage paperback).

Anthony Lewis, ed., *The Warren Court: A Critical Evaluation,* New York, Chelsea House, 1970.

Wallace Mendelson, ed., *Felix Frankfurter: A Tribute,* New York, Reynal, 1964.

G. Theodore Mitau, *Decade of Decision: The Supreme Court and the Constitutional Revolution, 1954–1964,* New York, Scribner's, 1967 (paperback).

Walter F. Murphy, *Congress and the Court,* Chicago, University of Chicago Press, 1962 (paperback).

Benjamin Muse, *Ten Years of Prelude: The Story of Integration Since the Supreme Court's 1954 Decision,* New York, Viking Press, 1964.

Arthur A. North, *The Supreme Court: Judicial Process and Judicial Politics,* New York, Appleton-Century-Crofts, 1966 (paperback).

C. Herman Pritchett, *The American Constitution,* 2nd ed., New York, McGraw-Hill, 1968.

C. Herman Pritchett, *Congress Versus the Supreme Court, 1957–1960,* Minneapolis, University of Minnesota Press, 1961.

John P. Roche, *Courts and Rights: The American Judiciary in Action,* 2nd ed., New York, Random House, 1966 (paperback).

Bernard Schwartz, *A Commentary on the Constitution of the United States: Part III, Rights of the Person,* New York, Macmillan, 1968, 2 vols.

Martin Shapiro, *Freedom of Speech: The Supreme Court and Judicial Review,* New York, Prentice-Hall, 1966 (Spectrum paperback).

Martin Shapiro, *Law and Politics in the Supreme Court,* New York, Free Press, 1964.

George W. Spicer, *The Supreme Court and Fundamental Freedoms,* 2nd ed., New York, Appleton-Century-Crofts, 1967 (paperback).

William Spinrad, *Civil Liberties,* Chicago, Quadrangle Books, 1970.

Stephen P. Strickland, ed., *Hugo Black and the Supreme Court: A Symposium,* Indianapolis, Bobbs-Merrill, 1967.

William F. Swindler, *Court and Constitution in the Twentieth Century: The New Legality, 1932–1968,* Indianapolis, Bobbs-Merrill, 1970.

Helen Shirley Thomas, *Felix Frankfurter: Scholar on the Bench,* Baltimore, Johns Hopkins University Press, 1960.

John D. Weaver, *Warren: The Man, the Court, the Era,* Boston, Little, Brown, 1967.

Index

773. 41
.579s
2./(P)

A Note on the Editor

Leonard W. Levy is William W. Clary Professor of United States History and Chairman of the Graduate Faculty in History at Claremont Graduate School, Claremont, California. He served for many years as Earl Warren Professor of American Constitutional History at Brandeis University. His most important books are *The Law of the Commonwealth and Chief Justice Shaw; Legacy of Suppression: Freedom of Speech and Press in Early American History; Jefferson and Civil Liberties: The Darker Side;* and *Origins of the Fifth Amendment: The Right Against Self-Incrimination,* which won the Pulitzer Prize for History in 1969.